TRAUMA AND MENTAL HEALTH SOCIAL WORK WITH URBAN POPULATIONS

Addressing the social problems associated with trauma and mental health amongst African Americans in urban environments, this book uses an African-centered lens to critique the most common practice models and interventions currently employed by social workers in the field.

Divided into four parts and grounded in traditional African cultural values, it argues that basic key values in a new clinical model for mental health diagnosis are:

- A spiritual component
- Collective/group approach
- Focus on wholeness
- Oneness with Nature
- Emphasis on truth, justice, balance, harmony, reciprocity, righteousness, and order

Being free from racism, sexism, classism, and other forms of oppression, this African-centered approach is crucial for working with people of African origin who experience daily "trauma" through adverse living conditions.

This book will be key reading on any practice and direct service course at both BSW and MSW level and will be a useful supplement on clinical courses as well as those aimed at working with diverse populations and those living in urban environments.

Rhonda Wells-Wilbon, DSW, LICSW, LCSW-C is a tenured Associate Professor and former Chair, Master of Social Work Program. She currently serves as a faculty member in the PhD Program, School of Social Work, Morgan State University, Baltimore, MD. She is Founder and CEO of Rhonda Wilbon Consulting LLC and Co-Founder of Empowered Wellness LLC. Her professional articles have appeared in several journals. Dr Wilbon has contributed to the professional literature with training curriculums, research reports, conference presentations, and book chapters. Her primary practice and research areas include domestic violence and adult survivors of child sexual abuse and sexual assault.

Anthony Estreet, PhD., LICSW, is a tenured Associate Professor and Chair of the Addiction area of specialized practice in the Master of Social Work Program, School of Social Work, Morgan State University, Baltimore, MD. He is CEO/Executive Director of a behavioral health consulting and treatment center – Next Step Treatment Center, LLC. Fueled by his strong desire to address health and mental health disparities through policy and practice efforts, he continues to develop key partnerships with various community-based organizations, hospitals, and universities across the United States and globally to provide ongoing training and technical assistance focused on improving behavioral health treatment-related outcomes.

TRAUMA AND MENTAL HEALTH SOCIAL WORK WITH URBAN POPULATIONS

African-Centered Clinical Interventions

Edited by
Rhonda Wells-Wilbon and Anthony Estreet

Routledge
Taylor & Francis Group

LONDON AND NEW YORK

Cover image: © Getty Images

First published 2022
by Routledge
4 Park Square, Milton Park, Abingdon, Oxon OX14 4RN

and by Routledge
605 Third Avenue, New York, NY 10158

Routledge is an imprint of the Taylor & Francis Group, an informa business

British Library Cataloguing-in-Publication Data
A catalogue record for this book is available from the British Library

Library of Congress Cataloging-in-Publication Data
A catalog record for this book has been requested

ISBN: 978-0-367-22733-3 (hbk)
ISBN: 978-0-367-22734-0 (pbk)
ISBN: 978-0-429-27661-3 (ebk)

DOI: 10.4324/9780429276613

Typeset in Bembo
by Apex CoVantage, LLC

We dedicate this book to our ancestors who were sold into slavery, stolen from our homeland on the continent of Africa, survived or died during the middle passage, enslaved for hundreds of years, and yet had the spiritual capacity and fortitude to maintain family in the midst of the MAAFA "Great Disaster." We give thanks to God for you, we are because you were, we honor your sacrifice, and we will continue to thrive and illuminate your brilliant light, until we meet on the other side. For our children and the generations of our children, yet to come . . .

Always know that to Be African is An Absolute Gift!

CONTENTS

FIGURES AND TABLES

Figures

Tables

CONTRIBUTORS

Paul Archibald, DrPH, LCSW-C School of Health Sciences, Department of Social Work, College of Staten Island, CUNY, Staten Island, New York.

Jazlyn A. Bain, BA MSW Candidate School of Social Work, University of North Carolina Wilmington, Wilmington, North Carolina.

Tricia Bent-Goodley, PhD, LICSW, LCSW-C Professor Emeritus, School of Social Work/ Graduate Professor, Department of Public Health, Graduate School, Howard University, Washington, DC.

Yolanda Bogan, PhD Professor of Psychology, Department of Educational Leadership and Human Services, Florida Agricultural & Mechanical University, Tallahassee, Florida.

Terra L. Bowen-Reid, PhD Associate Professor of Psychology, Department of Psychology, Morgan State University, Baltimore, Maryland.

Janeen Cross, DSW, MSW, MBA, LICSW, LCSW-C Assistant Professor, School of Social Work, Howard University, Washington, DC.

Kevin Daniels, PhD Associate Professor, Morgan State University, School of Social Work, Baltimore, Maryland.

Anthony Estreet, PhD, LCSW-C, LCADC Associate Professor, School of Social Work, Morgan State University, Baltimore, Maryland.

Chelsey Henderson, MSW, LICSW Doctoral Candidate, School of Social Work, Morgan State University, Baltimore, Maryland.

Loren Henderson, PhD, MA Associate Professor, School of Sociology, Anthropology, Public Health, University of Maryland Baltimore County, Baltimore, Maryland.

Lennon Jackson, MEd, MSW Office of the Vice President for Student Affairs, Howard University, Washington, DC.

Georgia Jennings-Dorsey, DSW, LCSW-C Assistant Professor, School of Social Work, Morgan State University, Baltimore, Maryland.

Korey Johnson, JD PhD Student, School of Social Work, Morgan State University, Baltimore Maryland.

Nia Johnson, PhD Assistant Professor, College of Education and Social Work, West Chester University, Westchester, Pennsylvania.

Tina Jordan, PhD, MSW Associate Professor, School of Social Work, Bowie State University, Bowie, Maryland.

Tiffany Y. Lane, PhD, MSW Associate Professor & BSW Coordinator, School of Social Work, University of North Carolina Wilmington, Wilmington, North Carolina.

Paula Langford, DMin CEO, The Healing Institute, Baltimore, Maryland.

Deidre McDaniel, MSW, LCSW President & Founder, Health Equity Resources & Strategies/ Doctoral Candidate, School of Social Work, Morgan State University, Baltimore, Maryland.

David Miller, MEd Doctoral Candidate, School of Social Work, Morgan State University, Baltimore, Maryland.

Natalie Muñoz, LMSW Doctoral Student School of Social Work, Howard University, Washington, DC.

Cashmere O'Neal, LCSW-C, LICSW CEO, Leading Men Toward Fatherhood of Authenticity and Omnipresence/Adjunct Professor/PhD Student, Morgan State University, School of Social Work.

Stephanie Oyler, MSW, LSW Founder & CEO, Adoptee LIT, LLC, Kennett Square, Pennsylvania.

Tonya C. Phillips PhD, LCSW-C, LCADC Founder & CEO, Team Phillips Consulting Group, Gwynn Oaks, Maryland.

Rhea C. Porter, PhD Project Coordinator, Supporting Through Empowerment and Prevention (STEP), School of Social Work, Morgan State University, Baltimore, MD.

Len Price, MSW PhD Student, School of Social Work, Morgan State University, Baltimore Maryland.

S. Rasheem, PhD Independent Scholar, S. Rasheem Presents, Baltimore, Maryland.

Sakima Romero-Chandler MEd, MDiv Project Manager, Domestic Violence Homicide Prevention, School of Social Work, Howard University, Washington, DC.

Noelle St. Vil, PhD Assistant Professor, School of Social Work, University at Buffalo, Amherst, New York.

LaTanya N. Townsend, PhD, LCSW-C Founder & CEO, Radical Restorations, Towson, MD.

Ingrid K. Tulloch PhD Assistant Professor of Psychology, Director, Animal Research Facility & Neurobiology of Risky Health Behavior Lab, Morgan State University, Baltimore, Maryland.

Jordan White, PhD, MSW Assistant Professor, School of Social Work, Morgan State University, Baltimore, Maryland.

Rhonda Wells-Wilbon, PhD, LCSW-C, LICSW Associate Professor, School of Social Work, Morgan State University, Baltimore, Maryland.

Aaliah Zonicle, MSW PhD Student, School of Social Work, Howard University, Washington, DC.

PEER-REVIEWERS

Kelly Costner, EdD Dean, Social Science Programs, Walden University, Baltimore, Maryland.

Ann Dillard, LMFT, DWCF Brainspotting Therapist/President, K.I.P. Consulting Services, Decatur, Georgia.

Tara Doaty, PhD CEO & Lead Consultant, Sage Wellness Group, Baltimore, Maryland.

Fran K. Franklin, PhD, LCSW Associate Professor, Department of Social Work, College of Health and Behavioral Sciences, Delaware State University, Dover, Delaware.

Ruby Gourdine, DSW Chair, Direct Practice Concentration, Co-Chair, Human Behavior & Social Environment Sequence, School of Social Work, Howard University, Washington, DC.

Nyasha Grayman-Simpson, PhD Henry S. Dulaney Professor, Associate Professor of Psychology and Africana Studies, Goucher College, Baltimore, Maryland.

Kimetta R. Hairston, PhD Associate Professor, Administration, Academics and Virtual Engagement, Bowie State University, Bowie, Maryland.

Denise Hayes, PhD Assistant Vice Provost for Student Affairs Director, Counseling and Psychological Services, Indiana University Bloomington, Bloomington, Indiana.

Adrianne Jackson, PhD United States Air Force Specialist, Primary Prevention of Violence, Valdosta, Georgia.

Sharon Jennings-Rojas, DOM Chair Integrative Medicine, Maryland University of Integrative Health, Laurel, Maryland.

Pia King, PhD, MSW, LMSW Financial Wellness Coach, Wealth Services, LLC, Washington, DC.

Katrina Bell McDonald, PhD Adjunct Instructor, Department of Humanities and Social Sciences, College of Health Sciences California Northstate University, Elk Grove, California.

Vonzella Renee McQueen, MA Staff Assistant to the Dean, College of Professional Studies, Bowie State University/Adjunct Professor, Community College of Baltimore County, Baltimore, Maryland.

Ruby Mendenhall PhD Associate Professor in Sociology, African American Studies, Urban and Regional Planning, and Social Work, University of Illinois Urbana-Champaign, Champaign, Illinois.

Shaeeda Mensah, PhD Visiting Assistant Professor, Department of Philosophy, Franklin and Marshall College, Lancaster, Pennsylvania.

Selena T. Rodgers, PhD, LCSW-R Associate Professor & Founding Director, MSW Program, School of Health Sciences and Professional Programs, Department of Social Work, York College of the City University of New York, Jamaica, New York.

Belinda Davis Smith, PhD, MSW Associate Professor, College of Public Service, School of Social Work, Jackson State University, Jackson, Mississippi.

Cudore L. Snell, MSW, DSW, LICSW Professor, School of Social Work, Howard University, Washington, DC.

Kesslyn Brade Stennis, PhD, MDiv, MSW Professor, School of Social Work, Coppin State University, Baltimore, Maryland.

Sandra Stukes Chipungu, PhD, MSW, MA Interim Dean 2018–2019, Chair Doctoral Program Retired 2019, School of Social Work Morgan State University, Baltimore, Maryland.

Bernadine Waller, LMHC, PhD Candidate Associate Director of Experiential Learning, The Center for Career and Professional Development/Adjunct Professor, School of Social Work, Adelphi University, Garden City, New York.

Anita M. Wells, PhD Associate Professor, Department of Psychology, Morgan State University, Baltimore, Maryland.

PREFACE

This first edition of the book is timely for the social work profession and comes at a time when there is an increased need to address trauma and mental health among Black or African American people. As a result of the COVID-19 pandemic and the increased focus on addressing social justice such as police brutality and racism, this book serves as a starting point for social workers and other mental health professionals who want to learn more about working with and helping to address trauma and mental health in the African American community. While it is still too soon to know the long-term impacts of COVID-19 on the health and mental health of the Black community, we do know that African Americans continue to be impacted by increased rates of trauma and mental health concerns such as anxiety and depression. Much of the trauma and mental health challenges experienced by the Black community do not exist inside a vacuum; they exist within the context of complex intersections with racism, discrimination, classism, health equity, economic insecurity and the associated experiences, violence, and criminal justice which compounds the mental health disparities within the Black community. While social workers represent the largest behavioral health profession in the United States and many other countries, the field of social work lacks a leading resource to help ensure social workers receive training based on the best available knowledge and intervention to address trauma and mental health within urban populations. As social workers and the overall profession have increased its interest in anti-racist work through presentations, course development, certification programs, and peer-reviewed articles, this book fills the gap by providing a comprehensive evidence-based guide that can serve as the cornerstone for anti-racist and clinical courses in social work.

Editing this book has provided a wonderful opportunity for us to reflect on the work that Black scholars have contributed toward developing and implementing African-centered practice models for addressing trauma and mental health. It has also provided an opportunity to see where more work is needed for implementation and moving toward the threshold of "evidence based practice." With approximately 13% of the U.S. population identifying as Black or African American and the increased rates of mental health within the Black community, we believe that many of the interventions and practice approaches available today do not address the complexity of historical trauma and mental health in a culturally responsive and healing-centered way. This book hopes to provide a starting point for social workers to begin thinking about and practicing in a way that takes into consideration the complexity of many of these issues. We have included some exciting new directions and opportunities for the profession that are inclusive, wholistic, and represent changes that are occurring in the field.

This book is divided into four parts which we felt helped to organize the overall flow of the book. The introductory Part 1 provides some level setting which encourages us to rethink trauma and mental health for people of African ancestry. Within this section, we lay the groundwork for understanding that true social justice and wholeness for the African American community will not be realized until we start to address the trauma and mental health disparities. We recognize that wholeness within this regard is inclusive of mental health, physical health, and the overall improvement in quality-of-life satisfaction. Part 2 offers social work practitioners a foundation of knowledge regarding four major areas: vicarious trauma, spirituality, supervision, and Brainspotting. These areas are critical as they recognize the importance of addressing vicarious trauma as police brutality is more publicized via social media and in the wake of health disparities related to COVID-19. It also highlights the importance and healing benefits of spirituality as an African-centered principle. As we encourage more Black social workers to enter the profession, the importance and requirement (for new social workers) of supervision becomes an area where many African and health-centered principles can be applied. The incorporation of the supervision chapter acknowledges the duality and importance of balancing one's own experiences as a Black person but also working in a profession as a helping professional. Lastly, this section looks toward innovation with a critique of somatic psychotherapy, eye movement desensitization and reprocessing (EMDR), and Brainspotting, looking toward how these newly developing models can be honed to include the cultural needs of the Black community. Part 3 focuses on trauma and the legacy of the Black experience. It offers an exploration and critique on practice approaches addressing trauma, intimate partner violence, sexual assault, working with Black youth, mothering daughters, and racialized gender trauma. Part 4 examines areas that we felt were inclusive and important within the Black community as they represent areas where Black people have historically been disproportionately represented. These areas include informal caregiving, Black male youth and police encounters, foster care and adoption, substance use and addiction, HIV/AIDS, and incarceration.

This book is aimed at both beginning and experienced social work practitioners, and all the chapters are written by experts who have experience in the field, working with trauma and mental health people within the Black community. As a point of transparency, this book is not for everyone. However, if you are a social worker who is concerned with gaining a better understanding and improving your work with the Black community, then this book is for you. We provide meaningful solutions that address some of the most complex issues as it relates to trauma and mental health. Given the ongoing issue of health and mental health disparities in the Black community, it is our hope that this book contributes to increased effectiveness by social workers in this often-neglected area of practice.

Working on this book has been a great joy but it has also been a community effort. We would like to thank our community of contributors, peer reviewers, and advisors who helped tremendously with the conceptualization and organization of this book. With their support, the overarching theme of the diversity of African-centered ideas has been our guiding light, and central to this book is the fact that mental health is fundamental to the health, wellness, and wholeness of the Black community.

Anthony Estreet
Rhonda Wells-Wilbon

ACKNOWLEDGMENT

The editors would like to thank Deirdre McDaniel, our PhD graduate assistant, for her consistent work over the past two years of managing this project. Writing an edited book is a major undertaking and having a skilled person managing the process and authors reduces the stress on editors. In our case, this book would not be possible without her.

Additionally, Dr Rhea C. Porter came on board during the final stretch to help edit down chapters, so we could stay within our contracted word limit. Jamilia Simmons our PhD graduate assistant who created the index and managed the process of putting it together with some assistance from Adrienne Dezurn one of our MSW students.

PART 1

Introduction

Rethinking trauma and mental health for people of African ancestry

1

RECLAIMING OUR RIGHT TO WHOLENESS AND WELLNESS

Rhonda Wells-Wilbon

Being the descendant of a group of people who were literally taken from one continent to be enslaved on another continent for over 400 years is not an easy legacy to inherit. But, when you know that the place your ancestors were taken from is vast and beautiful and filled with traditions and values and people who look like you, the process of healing is something you can begin to believe is possible. Knowing that "to be African" is a gift, (Gallman, Ani, & Williams, 2003) is a rich heritage that those who were taken across the Atlantic Ocean to be enslaved were literally physically and psychologically disconnected from. While many thrive, in spite of a legacy of enslavement, the harm caused from racism, oppression, and consistent hatred cannot be underestimated (Graham, 2005).

One of the most difficult things someone can be faced with doing is to coexist and live in the same space with someone who has been abusive to them. In fact, in the field of interpersonal violence (IPV) victims are removed or encouraged to leave these harmful relationships (Yoshioka & Choi, 2005). IPV is defined as any behavior within the relationship that causes physical, psychological, or sexual harm to those in the relationship (Waters, Hyder, Rajkotia, Basu, & Butchart, 2005). The interpersonal relationship between Blacks and whites, particularly in the United States, is one riddled with the same patterns of behavior (physical, psychological, and sexual abuse) considered so damaging in IPV relationships (Briere & Jordan, 2004), and yet, little has been done to address the horrific attack against Black humanity or reconcile the imbalance of power. In IPV relationships both the victims of the abuse and the abuser are challenged to go through counseling to seek help and support with the hope that healing can take place. Anger management and other cognitive behavior therapies are recommended for abusers, while the victims of IPV are given refuge, counseling, and resources to help them restore their lives (Briere & Jordan, 2004). But for African Americans and other Blacks the

DOI: 10.4324/9780429276613-2

question remains, as to what will be done to heal the deep wounds caused by the European slave trade.

African Americans and Black people across the globe, who are descendants of those who were taken from the continent of Africa have suffered great losses and have a right to their anger and pain. They also have a right to reclaim wholeness and be well (Fairfax, 2020). And, each individual person can only be in whatever space they are in, thus we see the diversity of where different people may be for example (economically, educational attainment, family stability, literacy, physical and mental health, etc.) within the Black community. Putting parameters and guidelines around how someone should respond to being oppressed is at best unfair, at worst inhumane, and is in fact itself abusive. The audacity of the idea. The arrogance, control, and privilege one must be overflowing with to assume such a right, to tell those who you oppressed how to respond to their oppressive conditions. And yet, the oppressor attempting to control the narrative of the oppressed is actually the norm (Wallis, 2016).

Crying out or fighting back when attacked is normal behavior, but Blacks are often denied even this basic right without fear of retribution or actual retribution; thus, the deep-rooted wound resulting in Black pain (Williams, 2009). And the outcomes are as tragic: physical and mental illness, self-hate, poverty, poor learning outcomes, violence, addictions, and the list goes on and on marking the dysfunctional results of a difficult past (Lindblad-Goldberg & Dukes, 1985). It is a miracle anyone at all escaped into even the possibility to thrive and be well.

Why focus on urban populations and urban social problems?

Throughout the world, you will find large populations of people of African descent living and working in urban centers. There are a variety of reasons for this clustering. Urban areas often have the potential for access to more needed resources and services, such as transportation, and more outlets for social engagement. But these environments also come with their challenges (Wells-Wilbon, McPhatter & Vakalahi, 2016). Overcrowded conditions, violence, food deserts, low-performing public school systems, environmental concerns, poverty, and substance use disorders are some of the big challenges in urban communities (Wells-Wilbon, McPhatter & Vakalahi, 2016). Perhaps, one of the greatest challenges is the gap between the haves and the have-nots (Farley & Frey, 1994), making the sting of racism and poverty and marginalization felt even more profoundly.

In spite of the fact that Blacks in the United States may live in some of the most challenging areas and neighborhoods in urban environments, urban centers are also places where there are a lot of opportunities. Not only do poor people live in these areas, but people who are highly educated, gainfully employed, pursuing professional careers, committed to service and volunteerism, and community activists are also urban dwellers (Wells-Wilbon et al., 2016). This combination of people, the haves and the have-nots, makes for great opportunities to work collaboratively and engage in social change regardless of socioeconomic background, if the residents of these various communities in environments are willing to build alliances.

Africa and spirituality

Central to the African way of life is spirituality. In fact, many would say that there is nothing greater than spirit. And, while people of African ancestry are very religious, spirit and a connection with spirit is more central and more universal to the way of life of African people than religions (Martin & Martin, 2002). Perhaps, this is an area where Blacks who were not born or raised on the continent of Africa experience some disconnection. Distinguishing between religion and spirituality, as if there is a need to choose between one and the other, not knowing that spirit is so ingrained in the DNA of African people, nothing even enslavement can separate Africans from the God force that is within.

African-centered, what do we mean?

Traditional African values are rooted in wellness (Ani, 2004). Unfortunately, the average Black person who wasn't born and raised on the continent of Africa is unaware of these core values. Before technology put information right at our fingertips, many Black scholars – Asante (1991); Kambon (1992); Harvey (2018); Schiele (1996); Bent-Goodley, Fairfax & Carlto-LaNey (2017); Bent-Goodley & Rodgers (2018); Carlton-LaNey (1999) – to name a few, devoted their work to reeducating us all. There is a debt of gratitude owed to these great intellectual warriors. In Africa, you rarely hear words like African-centered, Afrocentric, Africentric, and Afracentric. It is not because Africans who live on the continent don't value these concepts. It is because what these concepts represent in Africa, is such a way of everyday life, there is no reason to call it anything but living.

Unfortunately, for African Americans and other Black people, such as in the Caribbean, whose ancestors were taken from Africa on ships across the Atlantic Ocean to be enslaved, there was a disruption (Kambon, 2012). Mama Dr Marimba Ani (1994) identified this disruption as the *Maafa*, a Swahili word that means "Great Disaster." Because of the great disaster of the European slave trade, African Americans and African Caribbeans have been in a constant cycle of reclaiming the wholeness of what it means to be who they are, African.

In "Mental and Emotional Wellness Among African Americans in Urban Environments: What Do We Know? How Can We Improve Outcomes?," a chapter from the book *Social Work Practice with African Americans in Urban Environments* (Wells-Wilbon, et al., 2016), there is an Asili Ma'at restoration model which shows the utilization of the virtues of *Ma'at* to assist African Americans toward mental health and well-being. The principles of *Ma'at* are a guide for finding balance and practicing rightness and order as a way of life for optimum wellness.

Before we really knew much about *Ma'at* and other traditional African values, Afro American studies' professor Maulana Ndabezith Karenga created an African

American cultural holiday known as *Kwanzaa* in 1966. The seven principles of *Kwanzaa*, also referred to as the *Nguzo Saba*, are values rooted in African cultural values (Karenga, 2007). This was a time when Blacks in the United States were under intense attack during the civil rights movement and *Kwanzaa* was a reminder of the collective communal values shared by Black people, it was a challenge to come together. Each year hundreds of Black families celebrate *Kwanzaa* starting the day after Christmas and ending on New Year's Day. Practicing the principle of *Kwanzaa* is an investment in the Black family and Black community. It's a reminder of a collective identity and connection, one to the other.

The basic key values utilized throughout the book guide the African-centered lens, analyzing and diagnosing mental health needs. The clinical model/approach best fit when working with various African American urban populations include 1) a spiritual component; 2) collective/group approach; 3) focus on wholeness; 4) oneness with nature; and 5) emphasis on truth, justice, balance, harmony, reciprocity, righteousness, and order. Authors offer modifications to interventions/models using a more African-centered approach, where needed.

The African-centered lens represents the varied cultural values commonly identified as grounded in traditional African ways of being and functioning. Authors draw from their own scholarship, teaching, and practice knowledge and experience, guided by what the literature says about what it means to be African-centered. This is what African-centered scholars and practitioners know is important:

- De-emphasize pathology
- Anchored in Kemetic system of *Ma'at*: divinity (connection with the universe); teach-ability (capacity to learn and show knowledge); perfectibility (being present in the moment, but goal- and future-oriented); free will (consciously choosing to respond to what is real); responsibility (relationships guided by what is moral and socially responsible)
- Honoring: spirituality, interconnectedness, the precedence of the collective over the individual, self-knowledge, and self-healing power that is believed to be within us all
- Honoring: strengths, emphasizing wisdom, faith, and intelligence, wholistic, oneness with nature
- Connecting with the client, facilitating awareness, setting, and working on goals
- Taking action and instigating change
- Assessment/evaluation for purpose of providing client feedback and knowing what works with various client populations
- Processing feedback and monitoring accountability/order

African-centered theoretical perspectives are free from racism, sexism, classism, and other forms of oppression. The more African-centered scholars and practitioners are given opportunities to practice, conduct research, and produce scholarly literature, the more knowledge and information will be available to further enhance

African-centered theory, practice, and research development (Bent-Goodley, Fairfax, & Carlton-LaNey, 2017).

This book helps to answer the question of how an African-centered perspective philosophical and theoretical viewpoint can assist people who have and continue to experience daily "trauma" through adverse living conditions. Attempting to put what it means to be African in a box, in many ways takes away from "what it means to be African"; thus, the book utilizes some qualitative skills which will allow African-centered techniques and methods to evolve and be discovered, even when the practitioner themselves may not even know they are applying such components.

African-centered clinical interventions: in the spirit of Sankofa

Today, there is a great opportunity to take what we've learned from the past and combine it with real-life experiences of Black people throughout the diaspora. African-centered scholars and practitioners have an opportunity now to "go back and fetch" (Ani, 2004) what is known from the past and build the interventions, practices, and approaches that put Black people at the center of their own wellness. The *Maafa* was in fact a great disaster, but the resilience of the people of African ancestry has been demonstrated and proven over and over again (Ani, 2004). The cycle of returning to wholeness will in fact ensure that the circle is never ever broken.

There are some opportunities to learn from African-centered scholars. They are scattered around the country and teach in various academic disciplines. There are also programs at a few universities that are well respected, including the African Studies Program at Temple University and the Africana Studies Program at Howard University. The National Association of Black Social Workers Academy for Africa-Centered Social Work is a year-long study program where students learn from a collection of African-centered social work scholars (Reid-Merritt, 2010).

About this book

This book provides a critical analysis of many of the common interventions used in psychotherapy and mental health services when working with populations that experienced trauma, through the lens of multiple African-centered core values (Kambon, 2012). Each chapter is unique in its approach to critiquing existing clinical models. The authors are very creative in their critiques and applications, using their own area of expertise as the skill, population, or social problem to demonstrate the African-centered application. While the urban experience is the contextual framework for offering the analysis, the approaches discussed here can be used in any environment.

There is a focus on diverse communities and experiences of people of African ancestry; the authors consider individual and community experiences more openly and broadly. The book can be used broadly. It is useful for any practice/direct service course at both the undergraduate and graduate levels. It can be useful as a supplement for clinical courses. In addition, it is a good resource for practitioners, as it has case studies, activities, and assignments designed for both students and clients. It is not limited to social workers; it is useful for psychologists, counselors, and other mental health professionals, as well as a training tool for direct service models for students and staff.

The editors have made an effort not to box in anyone's ideas. So, readers will see varied language that can be used in many cases interchangeably, for example: holistic and wholistic; African-centered, Afrocentric, Africentric, and Afracentric; Black, African American, Caribbean, Afro Caribbean, and African. You will also see ideas, concepts, values, and principles used differently from chapter to chapter. After all, the experiences of African people throughout the diaspora are diverse and vast, there is no one way to approach healing, wellness, and what it means to be whole without celebrating the uniqueness of individual and collective experiences. And, the best approach is always the one that works and leaves people with their own sense of self and power.

Terms such as race, racism, oppression, vicarious, spirituality, cultural sensitivity, ethical practice, NTU, intersectionality, poverty, MAAT, *Nguzo Saba*, racial profiling, rites of passage, new slavery, sacred spaces, healing centered, legacy, and others will be key to understanding the implication of this book for empowered clinical practice.

The hope is to challenge those who say they are interested in helping Black populations to use knowledge, values, and skills that embrace the wholeness of who African people are, no matter where they are in the universe. There should not be a struggle to coexist in the world with differentness. In fact, much of what is known about core African values is that they are wholistic in nature and can be applied to people from all cultural backgrounds. Now is the time in human history for introspective-civility to be understood, practiced, and celebrated.

References

Ani, M. (1994). *Yurugu: An African-centered critique of European cultural thought and behavior.* Trenton, NJ: African World Press.

Ani, M. (2004). *Let the circle be unbroken: The implications of African spirituality in the diaspora.* New York, NY: Nkonimfo Publication.

Asante, M. K. (1991). The Afrocentric idea in education. *The Journal of Negro Education, 60*(2), 170–180.

Bent-Goodley, T. B., Fairfax, C. N., & Carlton-LaNey, I. (2017). The significance of African- centered social work for social work practice. *Human Behavior in the Social Environment, 27*(1–2), 1–6. https://doi.org/10.1080/10911359.2016.1273682

Bent-Goodley, T. B., & Rodgers, S. T. (2018, October). What social workers do during difficult times. *Social Work, 63*(4), 293–296. https://doi.org/10.1093/sw/swy035

Briere, J., & Jordan, C. E. (2004). Violence against women: Outcome complexity and implications for assessment and treatment. *Journal of Interpersonal Violence, 19*(11), 1252–1276.

Carlton-LaNey, I. (1999). African American social work pioneers' response to need. *Social Work, 44*(4), 311–321.

Fairfax, C. N. (2020). The need to be. *Phylon (1960–)*, *57*(1), 56–75.

Farley, R., & Frey, W. H. (1994). Changes in the segregation of whites from blacks during the 1980s: Small steps toward a more integrated society. *American Sociological Review*, 23–45.

Gallman, B. K., Ani, M., & Williams, L. O. (2003). *To be African*. Snellville, GA: M.A.A.T., Inc.

Graham, M. (2005). An African-centered paradigm for psychological and spiritual healing. *Integrating Traditional Healing Practices into Counseling and Psychotherapy*, 210–233.

Harvey, A. R. (2018). *A reader of Afri-centric theory and practice: Philosophical and Humanistic writings of Aminifu R. Harvey*. Chicago, IL: Third World Press Foundation.

Kambon, K. K. (1992). *The African personality in America: An African-centered framework*. Tallahassee, FL: Nubian Nation Publications.

Kambon, K. K. (2012). *African/Black psychology in the American context: An African-centered approach*. Tallahassee, FL: Nubian Nation Publications.

Karenga, M., & Karenga, T. (2007). The Nguzo Saba and the Black family. *Black Families*, 7–28.

Lindblad-Goldberg, M., & Dukes, J. L. (1985). Social support in black, low-income, single-parent families: Normative and dysfunctional patterns. *American Journal of Orthopsychiatry*, *55*(1), 42–58.

Martin, E. P., & Martin, J. M. (2002). *Spirituality and the Black helping tradition in social work*. Washington, DC: NASW Press.

Reid-Merritt, P. (2010). *Righteous self-determination: The Black social work movement in American*. Imprint Edition. Baltimore, MD: Black Classic Press.

Schiele, J. H. (1996). Afrocentricity: An emerging paradigm in social work practice. *Social Work*, *41*(3), 284–294.

Wallis, J. (2016). *America's original sin: Racism, white privilege, and the bridge to a new America*. Ada, MI: Brazos Press.

Waters, H. R., Hyder, A. A., Rajkotia, Y., Basu, S., & Butchart, A. (2005). The costs of interpersonal violence – An international review. *Health Policy*, *73*(3), 303–315.

Wells-Wilbon, R., Jones, K., & Rich, T. (2016). Mental and emotional wellness among African Americans in urban environments: What do we know? How can we improve outcomes? In R. Wells-Wilbon, A. R. McPhatter, & H. F. Vakalahi (Eds.), *Social work practice with African Americans in urban environments*. New York, NY: Springer Publishing Company.

Wells-Wilbon, R., McPhatter, A. R., & Vakalahi, H. F. (Eds.). (2016). *Social work practice with African Americans in urban environments*. New York, NY: Springer Publishing Company.

Williams, T. M. (2009). *Black pain: It just looks like we're not hurting*. New York, NY: Simon and Schuster.

Yoshioka, M. R., & Choi, D. Y. (2005). Culture and interpersonal violence research: Paradigm shift to create a full continuum of domestic violence services. *Journal of Interpersonal Violence*, *20*(4), 513–519.

PART 2

Conceptualizing urban practice and mental health

2

LIVING WHILE BLACK

The psychophysiological health implications of vicarious racial trauma

Terra L. Bowen-Reid, Ingrid K. Tulloch

Acknowledgment: This work was supported in part by NIH-NIGMS ASCEND BUILD Student Training Grant # 5TL4GM118974–05 and Faculty Development Core Grant # RL5GM 118972 awarded to Morgan State University. The content is solely the responsibility of the authors and does not necessarily represent the official views of the National Institutes of Health.

The health status of Black/African Americans warrants critical attention in identifying those barriers and prevention strategies to improve their quality of life and life span. Consistent reports show that race and ethnicity are important risk markers for underlying health conditions and mortality (CDC, 2020; Frank, 2007; Chen et al., 2020). Blacks/African Americans, Hispanics/Latinx, and Native Americans share the burden of the nation's leading physical, psychological, and social problems (CDC, 2020). Uncovering meaningful solutions and prevention strategies to mitigate racial/health disparities must move beyond the myopic representations of race-based theories and socioeconomic determinants.

A significant segment of biomedical and social science research has applied a race-comparative paradigm to explain Black–white health differences (e.g., Cockerham, Baldry, Hambry, Shikany, & Bae, 2017; Hogarth, 2019. This perspective suggests that Blacks are a monolithic group, while rarely utilizing a theoretical framework that addresses the unique cultural experiences of people of African descent. The preferred race-comparative approach assumes that African Americans and Euro-Americans share a similar sociocultural reality or universal human experience. Although there are some shared similarities between racial/ethnic groups, the cultural and historical experiences of African Americans have outcomes that are significantly different from that of their white counterparts. Subsequently, any concerted attempt to understand and improve the health status of Blacks must consider the historical context that has perpetuated damaging ideologies about innate race differences (Hogarth, 2019).

DOI: 10.4324/9780429276613-4

Overview of Black American mental health

For over 400 years, the mental health of Blacks has been under attack. The magnanimous effects of the *Maafa* (also known as the African Holocaust) and the enslavement of African people cannot be underestimated. Some mental health practitioners and researchers recognize the deep-rooted scarring of the enslavement era that has resulted in conditions referred to as post-traumatic slave disorder/ syndromes (PTSD/S) (DeGruy, 2017; Halloran, 2018; Kambon, 2012). PTSD/S represent the residual traumatic effects of African enslavement through the intergenerational transmission and perpetuation of systemic racism, hostile race relations, and oppression (DeGruy, 2017; Halloran, 2018; Kambon, 2012). This disorder or syndrome provides one contextual understanding of the etiology of Blacks' maladaptive behaviors (e.g., abuse, anger, destructive outlook, skin bias, n-word usage, etc.) that emanated from experiences endured from the middle passage, centuries of enslavement into modern-day racial trauma and injustices (DeGruy, 2017).

Despite historical and anecdotal evidence supporting the relationship between PTSD/S and African Americans' mental health conditions (DeGruy, 2017; Halloran, 2018), there is no clinical diagnosis of such disorders or syndromes in the *Diagnostic and Statistical Manual of Mental Disorders* (*DSM*). PTSD/S are often unrecognized, misdiagnosed, and poorly understood in mainstream clinical settings compared to the *DSM* description and definition of post-traumatic stress disorder. This exclusion may be attributed to several factors, such as lack of awareness and cultural competency among mental health practitioners and few, if any, validated assessments of PTSD/S (Williams, Metzger, Leins, & DeLapp, 2018).

Role of race and systemic racism on Black mental health

Racism is like a mutant virus that evolves in different toxic forms. One of the most insidious forms of racism is systemic or structural racism that permeates every facet of institutional practices, public policies, and cultural norms. Systematic racism provides a contextual framework for how social determinants can lead to diminished health, life spans, and higher mortality rates among Blacks (O'Brien, Neman, Seltzer, Evans, & Venkataramani, 2020). Systemic racism is defined as "the foundational, large-scale and inescapable hierarchical system of U.S. racial oppression devised and maintained by whites and directed at people of color" (cited in Feagin & Elias, 2013, p. 936). At a fundamental level, systemic racism denies Blacks and other minorities similar opportunities, privileges, access, and rewards offered to white Americans (Feagin, 1999).

The connotation of race is at the root of systemic racism. The major proxy of race is characterized by phenotypic characteristics, such as skin color, facial features, and hair texture. Beyond the scope of this chapter, disparaging treatment of Blacks based on skin color, or what some scholars refer to as colorism, is well documented (see Guthrie, 1998). From the time of slavery, race was conceptualized and emerged as a social construct encompassing a sociopolitical power structure to maintain the status quo and legacy of inferiority among people of African descent. The popular societal belief, however, purports that different races are due to biogenetic differences. Scientific evidence supports that race is a dynamic, malleable, and socially constructed concept (Richeson & Sommers, 2016). The Human Genome Project examined three billion base pairs of genetic letters in humans that were 99.9 percent identical in every person (Collins, Green, Guttmacher, & Guyer, 2003). Sequence comparisons between humans and other organisms were used to identify regions of similarity and differences and provide clues about specific gene structures and functions (Collins et al., 2003).

This research shows that there is no "Black race gene" or "white race gene." Genes linked to specific cultural groups indicate that a particular gene variant appears in a quantified detectable frequency in a particular geographic region rather than a specific race (Chou, 2017). Greater racial differences are evident within, rather than between, racial groupings. Nonetheless, race is often used as a way of categorizing individuals into distinct homogenous groupings. The stratification of races serves as a convenient tool to rationalize unwarranted and strategic biases against people of color. Characterizing one's attributes based on the superficial designation of race remains a significant problem for Blacks in the United States, who are more likely to experience racial profiling, police brutality, and fatality due to unsubstantiated assumptions associated with the color of their skin (Alang, McAlphine, McCreedy, & Hardeman, 2017; Monk, 2018).

Vicarious racial trauma on Black mental health

The implicit and explicit biases associated with race continue to be weaponized in the treatment of Blacks. Among the institutions that have threatened, demoralized, and extinguished many African Americans' lives and rights is the criminal justice system, especially law enforcement (Waxman, 2017). The devaluing of Black lives has led to a vicious cycle of violence, abusive, and racist practices in police practices. The disparities seen in the over-policing of Black communities, excessive police violence, and harsher outcomes of interactions with police is indicative of the pervasive cycle of systemic racism embedded in the cultural fabric of this country. Further research efforts are warranted to examine the link between PTSD/S and multigenerational exposure to structural violence and psychological malice toward Blacks in this country. One factor of particular concern related to PTSD/S is the enduring trauma of repeatedly experiencing and witnessing the deaths of innocent Black citizens at the hands of police (DeGruy, 2017).

Research across multiple disciplines has documented the disparaging treatment and racist police practices toward African Americans. Police are more likely to stop, harass, and interrogate Black citizens more than their white counterparts (e.g., Pierson et al., 2020). Excessive and deadly force are common forms of behavioral compliance methods used with Black suspects. Evidence shows "Black Americans account for 24 percent of those fatally shot and killed by the police despite being just 13 percent of the U. S. population" (Lowery, 2016), and unarmed Blacks are five times more likely to be shot and killed by a police officer. The highest risk of death by police officers is more frequent with Black boys and men. Young Black men are 9 times more likely than other Americans to be killed by police officers (Alang et al., 2017). Another recent study found that "people of color face a higher likelihood of being killed by police than do white men and women, that risk peaks in young adulthood, and that men of color face a nontrivial lifetime risk of being killed by police" (Edwards, Lee, & Esposito, 2019).

Abusive policing of Black communities has only amplified the incidence of vicarious community violence (Lipscomb et al., 2019). These experiences are hypothesized to have significant mental and behavioral health consequences for victims. In witnessing racially traumatic events, Blacks intuitively self-identify with the victim. For example, following the fatal shooting of Trayvon Martin, former President Barack Obama made a comment that "If I had a son, he'd look like Trayvon. When I think about this boy, I think about my own kids" (Tau, 2012). For some Black individuals, the sensationalized police killings may signify another tragic death of a Black man. Many, however, may internalize the tragedy, whereby they are psychologically traumatized with searing fatalistic thoughts and nightmares about another killing. The harrowing experience of these racially traumatic events permeates the psyche in a way that can potentially alter the cognitive schema. Although community violence as a construct is well studied in the literature, it is less explored in terms of the long-term psychological and physiological consequences and its relationship to past, current, and vicarious exposure to police violence toward Black individuals.

Racially traumatic incidents are defined as a significant clinical construct of incidents that lead to distress or profound sense of danger related to real or perceived experiences due to one's race (Bryant-Davis & Ocampo, 2006). Self-report studies suggest that experiences of racial trauma are correlated with an increase of psychological and physical symptoms in Blacks (e.g., Comas-Diaz, Hall, & Neville, 2019). Those experiencing racial trauma exhibit psychological symptoms, such as anxiety, hypervigilance to threat, or hopelessness. Consequently, racially charged stimuli can affect general cognitive functioning. Tran's (2012) research suggests that a range of race-related stimuli has the potential to induce emotional stress, and in turn, heavily draw on an individual's limited cognitive resources.

Physiological implications of vicarious racial trauma

Vicarious exposure to racial trauma can be a chronic stressor in the lives of Black people that affects physical outcomes. Earlier research has found that African Americans exhibit distinct patterns of physiological arousal and an increase in negative emotions when encountering racist stimuli (e.g., Bowen-Reid & Harrell, 2002; Harrell, Hall, & Taliaferro, 2003). Physiological responses to stress are caused by neuroendocrine activity. According to Lundberg (2005), in response to stress the body's adrenal gland releases stress chemicals called epinephrine and cortisol. Accelerated heart rate, blood pressure, tense muscles, sweating/diaphoresis, and increased respiratory rate are additional short-term physical "fight or flight" responses to stress (Goldstein, 2010).

Repeated stress is considered a threat to the homeostasis of one's body. Homeostasis is a necessary process for maintaining normal bodily functions, such as glucose, temperature, blood pressure, pH levels, and clearing toxins among other functions (McEwen & Stellar, 1993). The frequent stressful encounters of the body and its corresponding fight or flight response then affects homeostasis because it shifts from organ systems' maintenance to vigilance and protection from external threats. The frequent triggering of stress responses is called allostasis or allostatic loading. Allostatic loading is "the cost of chronic exposure to fluctuating or heightened neural or neuroendocrine response resulting from repeated or chronic environmental challenges that an individual reacts to as being particularly stressful" (McEwen & Stellar, 1993). Ultimately, allostasis can further alter vascular function, leading to conditions like high blood pressure, stroke, cognitive dysfunction, and cardiac arrests (Juster, McEwen, & Lupien, 2010).

In the case of racial stressors, the body will continue to release stress hormones. As the frequency of these racial stressors increases, the body's healthy response to stress weakens, which is reflected in emotional desensitization as organ systems begin to deteriorate (Duru et al., 2012; Mrug, Madan, Cook, & Wright, 2015). Blood pressure and heart rate have been used as biomarkers to further understand the physiological response to violent stimuli (Harrell et al., 2003; Mrug et al., 2015). Increasingly, immune biomarker levels are reported to correlate with anxiety, depression, and suicide and hypothesized to be impacted by traumatic racial stressors (Santoft et al., 2020).

Inflammatory cytokines are immune molecules and a possible biological mechanism by which racial trauma might affect mental health. These small signaling proteins are released in response to any stressor (Gulati, Guhathakurta, Joshi, Rai, & Ray, 2016). Notably, racial stress, such as witnessing and experiencing police brutality, racial profiling, being called racial slurs, and public racial humiliation, can elicit cytokine release as part of the previously mentioned short-term physiological responses (Utsey et al., 2013). Subsequent cytokine releases are likely to play a pathophysiological role in long-term effects and poor health outcomes, as they are associated with many health conditions disproportionately affecting Blacks and other marginalized individuals in the United States (Phillips, Park, Robinson, & Jones, 2020).

As Black Americans increasingly fall victim to discriminatory and racially stressful practices, this further compounds the allostatic load. While there are many external factors affecting allostatic load, exposure to vicarious racial trauma might place Blacks at a higher risk for health disparities, such as the prevalence of morbidity due to aging-related neurological and cardiovascular diseases. Studies of allostatic loading suggest a variety of emotional and physiological reactions to violent or traumatizing media. These reactions include heart rate, blood pressure, respiration, and galvanic skin response (GSR) changes (e.g., Brumbaugh, Kothuri, Marci, Siefert, & Pfaff, 2013). GSR is skin conductance of electrodermal activity due to variation of electrical resistance across two regions of the skin. GSR is also a rapid response during mental, physical, and emotional arousal (Keil et al., 2008). Low emotional arousal or GSR response to stimuli suggests emotional desensitization; however, few studies explicitly include race-based vicarious violence as a correlate of GSR.

Research gap

A necessity for increasing empirical evidence among understudied demographics most affected by vicarious racial trauma is to study students of color who might be at greater risk. Social media platforms are heavily and most often used by Black youth and young adults to vehemently speak out against police abuse and racial injustice. In many instances, young Black viewers are of similar age and can self-identify with the assaulted or murdered victims. Consequently, there is an aspect of watching these racially traumatic videos that might be commonly overlooked: What are the lingering psychological and physiological implications of watching these racially traumatic events on social media or other media platforms?

To address this question, a series of studies were conducted at a historically Black college and university (HBCU) in the mid-Atlantic region. Each of the investigations assessed participants' health status, mood, and physiological reactions to racially motivated police violence. Previous studies suggest that elevated blood pressure responses may be possible indicators for future cardiovascular and cognitive dysfunction (Bowen-Reid & Harrell, 2002; Mrug et al., 2015) and cognitive decline (De Menezes et al., 2021). Therefore, it is critical to identify specific factors that alter these responses. The following two studies briefly describe empirical efforts to assess the psychophysiological implications of vicarious racial trauma.

Study 1

Approximately 60 Black female undergraduate students were recruited from a HBCU to study psychophysiological reactions to social situations. Past studies have found that males have higher blood pressures than females, especially before age 50 (Reckelhoff, 2001). Given this extraneous factor, only females were targeted in Study 1. Informed consent and a prescreening survey were taken before starting the experimental condition. Each participant was positioned in a recliner chair with an appropriately sized blood pressure cuff attached to the left arm brachial artery and seated in front of a laptop monitor. Before exposure to the video stimulus, the participant engaged in a three-minute guided meditation to reduce the blood pressure and heart rate to resting levels. Participants were then shown one of two videos of police officers shooting either 1) a Black victim or 2) a white victim. Participants' cardiovascular responses were taken at two intervals: 1) during viewership of the 60-seconds video clip and 2) following a second resting period. The videos were real-life occurrences of incidents shown on social media. Prior viewership was controlled. Data were also collected on self-reports of mood, post-traumatic stress symptoms, perceptions of racial stress, and sociodemographic characteristics.

Findings revealed significant cardiovascular reactivity from resting to each video stimulus. Subsequently, there were no significant psychological or physiological differences between the two video conditions. The findings might suggest habituation or desensitization, as the race of the victim did not seem to play a factor in reactivity. Participants displayed similar reactions to each traumatic event. Other findings showed that increased social media consumption was associated with higher self-reports of post-traumatic stress symptoms and bodily alarm response, which is how the body naturally reacts to stressors.

Study 2

Approximately 63, primarily Black female (approximately 90.7%) participants were recruited from the same population in Study 1. After providing informed consent, participants completed a community violence exposure survey. Participants performed a relaxed breathing exercise followed by pre-video blood pressure and GSR measurements similar to Study 1. Participants then viewed one of two randomly assigned video stimuli taken from a documentary film on violence. The vicarious trauma video consisted of a two-minute video clip depicting assaults by groups of Black and Hispanic men as police lights and sirens blared in the background. It ended with the same men running from the police. The neutral video of the same length consisted of a narrator discussing violence but without police or any violence shown. Blood pressure (BP) and GSR measurements were then taken post-video along with a mood assessment. Although less than half of the participants reported high levels (>35 events) of prior community violence exposure, a significant proportion of the sample experienced some level of community violence associated with trauma. Participants who viewed the neutral video and had relatively lower community violence exposure had the highest positive emotion scores. These participants also had the highest negative affect scores as expected for participants who are not desensitized to the violence. Participants with high levels of past community violence had a lower negative emotion score, as would be expected if they were desensitized. These differences were only marginal when statistically analyzed using a two-way ANOVA $(p = .051)$. The physiological outcomes revealed desensitization responses (lowered BP) only for diastolic blood pressure (DBP).

All participants in the vicarious trauma condition (violent video) had lower post-video DBP than participants in the neutral video condition. The lowest post-video DBP observed were for participants with high prior community violence exposure and who viewed the vicarious violence video. Taken together, the findings suggest that cardiovascular and emotionally desensitized responses to vicarious violence occurred among individuals with prior violent trauma experiences.

Summary

The current investigations suggest that individuals exposed to traumatic events exhibit distinct cardiovascular reactivity from a resting state. An immediate sign of stress response activation is raised BP and heart rate (McEwen, 1993). Although these reactions to trauma are normal, prolonged physiological arousal is harmful because the body seeks homeostasis by downregulating the normal activation response (Juster et al., 2010). Furthermore, the amygdala, which alerts your body that it is under attack, cannot distinguish between actual and perceived events (Siever, 2008). These processes are believed to underlie the dysregulated responses to perceived threats observed in post-traumatic stress disorder (Ousdal et al., 2020).

Contrary to a prediction of Study 1 that suggested Black participants would identify and show more exaggerated responses to the Black victim compared to the white victim, there were no discriminant differences in psychological and physiological responses between the races of the victim experiencing the traumatic event in the video. For Black viewers, exaggerated cardiovascular reactivity was exhibited across conditions. The Social Identity Theory provides one explanation for this finding. The Social Identity Theory posits that individuals connect to others based on their membership in social groups (Tajfel et al., 1979), in this case, the status of the victim. This theory is predictive of socially influenced changes in physiological states, subjective emotions, cognitions, and behavior.

In Study 2, GSR did not differ from controls as predicted, and heart rate effects were not exaggerated. The lack of reactivity might be attributed to desensitization or a form of amygdala habituation (the change over time in response to repeated stimuli) (Kim et al., 2019). Since police violence is deemed a normal occurrences, Black and Brown individuals may show less physical and emotional energy to the situation (Calvert, Brady, & Jones-Webb, 2020). Individuals repeatedly exposed to media depiction of violence by and against Black and Brown individuals might cognitively interpret the videos as the norm. Consequently, this decreased reactivity is reflective of an unconscious avoidant coping style, which is predictive of poorer mental health and low survival after heart failure (Fang, Chung, & Wang, 2020). If cognitive appraisal conforms to expected outcomes, then less dramatic arousal during the acute phase of the response will result (Alhurani et al., 2018), similar to what was observed in both studies. Given that multiple factors influence defense mechanisms or specific types of cognitive appraisals and coping with a threatening stimulus, the consequences are not always direct or immediately observable.

Whether actual or perceived, the magnitude of vicarious racial trauma might be greater than what is articulated. There are limited data on police violence and killings due to inconsistent documentation and longitudinal follow-up for victims (Nix, 2020). The short- and long-term causal effects of these traumas on the pathophysiological mechanisms that lead to adverse health consequences for Blacks require additional studies because racial violence might influence those outcomes (e.g., Woodson, Hives, & Sanders-Phillips, 2010). Given these issues, it is difficult to understand the true impact of racial trauma among African Americans in this country. Longitudinal studies and experimental research designs are further needed to support interventions and policy. Assessing the cognitive, behavioral, and physiological outcomes with these study designs might provide convincing evidence of the causal psychophysiological mechanisms by which viral viewing of racial trauma lead to mental and physical health disparities.

Investigations of immediate and long-term responses to potentially traumatic stimuli are further needed. Acute and long-term measures of inflammatory cytokines levels and cognitive behavioral responses that account for personality factors should be examined. These types of outcome measurements would reflect the multifaceted nature of how race-based trauma likely affects short- and long-term mental health outcomes. Additionally, empirical assessments of cultural and other psychosocial factors that can mitigate these effects are warranted because desensitization to violence might cause or exacerbate health risks (Mrug et al., 2015).

Conclusion

We conclude this chapter with implications for practice, research, and policy. Understanding the varied methods by which Blacks/African Americans experience race-based injustices and their mental health consequences necessitate a transdisciplinary approach to research and practice. It is near impossible to avoid exposure to racial violence living while Black in the United States. Media sources will continue to sensationalize and repeatedly present images of violence in cities with significant Black populations. Traumatically violent encounters against members of the Black community are not only shared via news reports and documentaries but also repeatedly re-shared on social media. The two studies briefly described in the chapter explicitly depicted or implied police encounters. This is just one type of traumatizing experience. Laboratory evidence, however, should be interpreted with caution. Real-life experiences will yield stronger reactions. Nonetheless, the current evidence adds to the research and theoretical considerations on the implications of experiencing vicarious racial trauma.

Black mental health consequences due to racial trauma necessitates a multidimensional approach to mitigating its effects. Empirical research that informs practice and policy must focus on understanding the scope of the problem across multiple domains: behavioral, cognitive, emotional, physiological, and social. Increases in use of existing interventions that are protective or enhance resilience are also needed. Effective interventions must also incorporate knowledge from culturally relevant trauma-informed research (Blitz, Anderson, & Saastamoinen, 2016). We further advance that research and testing of culturally relevant, trauma-informed biopsychosocial interventions must inform policy that increases mental health care access for Black individuals. It is hoped that such policies in a nation steeped in repeated actual and vicarious trauma can authentically address the mental health consequences associated with race-based violence.

References

Alang, S., McAlpine, D., McCreedy, E., & Hardeman, R. (2017). Police brutality and Black health: Setting the agenda for public health scholars. *American Journal of Public Health*, *107*(5), 662–665. https://doi.org/10.2105/AJPH.2017.303691.

Alhurani, A. S., Dekker, R., Ahmad, M., Miller, J., Yousef, K. M., Abdulqader, B., . . . Moser, D. K. (2018). Stress, cognitive appraisal, coping, and event free survival in patients with heart failure. *Heart & Lung: The Journal of Critical Care, 47*(3), 205–210. https://doi.org/10.1016/j.hrtlng.2018.03.008

Blitz, L. V., Anderson, E. M., & Saastamoinen, M. (2016). Assessing perceptions of culture and trauma in an elementary school: Informing a model for culturally responsive trauma-informed schools. *Urban Review, 48*, 520–542. https://doi-org.proxy-ms.researchport.umd.edu/10.1007/s11256-016-0366-9

Bowen-Reid, T. L., & Harrell, J. P. (2002). Racist experiences and health outcomes: An examination of spirituality as a buffer. *Journal of Black Psychology, 28*(1), 18–36. https://doi.org/10.1177/00957984020280012.

Brumbaugh, C. C., Kothuri, R., Marci, C., Siefert, C., & Pfaff, D. D. (2013). Physiological correlates of the big 5: Autonomic responses to video presentations. *Applied Psychophysiology and Biofeedback, 38*(4), 293–301. https://doi.org/10.1007/s10484-013-9234-5

Bryant-Davis, T., & Ocampo, C. (2006). A therapeutic approach to the treatment of racist-incident-based trauma. *Journal of Emotional Abuse, 6*(4), 1–22. https://doi.org/10.1300/j135v06n04_01.

Calvert, C. M., Brady, S. S., & Jones-Webb, R. (2020). Perceptions of violent encounters between police and young Black men across stakeholder groups. *Journal of Urban Health, 97*, 279–295. https://doi.org/10.1007/s11524-019-00417-6

Center for Disease Control. (2020). *CDC in review.* Department of Health and Human Services. Retrieved from www.cdc.gov/media/releases/2020/p1229-cdc-2020-review.html

Chen, Y., Freedman, N. D., Rodriquez, E. J., Shiels, M. S., Napoles, A. M., Withrow, D. R., . . . Berrington de González, A. (2020). Trends in premature deaths among adults in the United States and Latin America. *JAMA Network Open, 3*(2), e1921085. doi: 0.1001/jamanetworkopen.2019.21085. PMID: 32049297; PMCID: PMC8268086.

Chou, V. (2017, April 17). *How science and genetics are reshaping the race debate of the 21st century.* Retrieved from https://sitn.hms.harvard.edu/flash/2017/science-genetics-reshaping-race-debate-21st-century/

Cockerham, W. C., Baldry, S., Hambry, B. W., Shikany, J. M., & Bae, S. A. (2017). A comparison of Black and White racial differences in health lifestyles and cardiovascular disease. *American Journal of Prevention Medicine, 52*(1S1), 56–62. https://doi.org/10.1016/j.amepre.2016.09.019

Collins, F., Green, E., Guttmacher, A., & Guyer, M. S. (2003). A vision for the future of genomics research. *Nature, 42*, 835–847. https://doi.org/10.1038/nature01626

Comas-Diaz, L., Hall, G., N., & Neville, H. A. (2019). Racial trauma: Theory, research, and healing: Introduction to the special issue. Special issue of *American Psychologist, 74*(1), 1–5.

DeGruy, J. D. (2017). *Post-traumatic slave syndrome: America's legacy of enduring injury and healing.* Milwaukie, OR: Uptown Press.

De Menezes, S. T., Giatti, L., Brant, L., Griep, R. H., Schmidt, M. I., Duncan, B. B., . . . Barreto, S. M. (2021). Hypertension, prehypertension, and hypertension control: Association with decline in cognitive performance in the ELSA-Brasil cohort. *Hypertension (Dallas, Tex.: 1979), 77*(2), 672–681. https://doi.org/10.1161/HYPERTENSIONAHA.120.16080

Duru, O. K., Harawa, N. T., Kermah, D., & Norris, K. C. (2012). Allostatic load burden and racial disparities in mortality. *Journal of the National Medical Association, 104*(1–2), 89–95. https://doi.org/10.1016/s0027-9684(15)30120-6

Edwards, F., Lee, H., & Esposito, M. (2019). Risk of being killed by police use of force in the United States by age, race-ethnicity, and sex. *Proceedings of the National Academy of Sciences of the United States of America, 116*(34), 16793–16798. https://doi.org/10.1073/pnas.1821204116

Fang, S., Chung, M. C., & Wang, Y. (2020). The Impact of past trauma on psychological distress: The roles of defense mechanisms and alexithymia. *Frontiers in Psychology*, *11*, 992. https://doi.org/10.3389/fpsyg.2020.00992

Feagin, J. (1999). Excluding Blacks and others from housing: The foundation of White racism. *Cityscape: A Journal of Policy Development and Research*, *4*(3), 79–91.

Feagin, J., & Elias, S. (2013). Rethinking racial formation theory: A systemic racism critique. *Ethnic and Racial Studies*, *36*(6), 931–960. Doi.org/10.1080/01419870.2012.669839.

Frank, R. (2007). What to make of it? The (Re) emergence of a biological conceptualization of race in health disparities research. *Social Science & Medicine*, *64*(10), 1977–1983. https://doi.org/10.1016/j.socscimed.2007.01.01.010

Goldstein, D. S. (2010). Adrenal responses to stress. *Cellular and Molecular Neurobiology*, *30*(8), 1433–1440. Doi.org/10.1007/s10571-010-9606-9.

Gulati, K., Guhathakurta, S., Joshi, J. C., Rai, N., & Ray, A. (2016). Cytokines and their Role in Health and Disease: A Brief Overview. *MedCrave Online Journal of Immunology*, *4*(2), 00121. https://doi.org/10.15406/MOJI.2016.04.00121

Guthrie, R. V. (1998). *Even the Rat was White: A Historical View of Psychology*. Boston: Allyn & Bacon.

Halloran, M. J. (2018). African American health and post traumatic slave syndrome: A terror management theory account. *Journal of Black Studies*, *50*(1), 45–65. https://doi.org/10.1177/0021934718803737

Harrell, J. P., Hall, S., & Taliaferro, J. (2003). Physiological responses to racism and discrimination: An assessment of the evidence. *American Journal of Public Health*, *93*(2), 243–248. https://doi.org/10.2105/ajph.93.2.243

Hogarth, R. A. (2019). The Myth of innate racial differences between White and Black people's bodies: Lessons from the 1793 yellow fever epidemic in Philadelphia, Pennsylvania. *American Journal of Public Health*, *109*, 1339–1341. https://doi.org/10.2105/AJPH.2019.305245

Juster, R., Mcewen, B. S., & Lupien, S. J. (2010). Allostatic load biomarkers of chronic stress and impact on health and cognition. *Neuroscience & Biobehavioral Reviews*, *35*(1), 2–16. https://doi.org/10.1016/j.neubiorev.2009.10.002

Kambon, K. K. (2012). *African/Black psychology in the American context: An African centered approach*. Tallahassee, FL: Nubian Nations Publications.

Keil, A., Smith, J. C., Wangelin, B. C., Sabatinelli, D., Bradley, M. M., & Lang, P. J. (2008). Electrocortical and electrodermal responses covary as a function of emotional arousal: A single-trial analysis. *Psychophysiology*, *45*(4), 516–523. https://doi.org/10.1111/j.1469-8986.2008.00667.x

Kim, J. Y., van Rooij, S., Ely, T. D., Fani, N., Ressler, K. J., Jovanovic, T., & Steven, J. S. (2019). Association between posttraumatic stress disorder severity and amygdala habituation to fearful stimuli. *Depress Anxiety*, *36*(7), 647–658. https://doi.org/10.1002/da.22928

Lipscomb, A. E., Emeka, M., Bracy, I., Stevenson, V., Lira, A., Gomez, Y. B., & Riggins, J. (2019). Black male hunting! A phenomenological study exploring the secondary impact of police induced trauma on the Black man's psyche in the United States. *Journal of Sociology*, *7*(1), 11–18.

Lowery, W. (2016, July 11). Aren't more white people than black people killed by police? Yes, but no. *The Washington Post. Online Edition*. Retrieved from www.washingtonpost.com/news/post-nation/wp/2016/07/11/arent-more-white-people-than-black-people-killed-by-police-yes-but-no

Lundberg, U. (2005). Stress hormones in health and illness: The roles of work and gender. *Psychoneuroendocrinology, 30*(10), 1017–1021. https://doi.org/10.1016/j.psyneuen.2005.03.014

McEwen, B., & Stellar, E. (1993). Stress and the individual. Mechanisms leading to disease. *Archives Internal Medicine.* https://doi.org/153:2093–2101

Monk, E. P. (2018). The color of punishment: African Americans, skin tone, and the criminal justice system, *Ethnic and Racial Studies*, 1–21. Doi.org/10.1080/01419870.2018.15 08736.

Mrug, S., Madan, A., Cook, E. W., 3rd, & Wright, R. A. (2015). Emotional and physiological desensitization to real-life and movie violence. *Journal of Youth and Adolescence, 44*(5), 1092–1108. https://doi.org/10.1007/s10964-014-0202-z

Nix, J. (2020). On the challenges associated with the study of police use of deadly force in the United States: A response to Schwartz & Jahn. *PloS One, 15*(7), e0236158. https://doi.org/10.1371/journal.pone.0236158

O'Brien, R., Neman, T., Seltzer, N., Evans, L., & Venkataramani, A. (2020). Structural racism, economic opportunity and racial health disparities: Evidence from U.S. counties. *SSM – Population Health, 11*(100564). IISSN 2352-8273. https://doi.org/10.1016/j.ssmph.2020.100564

Ousdal, O. T., Milde, A. M., Hafstad, G. S. Hodnelande, E., Dyb, G., Grave, A. R., . . . Hugdahl, K. (2020). The association of PTSD symptom severity with amygdala nuclei volumes in traumatized youths. *Translational Psychiatry, 10*(1), 288. https://doi.org/10.1038/s41398-020-00974-4

Phillips, N., Park, I. W., Robinson, J. R., & Jones, H. P. (2020). The perfect storm: COVID-19 health disparities in US Blacks. *Journal of Racial and Ethnic Health Disparities, 382*(26), 2534–2543. https://doi-org.proxy-ms.researchport.umd.edu/10.1007/s40615-020-00871-y

Pierson, E., Simiou, C., Overgoor, J., Corbett-Davies, S., Jenson, D., Shoemaker, A., . . . Goel, S. (2020). A large-scale analysis of racial disparities in police stops across the United States. *Nature Human Behaviour, 4*, 736–746. https://doi.org/10.1038/s41562-020-0858-1

Reckelhoff, J. F. (2001). Gender differences in the regulation of blood pressure. *Hypertension, 37*(5), 1199–1208. https://doi.org/10.1161/01.hyp.37.5.1199

Richeson, J. A., & Sommers, S. R. (2016). Toward a social psychology of race and race relations for the twenty-first century. *Annual Review of Psychology, 67*, 439–463. https://doi.org/10.1146/annurev-psych-010213-115115

Santoft, F., Hedman-Lagerlöf, E., Salomonsson, S., Lindsäter, E., Ljótsson, B., Kecklund, G., . . . Andreasson, A. (2020). Inflammatory cytokines in patients with common mental disorders treated with cognitive behavior therapy. *Brain, Behavior, & Immunity – Health, 3.* Published. https://doi.org/10.1016/j.bbih.2020.100045

Siever, L. J. (2008). Neurobiology of aggression and violence. *The American Journal of Psychiatry, 165*(4), 429–442. https://doi.org/10.1176/appi.ajp.2008.07111774

Tajfel, H., Turner, J. C., Austin, W. G., & Worchel, S. (1979). An integrative theory of intergroup conflict. *Organizational Identity: A Reader*, 56–65.

Tau, B. (2012). *Obama: 'If I had a son, he'd look like Trayvon' Politico Blog.* Retrieved January 15, 2021, from https//politico44/2012/03/bama-if-i-had-a-son-hed-look-like-trayvon-118439

Tran, G-T. (2012). *"What's the big deal?": Recognition of racism and impairment of cognitive functioning.* Retrieved from the University of Minnesota Digital Conservancy. https://hdl.handle.net/11299/139704

Utsey, S. O., Belvet, B., Hubbard, R. R., Fischer, N. L., Opare-Henaku, A., & Gladney, L. L. (2013). Development and validation of the prolonged activation and anticipatory race-related stress scale. *Journal of Black Psychology, 6*, 532.

Waxman, O. B. (2017). *The history of police in America and the first force.* Retrieved from http://time.com/4779112/police-history-origins/

Williams, M. T., Metzger, I. W., Leins, C., & DeLapp, C. (2018). Assessing racial trauma within a DSM-5 framework: The Uconn Racial/Ethnic Stress & Trauma Survey. *Practice Innovations, 3*(4), 242–260. https://doi.org/10.1037/pri0000076

Woodson, K. M., Hives, C., & Sanders-Phillips, K. (2010). Violence exposure and health related risk among African American adolescent female detainees: A strategy for reducing recidivism. *Journal of Offender Rehabilitation, 49*(8), 571–584. https://doi.org/10.108 0/10509674.2010.519669

3

SACRED SPACES

Spirituality as a healing-centered modality for trauma in urban communities

Kevin Daniels, Georgia Jennings-Dorsey

The history of exposure to trauma of African American people living in the United States, particularly in urban environments, is not a new phenomenon. Since the cruel and brutal system of chattel slavery because of Eurocentric domination starting in the 17th century, it has been well documented that historical trauma has been a persistent epistemological theme to navigate for African Americans and people of color (Martin & Martin, 2002; Sefa Dei, 2017; Turner & Neville, 2020). Subsequently, the taxonomy of trauma categories, whether acute, chronic, or complex, impinged upon the totality of African American life has also been empirically studied, particularly as it also relates to the social determinants of health such as economic stability, neighborhood and physical environment, education, food, and access to healthy options, community, and social context, and the health care system (Archibald & Daniels, 2013; Daniels, Akers, Smith & Archibald, 2015). Moreover, with the recent rise of the COVID-19 pandemic in the United States that has been impacting multiple ethnic groups worldwide, it has further exacerbated trauma categories in the lives of African American people, especially living in urban communities. However, according to recent studies, it has left many to further and deeply reengage in the Afrocentric worldview of spirituality not only as a modality of healing but also for consciousness centering and stability (Gecewicz, 2020b). This chapter will provide a brief history of trauma among African American people in the United States, address the current issue across the intergenerational life span, along with common social work and other interventions and practice models, while providing a critique of those models from an African-centered lens, specifically offering for consideration an adapted model for spirituality as a healing-centered modality.

DOI: 10.4324/9780429276613-5

Brief history (trauma and spirituality)

As previously stated, historical trauma in the lives of African American people is defined as a deep woundedness that directly and indirectly impact the bio-psycho-social-spiritual domain categories of a person and or specific targeted groups. This deep woundedness has existed through colonization to the present contemporary moment (Lincoln & Mamiya, 1990; Pinn, 2002).

Given those historical markers, African Americans have had to be resilient and navigate antebellum and emancipation; aftermath of 13th, 14th, 15th amendments; Jim Crow; Civil Rights (1960s); deindustrialization of urban cities leading toward urban decay (1970s); crack cocaine (1980s); crime bill (1990s), and continued present-day social injustices such as racial unrest, police brutality, voting irregularities, economic wealth gap; continued health epigenetic intergenerational developmental disparities, and the recent COVID-19 worldwide health pandemic (Braithwaite & Taylor, 2001; Gecewicz, 2020a).

However, according to the Afrocentric paradigm (Asante, 2011; Schiele, 2000) through all of these historical periods, and because of sociocultural uniqueness, collectivism, and specifically the uplift of spirituality, people of color have always leaned on the unseen to gain an axiological, epistemological, and philosophical worldview for both stability and sustainability in the world. According to Martin and Martin (2002) and Sanders-Thompson, Bazile, and Akbar (2004), spirituality has been a strategic part of the fight for African American's liberation in America through the *moaning* of a historical past, through the *mourning* of present circumstances, but also a *morning* toward reimagining of a future prospect.

Contemporary trauma and spirituality

Subsequently, the historical periods in America for African Americans have left a well-documented trail of tears of Adverse Childhood Experiences (ACEs) (Ellis & Deitz, 2017), Adverse Cultural Experiences and Adverse Community Experiences (Ellis & Deitz, 2017) across the intergenerational life span, specifically for those living in urban communities. The intergenerational neglect, environmental instability, and abuse are normally associated with further adverse risky health behaviors, challenging mental health status, decreased life potential, and other adverse childhood abnormalities that show intergenerational continuity (similarly across parents and offspring) – the impact on well-being and health can reverberate across generational life spans and the social determinants of health (Ellis & Deitz, 2017).

The recent worldwide pandemic of the SARS-CoV-2 virus that causes COVID-19 has exacerbated the ACE categories in claiming the lives of people worldwide, specifically African Americans. According to the Center for Disease Control and Prevention (2020a), the COVID-19 pandemic has further exacerbated the already underlying conditions for people of color, specifically for those living in urban communities – it has brought social and racial injustice and inequity to the fore-front of public health concern. Although African Americans make up 12.5% of the U.S. population, they accounted for over 37.5% of confirmed COVID-19 cases (Centers for Disease Control and Prevention [CDC], 2020b).

According to McPhatter (2016), the *urban environment is defined in social work* literature as specifically and historically settings where people of color tend to reside.

Contextually, those navigating urban environment must be culturally competent in the underlying:

- *Assumptions, beliefs, and principles* take into consideration that *race, ethnicity, culture, gender, disability, the language of origin*, and *sexual orientation matter* and,
- *The Eurocentric worldview of this country's structural oppression, classism, racism, internalized oppression, as well as strengths and resilience* must be considered for people of African descent in the practice of social work.
- *Even the urban social work practitioner* must be *culturally competent as well as equipped to navigate liberation models, strong awareness of African-centered perspective, and awareness of disparities, and empowerment advocacy.*

Subsequently, and at the time of this writing, the Trump Administration was engaging in a political feud with the Center for Disease Control's (CDC) around the public health scientific methods surrounding COVID-19 and guidelines for the nation, while many people are navigating an *existential crisis*. An *existential crisis* is moments when individuals question their worldview, identity, whether their lives have meaning, purpose, or value and question who is really concerned – it is the moment when people normally grapple with and ask the moral question, *"Where is God?"*

According to a recent Pew poll, 56% of African Americans said their faith in spirituality of an ever-present higher power guiding toward an imagined future has grown stronger as a result of the coronavirus pandemic (women were more likely than men and older adults more than younger people). As previously discussed, historically, African Americans have always intentionally leaned on their spirituality as a panacea during very segregated, unequal, and unfair trying times in this country – spirituality has also been a part of the indigenous framework of African people from its origins well beyond this country. For many, their faith toward higher spiritual values are more than just what some call a *"mythical and magical"* belief in something or someone – faith is substantive and leads to both action and praxis. Faith is a belief in something and someone you have *reliable and valid reasons* to believe exist, and faith is not in an argument with science, but compatible – science is a part of the creator's creation to be explored (Daniels, 2020; Gecewicz, 2020b). Because African Americans have a worldview that includes a strong spiritual conscious, helping and liberating modalities against trauma must give adequate consideration in interventions and practice models of recovery.

Current interventions and practice models

Many of the current clinical interventions (i.e., engagement, assessment, planning, interventions, and evaluations) and practice models surrounding trauma for African Americans in social work are somewhat inadequate to fully resolve the depth of historical and cumulative challenges holistically. The current general and often used clinical and community interventions to address trauma are (Turner & Neville, 2020):

- *Cognitive behavioral therapy (CBT)*
- *Crisis intervention*
- *Narrative*
- *Problem solving*
- *Solution-focused*
- *Task-Centered*
- *DSM-V religious and spiritual categories and interventions (V-code 62.89)*
    - In the DSM-V (V-code 62.89), four categories have been determined to be the focus of clinical attention, which are:
        - *Religious problems*
        - *Spiritual problems*
        - *Combined religious and spiritual problems*
        - *Overlap of religious/spiritual problem and DSM-V disorder*

These approaches, along with the DSM-V, and the recent book (*Religious and Spiritual Issues in Psychiatric Diagnosis – A Research Agenda for DSM-V*) address trauma categories such as the following.

- Criteria A (single exposure)
- Criteria B (re-experience/intrusions)
- Criteria C (avoidant symptoms)
- Criteria D (negative alterations in mood or cognition)
- Criteria E (increased arousal symptoms)
- Criteria F, G, H (subtype and dissociation, depersonalization, derealization)

However, very little attention is given to the depth of historical and cumulative trauma of African Americans in the United States or the depth of indigenous spiritual modalities necessary to address these levels of trauma (American Psychiatric Association, 2013; Canda & Furman, 2010; Peteet, Lu, & Narrow, 2011). As a matter of fact, instead of spirituality and religion being a primary focus of clinical treatment for African Americans, spiritual and religious categories and indigenous treatment modalities are usually assessed through the culturally formulated process but never given the kind of regulatory value as other major diagnoses within the social work profession – it is only billable within the scope of other major diagnosable areas within the DSM-V (Peteet, et al., 2011).

Further, according to Ginwright (2018), many of these interventions and practices utilize the *problem* as a starting point but not a *preventative* healing-centered modality; it encompasses being trauma-informed as a pathology (trauma) but never well-being as a possibility (well-being) beyond the problem – in other words, it focuses primarily on harm, injury, and trauma. It is deficit-based rather than asset-driven; it presumes trauma as an individual experience rather than a collective one and how to fully address the root causes. African indigenous modalities should focus on well-being rather than symptoms needing to suppress, built upon a person's experience, knowledge, skills, and curiosity as positive traits needing to be enhanced – spiritual in scope and scale (Ginwright, 2018; Mbiti, 1970; Sefa Dei, 2017). Consequently, *spirituality*, which is defined by Canda and Furman (2010) and Martin and Martin (2002) as a more universal reach toward the ultimate reality beyond space, time, and matter, also encapsulates the search and quest for identity, meaning and purpose, destiny, and oneness with others. In contrast, *religion* addresses a more institutionalized and systematic symbols, behaviors, pattern of values shared by communities and transmitted over time in traditions – some say religion is the vestibule that leads to spirituality and the spiritual encounter with the highest.

Toward a new spiritual model of trauma recovery

According to Turner and Neville (2020), current indigenous treatment models must pay careful attention to reframing the experience from a Euro-colonialism perspective and rebuild a new rhythm from a settler, anti-colonial, and DE colonial prism to regain identity, meaning, and purpose and driven by destiny that is indigenously consistent with the ancestral genius of our origins. There are Afrocentric approaches currently in use that support this assertion.

Valandra (2007) explored healing and recovery from sexual violence within the context of an Afrocentric approach to magnify the personal experiences and perspectives of women recovering from prostitution. The program format at Breaking Free, a grassroots Afrocentric non-nonprofit organization in St. Paul, Minnesota acknowledges the cultural context and addresses the impact of systemic race, gender, and class-based oppression in the lives of African American women who are recovering from prostitution. Valandra discussed how

> [T]he spirituality theme was reflected as a source of support and strength, a factor in healing and recovery, and a factor in the decision to leave prostitution. Women referred to God, a higher power, or spirituality as a source of strength. Spirituality was experienced as an integral part of the physical world, interwoven with other sources of support.
>
> *(Valandra, 2007, p. 200)*

This Afrocentric recovery approach used a framework of prostitution as violence against women that is rooted in a historical system of institutional racial, class, and gender oppression served the recovery needs of this group of women and demonstrated the utility of spirituality.

Similarly, in 2003, the University of Memphis Relative Caregiver Program (RCP) designed a pilot mentoring group program named the Kuumba Group (Washington, Johnson, Jones, & Langs, 2007). The African American males, aged 9–17, selected for the RCP therapeutic mentoring group were living in impoverished violent communities and vulnerable to mental health problems. The primary goal was to assist and provide support for children being raised by relative caregivers, often women who were poor and single. A pre-/post-test evaluation outcome model was utilized to measure spirituality and the perceptions of the relative caregivers. A central strategy of the group intervention was infusing the themes of the *Nguzo Saba*, an Afrocentric perspective that concentrates on themes such as unity, spirituality, self-determination, and collectivity that are seen as crucial to the healthy identity development in African American male youth. The results of the post-intervention interviews with the relative caregivers indicate a perception that the functioning of the participants in school and at home had improved in the areas investigated. The participants developed better home behavior, family relationships improved, and a positive growth in attendance was seen, demonstrating the utility of Afrocentric-focused interventions.

The Afrocentric paradigm must take a preeminent place in highlighting the sociocultural significance, collectively vibrant, and spiritually intuitively and rationality in both thinking, feeling, and behaving (Ginwright, 2018; Lincoln & Mamiya, 1990). According to Martin and Martin (2002), Afrocentric spiritual interventions must consider the micro, mezzo, macro domains as a focus of intervention and use a starting point possibility over problem and pathology. A new model must go beyond the tenets of the definition of trauma-informed given by the *Substance Abuse and Mental Health Services Administration (SAMHSA)* that defines trauma-informed as *Realizing, Recognizing, Responding to prevent Re-traumatization, but it must include Reorienting and Reactivating toward new levels of reality.* The SAMHSA (2012) identifies a trauma-informed organization as one that encapsulates the following four tenets.

- *Realizes* the widespread impact of trauma and understands potential paths for recovery
- *Recognizes* the signs and symptoms of trauma in clients, families, staff, and others involved with the system
- *Responds* by fully integrating knowledge about trauma into policies, procedures, and practices; but must go further to further
- Seeks to actively resist *re-traumatization*
- *Emphasizes safety, trustworthiness and transparency, peer support, collaboration and mutuality, empowerment (voice and choice), and cultural/intergenerational/gender issues*

However, African-centered spiritual healing approaches toward dismantling trauma must include the next step before *re-traumatization* as *re-orientating and reactivating toward a* higher level of potentialities beyond the scope of just American life toward the indigenous ancestral lands of Africa and genius of the first people. Reorientation and reactivation must include a spiritual worldview that incorporates origins, meaning and purpose, morality, and destiny (solidifying an assurance of the future). This next step and addition are reflective in (Table 3.1). Inspired by Martin and Martin (2002) this reorients and reactivates deeper levels of awareness and purpose – it starts with possibilities vs problems, its objectives and goals reach beyond Maslow's self-actualization toward the highest and optimal levels well beyond peak performances toward interventions that fully saturate and transform well-beingness as a desired outcome on the three micro, mezzo, and macro levels.

Phases of reorientation and reactivation should take into consideration quantum techniques for healing-centered mind development. Whitehead (2001), McPhail and Smilkstein (2001), and Daniels et al. (2015) place the tenets of quantum physics as a development and literacy option within the philosophical and metaphysical grasp of African people. Historically, classical physics studies the movement of particles within the domain of time, space, and matter, but since the discovery of quantum physics by both Einstein and Max Planck, it now lends itself to the learning styles of African people in the Nile Valley who built some of the first major civilizations. The learning styles of African people then and now mimic the intuitive and rational tenets of quantum, which is the movement of wave–particle duality, superposition, and quantum electrodynamic thinking (i.e., interpretative/intuitive, uncertainty/certainty of matter and waves, and the interconnectedness of all space, time, and matter (Browder, 1992; Whitehead, 2001). Moreover, quantum emphasizes dimensional capacities of thinking beyond the four spatial space, time, and matter dimensions based upon Einstein's scientific string theory, which suggests that well beyond the four spatial space–time continuum there exist seven more dimensions. *The Reorientation and Reactivation phase explores* those dimensional capacities through discussion and practice techniques of meditation and contemplation.

Case example

John Brown is a 15-year-old African American male who has been attending a predominantly white private Jesuit-run Catholic boys' high school for five months. His family lost their housing when John's father lost his job. Neither of his parents finished high school. His mother works as a maid and cannot support the family adequately. His mother works all the time. His parents have always argued about money. John, his mother, and father recently moved to live with his maternal grandmother and step-grandfather in a community with food deserts, community violence, inadequate educational facilities, old and vacant housing stock, poverty, etc. John's older brother recently went to jail for distributing drugs. John feels isolated because he no longer has the support and companionship of friends from his old neighborhood. He lives in a dangerous new neighborhood. John is being bullied at his new school. He feels abandoned by his mentor from his middle school.

TABLE 3.1 Micro, Mezzo, and Macro Afrocentric Spiritual Interventions

	Human Nature	Target Group	Possibilities vs Problems	Objectives and Goals	Intervention Process / Method / Techniques	Desired Outcomes
Micro-Level Approach (Myer's Approach)	Spiritual/ natural with spirituality gaining ascendancy	African individual in general	Realizing, Recognizing, Responding, **Reorienting/ Reactivating,** releasing suboptimal fragmented or segmented thinking and worldviews that separate spirituality from material existence	To develop optimal cognition and worldviews that see the spiritual and the material as a unified whole	Cognitive Behavioral Therapy; cognitive restructuring techniques; dream analysis, relaxation exercises, readings in ancient African history and metaphysics (quantum literacy – wave/ particle techniques consistent with African thought)	Create a holistic, optimal worldview that leads to greater self-worth and identity, oneness of self: **a) safety, b) trustworthiness**
Mezzo-Level Approach (Hill's Approach)	Spiritual/ Natural with spirituality gaining ascendancy	Groups including young men, etc. (Hill's approach focused on young men but can be adapted to other groups.)	Realizing, Recognizing, Responding, **Reorienting/ reactivating** socialization that leads to mature behaviors and lifestyles	To build family through a sense of belonging and functionality within society	Use *Nguzo Saba* in lessons in spirituality, physical fitness, cooperative economics, use of African rituals, symbols, etc., use of elders as mentors and advisers	Create initiates who feel a sense of commitment to community, operate maturely and responsibly in society; relate positively to parents, peers, extended families, teachers, and elders; also, **a) peer support, b) collaboration and mutuality**

(Continued)

TABLE 3.1 (Continued)

	Human Nature	Target Group	Possibilities vs Problems	Objectives and Goals	Intervention Process/Method/Techniques	Desired Outcomes
Macro-Level Approach (Schiele's Macro Approach)	Spiritual/ natural spirituality gaining ascendancy	Policies that impact African American life	Realizing, Recognizing, Responding, *Reorienting/ reactivating* to reject political oppression, spiritual alienation, and cultural miss-orientation, that leads to excessive	To address social inequities and power disparities, promote spiritual wellness and development and a subjective view of God, and realign Black people with their Communalistic caregiving cultural heritage	Use MAAT principles of justice and advocacy for social policies that address societal inequities, development of empathy, building of strengths and collective responsibility	Create spiritually strong, culturally aligned, and conscious Africans with a sense of obligation to community and a strong commitment to the struggle for social change; **a) Empowerment of voice and choice, b) Cultural and intergenerational, gender issues**

John has conflicting feelings about his father. He wonders why he is not doing more to support the family. John is dissatisfied with his housing situation. John fears he will be stigmatized by classmates should they learn his brother is in jail. John is in danger of losing his scholarship because he is skipping class.

Application of Myer's Afrocentric spiritual intervention (micro level)

The Afrocentric paradigm posits

> [R]eality is at once spiritual and material; the material without a spiritual core is illusionary, temporal, and chaotic; Black people are inextricably connected to ancestors, nature, the community, and the yet unborn; and that it is through the process of human and spiritual networks that individuals achieve their goals.
>
> *(Martin & Martin, 2002, p. 235)*

Ms Michaels is the school social worker providing services for John. Ms Michaels performed a bio-psycho-social-spiritual assessment that provided background information on John, including the strengths and skills that had brought John to the private school. John is a good student who was initially proud that he had gotten a scholarship to attend the Catholic high school but now wishes he had gone to the same high school as his middle school friends. John is feeling depressed, alone, anxious all the time, angry, and worried. He is bullied at school because he is African American and poor. As a result, he started skipping class and came to the attention of school administrators. Ms Michaels validated John's concerns regarding his family, feelings, being bullied, living in a new community, and going to a new school. John was diagnosed with (F43.23) adjustment disorder with mixed anxiety and depressed mood, and housing, primary support group, education, other social, and environmental stressors.

Through her assessment, Ms Michaels *realized* that his adverse childhood, cultural and community experiences have negatively impacted John and *recognized* he would need multiple interventions to address his traumatic experiences. Also, Ms Michaels recognized the signs and symptoms of trauma that manifested John's DSM-V diagnosis and the impact of his family history. John was feeling disconnected from all aspects of his life, family, school, and community. Afrocentric assumptions are in direct conflict with suboptimal thinking that prevents the unification of the physical and transphysical (spiritual) self that would allow African Americans to understand the universe as a unified, interdependent, and integrated whole where they are one with themselves, their history, and community (Martin & Martin, 2002).

Teachers, administrators, and school social workers must create an environment that is user-friendly and culturally appropriate for African American male youth to motivate them to learn and strive toward academic and professional excellence

(Schiele, 2000). Besides, a strengths perspective demands individuals, families, and communities are seen in the light of their capabilities and composing a roster of resources existing within those entities (Saleebey, 1996).

To begin the process of *reorienting* and *reactivating* John's thinking and world-view, Ms Michaels worked on developing a trusting environment for the two of them to work. They worked on goals that would lead to John developing more positive thinking about himself, his family, and unifying the material with the spiritual. Ms Michaels used cognitive restructuring techniques to help John reframe his thinking about his situation and began to problem solve different aspects of his life. John felt he needed a male role model. Ms Michaels introduced John to Mr Robert Brown, the football coach. Mr Brown, an African American, had attended the Catholica high school as a youth and listened to John and gave him suggestions for connecting with other students and having better communication with his teachers. John decided to build on his academic strengths by going to coaching class. He joined the African American and Hispanic student unions. During their time together, Mr Brown taught John how to play chess, and he joined the chess team. Knowing how to play chess helped him develop friendships with Caucasian and other African American students. In January, John worked with Mr Brown to put together activities for Black History Month. John had an opportunity to develop his sense of African consciousness by reading about *Nguzo Saba*, an Afrocentric perspective that concentrates on themes such as unity, spirituality, self-determination, and collectivity that are seen as crucial to the healthy identity development in African American male youth and reinforce African American people's resiliency. John also went to Mass daily with the rest of the boys, and while he was not a proponent of the Catholic religion, he developed his sense of spirituality. This connectedness to something higher moved him to join the Baptist Church near his new neighborhood and feel there was a safe place for him in that community.

Outcomes related to using the Myers' Micro Level Spiritual Intervention were as follows: John could discuss his family problems with Bishop Lance Sails and get advice on developing deeper relationships with his family and navigating the community. John learned to read the Bible and find comfort in God's teachings. Mr Brown and the school administrators, who did not tolerate any type of bullying, were there for John as he navigated racist comments from a few students. John began to blossom in his classes and was more comfortable at school. He started to talk to his parents about his feelings and visited his brother in jail so they could stay connected as a family. Using this Micro Level Spiritual Intervention from the Model helped John to reaffirm his African American heritage while at the same time feeling part of a collective and receiving spiritual guidance and support. John's worldview has become more unified, interdependent, and integrated.

Conclusion

As aforementioned, African American life has been empirically studied, particularly as it also relates to the social determinants of health such as economic stability, neighborhood and physical environment, education, food and access to healthy options, community, and social context, and the health care system (Archibald & Daniels, 2013; Daniels et al., 2015). African Americans have a history of trauma documented through Adverse Childhood Experiences (ACEs), Adverse Cultural Experiences, and Adverse Community Experiences across the intergenerational life span, specifically for those living in urban communities (Ellis & Deitz, 2017). These experiences are the root causes of trauma faced by African Americans in the United States today. The recent rise of the COVID-19 pandemic in the United States has further exacerbated trauma categories in the lives of African American people. The current White House Administrations' refusal to heed CDC scientific methods to promote a healthier environment for African Americans and other Americans has led to a monumental loss of life felt more significantly among minority communities. The COVID-19 pandemic has left many to further and deeply reengage in the Afrocentric worldview of spirituality not only as a modality of healing but also for consciousness centering and stability (Gecewicz, 2020b).

The Afrocentric Spiritual Interventions Model, as adapted by Daniels (2020), is an asset-driven preventative healing-centered trauma treatment modality focused on the holistic well-being of African American people on three levels: micro, mezzo, and macro. The model addresses the historical and current collective ACES categories of adverse childhood, community, and cultural trauma African Americans experience in the United States that perpetuate social determinants of health such as economic stability, neighborhood and physical environment, education, food and access to healthy options, community, and social context, and the health care system (Archibald & Daniels, 2013; Daniels et al., 2015). Further, the Afrocentric Spiritual Interventions Model incorporates the tenants of *Substance Abuse and Mental Health Services Administration* (*SAMHSA*) definition of trauma-informed as *Realizing, Recognizing, Responding to prevent Re-traumatization*, and Daniels (2020) model includes necessarily *Reorienting* and *Reactivating* toward new levels of reality before the final phase of *Seeking* to actively resist Re-traumatization. The *Reorientation* and *Reactivation* phase explores dimensional capacities through discussion and practice techniques of meditation and contemplation as stated previously. Reorienting and reactivating quantum techniques align with indigenous literacy processes surrounding higher dimensional capacity, interpretation, uncertainty of matter, and interconnectedness of space, time, and matter. The model infuses evidence-based interventions such as Cognitive Behavioral Therapy and Cognitive Restructuring to enhance clinical outcomes. Further, using the Afrocentric Spiritual Interventions Model when working with African American populations can correct for culturally created deficits in evidenced-based models that promote Eurocentric worldviews.

References

American Psychiatric Association. (2013). *Diagnostic and statistical manual of mental disorders* (5th ed.). Arlington, VA: Author.

Archibald, P., & Daniels, K. (2013). Utilization of an intergenerational life stage model to promote community-based mental health initiatives among urban African-Americans in a faith based environment. Unpublished manuscript, Morgan State University, Baltimore, MD.

Archibald, P., Daniels, K., & Austin, S. (2016). Exploring urban faith-based/social work community collaboration for mental health promotion in urban African American communities. In R. Wells-Wilbon, A. R. McPhatter, & H. F. Vakalahi (Eds.), *Social work practice with African Americans in urban environments.* New York, NY: Springer Publishing Company.

Asante, M. (2011). *De-westernizing communication: Strategies for neutralizing cultural myths.* Cambridge: Polity.

Braithwaite, R. L., & Taylor, S. E. (2001). *Health issues in the Black community* (2nd ed.). San Francisco: Jossey-Bass.

Browder, A. (1992). *Nile valley contributions to civilization (exploding the myths).* New York: Karmic Guidance Publisher.

Canda, E. R., & Furman, I. (2010). *Spiritual diversity in social work practice.* New York, NY: Oxford University Press.

Centers for Disease Control and Prevention (CDC). (2020a, September 21). *Cases of coronavirus disease (COVID-19) in the U.S.* Retrieved from www.cdc.gov/coronavirus/2019-ncov/cases-updates/cases-in-us.html

Centers for Disease Control and Prevention (CDC). (2020b, September 21). *Provisional death counts for coronavirus disease (COVID-19): Data updates by select demographic and geographic characteristics.* Retrieved from www.cdc.gov/nchs/nvss/vsrr/covid_weekly/

Daniels, K. (2020, April). Faith in the midst of COVID-19. [Editorial]. *Afro Newspaper,* A18.

Daniels, K., Akers, A., Smith, S., & Archibald, P. (2015). Urban gangs: Epidemiology criminology as a theoretical framework for social work practice. In R. Wells-Wilbon, A. R. McPhatter, & H. F. Vakalahi (Eds.), *Social work practice with African Americans in urban environments.* New York, NY: Springer Publishing Company.

Ellis, W. R., & Dietz, W. H. (2017). A new framework for addressing adverse childhood and community experiences: The building community resilience model. *Academics Pediatrics, 17*(7), S86–S93. https://doi.org/10.1016/j.acap.2016.12.011. Retrieved from www.academicpedsjnl.net/article/S1876-2859(16)30552-6/pdf

Gecewicz, C. (2020a). *Amid pandemic, Black and Hispanic worshippers more concerned about safety of in-person religious services.* Washington, DC: Pew Research Center.

Gecewicz, C. (2020b). *Few Americans say their house of worship is open, but a quarter say their faith has grown amid pandemic.* Washington, DC: Pew Research Center.

Ginwright, S. (2018). *The future of healing: Shifting from trauma informed care to healing centered engagement.* Kinship Carers Victoria occasional paper 25. Retrieved from http://kinship carersvictoria.org/wp-content/uploads/2018/08/OP-Ginwright-S-2018-Future-of-healing-care.pdf

Lincoln, C., & Mamiya, L. (1990). *The Black church in the African-American experience.* Durham: Duke University Press.

Martin, E. P., & Martin, J. M. (2002). *Spirituality and the Black helping tradition.* Washington, DC: NASW Press.

Mbiti, J. S. (1970). *African religious and philosophies.* Garden City, NY: Anchor Brooks/Doubleday.

McPhail, I. P., McPhail, C., & Smilkstein, R. (2001). *Culture, style, and cognition: Expanding the boundaries of the learning paradigm for African-American learners in the community college.* Los. Angeles, CA: ERIC Clearinghouse for Community Colleges.

McPhatter, A. (2016). Urban social work with African-Americans: Critical perspectives, concepts, and theories. In R. Wells-Wilbon, A. R. McPhatter, & H. F. Vakalahi (Eds.), *Social work practice with African Americans in urban environments*. New York, NY: Springer Publishing Company.

Peteet, J. R., Lu, F. G., & Narrow, W. E. (2011). *Religious and spiritual issues in psychiatric diagnosis: A research agenda for DSM-V.* Arlington, VA: American Psychiatric Association.

Pinn, A. (2002). *The African-American church in the post-civil rights era.* Maryknoll, NY: Orbis Books.

Saleebey, D. (1996). The strengths based perspective in social work: Extensions and cautions. *Social Work, 41*(3), 296–305.

SAMHSA's National Center for Trauma-Informed Care. (2012). *Report of project activities over the past 18 months, history, and selected products.* Retrieved from www.nasmhpd.org/docs/NCTIC/NCTIC_Final_Report_3-26-12.pdf

Sanders-Thompson, V. L., Bazile, A., & Akbar, M. (2004). African-Americans' perceptions of psychotherapy and psychotherapists. *Professional Psychology: Research and Practice, 35*(1), 19–26.

Schiele, J. H. (2000). *Human services and the Afrocentric paradigm.* New York: The Haworth Press.

Sefa Dei, G. J. (2017). *Reframing Blackness and Black solidarities through anti-colonial and decolonial prisms.* Toronto, Canada: Springer International Publishing.

Turner, L., & Neville, H. A. (2020). *Frantz Fanon's psychotherapeutic approaches to clinical: practicing internationally with marginalized communities.* New York: Routledge Publisher.

Valandra. (2007). Reclaiming their lives and breaking free: An Afrocentric approach to recovery from prostitution. *The Journal of Women in Social Work, 22*, 195–208.

Washington, G., Johnson, T., Jones, J., & Langs, S. (2007). African American boys in relative care and a culturally centered group mentoring approach. *Social Work with Groups*, 45–68.

Whitehead, D. (2001). Quantum literacy. *Teaching in Higher Education, 6*(4), 519–526. https://doi.org/10.1080/13562510120078054

4

SOMATIC EXPERIENCING, EMDR, AND BRAINSPOTTING

An African-centered critique

Paula Langford

While access to mental health interventions has improved over time, there continues to be a lack of culturally appropriate interventions that are sensitive, relevant, and responsible when treating generations of African American trauma and mental illness. African American's historical distrust of medical and mental health systems, lack of affordable insurance, and access to appropriate therapy that has been long overdue continues to create barriers to mental wellness. This chapter will briefly discuss historical trauma of African Americans, barriers to mental health treatment, and an exploration of somatic psychotherapy, Eye Movement Desensitization and Reprocessing (EMDR), and Dr David Grand's (2013) neuro-experiential integrative model, Brainspotting (BSP) from an African-centered perspective and address implications for the use of these models in the treatment and healing of African Americans' trauma.

Historical trauma and the history of mental illness among African Americans

The trauma experienced before and during slavery to the present, with police brutality vibrating in the cellular memory of the people of African descent enhances the negative outcomes of trauma, thus impeding the success of Black communities. In *The Body Keeps the Score*, Van der Kolk (2015) examines the impact of war experiences on veterans' mental and physical health. No one associated with Europe or North America has escaped single or complex trauma. Van der Kolk (2015) maintains that trauma "leaves traces on our minds and emotions, on our capacity for joy and intimacy, and even on our biology and immune systems." For African Americans, physical and mental disease continue to affect epigenetics and cellular structure in DNA.

The history of African American trauma is well known but often goes unaddressed. While all people have experienced traumatic events, there is a collective

DOI: 10.4324/9780429276613-6

traumatic experience of African enslavement during the transatlantic slave trade by Europeans (Eyerman, 2001; Gump, 2010). From separation of families, cultural traditions, and language to watching men, women, and children being physically and sexually abused; to witnessing kinsmen being brutalized and lynched; trauma continues to vibrate in the cellular memory of African people throughout the world (Buonagurio, 2020).

According to Umeh (2019) John Galt, a physician and medical director in Virginia, offered this: "Blacks are immune to mental illness." Galt hypothesized that enslaved Africans could not develop mental illness because as enslaved people, they did not own property, engage in commerce, or participate in civic affairs such as voting or holding office," ridiculous of course, and yet medical and mental health professions continue to ignore Black and African people's physical and mental suffering or provide treatment interventions that are culturally appropriate. It has been well documented that historically white doctors discount Black pain when prescribing medication forcing Black patients to seek relief by other legal and illegal means to reduce their suffering (Umeh, 2019). Antebellum medical researchers promoted mental illness as the cause for enslaved Blacks to flee plantations or feel lethargy in response to enslavement (Umeh, 2019). It is no wonder that African Americans are distrustful of medical and mental health providers considering the following examples.

- The use of legal sterilization of African Americans misdiagnosed, imprisoned, or housed in mental institutions by southern states such as North Carolina.
- The mistrust of medical institutions with testing such as the Tuskegee Experiments and the use of cells of Baltimorean, Henrietta Lack, and many others have greatly impacted African Americans' use of medical and mental health treatment.
- The experiments performed on children for behaviors related to aggression and hyperactivity (Umeh, 2019).

Unaddressed intergenerational trauma or "Post Traumatic Slave Disorder" (Degruy-Leary, 1994; Mims, 2008) is now being considered by some practitioners in the assessment of mental illness of Africans and African Americans. Living in a perpetual state of flight, fight, or freeze has costly consequences and we see this with African Americans in their physical and mental health, with the higher prevalence of hypertension, cancer, anxiety, and depression than any other group in the United States.

Mental health stigma in the Black family

"What happens in the house stays in the house," is an adage heard in many Black households. It means that family secrets are to remain unspoken within the family but certainly never disclosed to outsiders. Throughout history, the Black community has maintained, even to our physical and mental detriment, secrets that have negatively affected our physical, mental, spiritual, and financial health (Jordan, 2020). It was not uncommon for family members who suffered from depression (known as melancholy), sexual abuse, and serious mental illness to go untreated and be locked away. Family members who experienced sexual abuse and other traumatic experiences learn to live in silence, self-medicate with drugs and alcohol, or dissociate, in order to get through or get relief (Jordan, 2020). When considering why such atrocities were not reported, include unfair treatment in judicial system, shame, being considered "loose" or promiscuous, ostracized, and or excommunication from Black church and other institutions.

The Black church

Historically, the Black church has played a pivotal role in the sustainability of the Black community. During the post slavery period, the Black church not only provided spiritual sustenance, but it was central in providing money, food, shelter, education, and often physical protection for Black communities. Professor James Small (2021) talks about "the Black church being the most formative weapon we have in the Black community as a sacred spiritual and learning system." According to Small (2021) African spirituality is how we experience and understand our place in the universe. The brutalizing colonization of African people is witnessed even in the dismantling and demonizing of traditional African spirituality and religious practices only to be replaced by European religions. With the acculturation into white America's religious systems, the Black church leaders caused great harm to the psyche of Black people by using biblical text to demonize and spiritualize mental illness, while failing to legitimize mental and physical health illnesses and asking parishioners to use prayer as the foundation of addressing psychosis, depression, and anxiety.

Current state of mental health

According to National Alliance on Mental Illness (NAMI) (Phillips, 2020), millions of people in the United States are diagnosed with mental illness. According to King-Wagner (2021), a child welfare trainer, approximately 48 million people are diagnosed with anxiety disorders and nine million are diagnosed with post-traumatic stress disorder (PTSD). Access to mental and behavioral health practitioners trained and certified in integrative models remains out of reach for African Americans (Wells-Wilbon, Porter, Geyton, & Estreet, 2021). According to national statistics, the ratio of mental health providers to clients is 1:529 (King-Wagner, 2021). Traditional psychotherapy has had its place in mental health. However, African Americans have not always had access to psychotherapy or other mental health modalities.

The Adverse Childhood Experiences (ACEs) Study (Merrick et al., 2017), developed by Kaiser Permanente in 1995, explored the correlation between early childhood trauma and physical and mental health. The study was conducted with 17,000 participants and examined participants who had four or more negative childhood experiences, that is, childhood trauma, mental illness, physical illness, and substance abuse. ACEs have shown a negative impact on education, job opportunities, and earning potential; subjects with higher ACEs scores are more likely to have experienced physical illnesses, poor academics, and increased propensity for substance abuse (Bernard et al., 2021). For those who have experienced ACEs, there have been several interventions that are known to improve their functioning that include therapy, meditation, and physical exercise (Greeson et al., 2014).

Access to clinicians of color: cultural sensitivity, attunement, and responsibility

Not only are historical trauma, stigma, poverty, and transportation reasons that impede access to mental health treatment, but African Americans may also feel a disconnection when receiving services from white mental health providers. The creation of organizations such as Clinicians of Color in Private Practice (COC), Black Therapists Rock (BTR), and Taraji P. Henson's Boris Lawrence Henson Foundation (BLHF) has increased access to Black mental health providers across the United States and abroad. These organizations actively recruit clinicians who are culturally sensitive, attuned, and responsible in improving access to practitioners and decreasing barriers to mental health services.

Lisa Savage-Phillips and Kim Knight created the Clinicians of Color (COC) Facebook group. The COC provides over 100 classes, expert training, resources, and support. The COC has created an online training academy offering clinicians discounts on training that Black clinicians generally would not have access to, such as EMDR, which can access trauma deep within the brain (Jefferies & Davis, 2012).

In her anthology, *Black Therapists Rock: A Glimpse Through the Eyes of Experts*, CEO of BTR, Deran Young mentions that BTR has become a movement that is passionate about speaking out about the varied truths that will begin healing emotional wounds that are multiple generations' deep (Young 2018). Young established BTR after recognizing "a gap between mentorship, knowledge, and unity among helping professionals."

The Boris Lawrence Henson Foundation (BLHF) increased its visibility at the onset of the COVID pandemic. Established by Actress Taraji P. Henson, the foundation initially provided free telehealth to women who struggled with finding a quality and affordable therapist. Now, BLHF has expanded mental services to include men and children. Henson has since become a national spokesperson and advocate for mental health presenting before the Congressional Black Caucus to help destigmatize mental illness, while increasing support for accessible mental health services.

Somatic and "power" mental health interventions

Somatic experiencing

Somatic experiencing (SE) is a form of trauma therapy that emphasizes guiding the client's attention to interoceptive, kinesthetic, and proprioceptive experience.

SE claims that this style of inner attention, in addition to the use of kinesthetic and interoceptive imagery, can lead to the resolution of symptoms resulting from chronic and traumatic stress symptoms (Payne, 2015).

SE focuses on resolving the symptoms of chronic stress and post-traumatic stress. SE differs from cognitive therapies in that its major interventional strategy involves bottom-up processing by directing the client's attention to internal sensations, both visceral (interoception) and musculo-skeletal (proprioception and kinesthesis) rather than primarily cognitive or emotional experiences. It specifically avoids direct and intense evocation of traumatic memories, instead approaching the charged memories indirectly and very gradually, as well as facilitating the generation of new corrective interoceptive experiences that physically contradict those of overwhelm and helplessness. When the nervous system has become "tuned" (Gellhorn, 1967) by repeated exposure to long-term stress or trauma, the result is manifest in the symptoms of post-traumatic stress symptoms (PTSS). Failure to resolve PTSS can evolve into multiple comorbidities involving the cognitive, affective, immune, endocrine, muscular, and visceral systems.

The emphasis in mindfulness meditation on remaining detached from discursive thought may sometimes encourage a remote or uninvolved attitude toward arising images, feelings, and insights. SE encourages an active, curious exploration of arising phenomena, which is nonetheless not conceptually based. We believe that a familiarity with this form of exploration can inform the practice of mindfulness. Moreover, it does so without diverting the practitioner into psychological analysis, which may be a significant diversion from the intent of body-focused and meditative practices.

In the 1994 study, the Department of Health and Human Services in posit to demonstrate how the methods of SE help restore functionality to the core response network CRN, and we emphasize the importance of taking into account the instinctive, bodily based protective reactions when dealing with stress and trauma, as well as the effectiveness of using attention to interoceptive, proprioceptive, and kinesthetic sensation as a therapeutic tool (National Center for Health Statistics (US), & National Center for Health Services Research, 1994).

African-centered critique

Exploring the SE model using the African-centered paradigm demonstrates the use of spirituality and communalism as elements in healing complex trauma and mental illness among African Americans. Utilizing sensing structural and movement Rolfing, yoga, spirituality, and SE led to the observation that even with highly efficient SE intervention processes in severe trauma, the client goes through a recovery. For that, one needs to redefine and restructure negative experience with a reasonable understanding of what happened and relieve and/or transform the emotional and physiological symptoms (Silva, 2014).

Traditionally, access to the spirit has been a central practice that has been used for guidance in areas such as parenting, conflict resolution, and business accomplishments. SE offers reconnection to physical bodily sensations through physical movement and access to the brain's limbic system including the hippocampus, location of long-term memory and grants access to unfathomable healing of individuals and communities with a decrease in emotional and physical activation and regaining of body resourcing through the parasympathetic nervous system responsible for rest, decrease in heart rate, and a balance of digestion. SE offers clients the ability to reconnect to spiritual rituals once thought lost. Without the use of traditional medication, SE, like EMDR and BSP, nurtures cellular healing not accessible with therapies such as Dialectical Behavioral Therapy (DBT) and Cognitive Behavior Therapy (CBT). Rather, SE promotes the use of the brain and body's intuition rather than cognitive processing to connect on higher spiritual level returning individuals to the natural homeostasis.

SE is a communal model that makes space and opportunity for dual attunement between the client and the therapist. Therapists trained in SE relax certainty about the client's use of behavioral reactions to traumatic events while embracing confidence that the client's system is aware of what is needed in the healing process. In SE, the therapist functions as the support for the client, thus engaging in physical contact with the client, is a necessary component of this approach.

EMDR

Developed by Dr Francine Shapiro in 2017, EMDR utilizes bilateral eye movement to access traumatic memory. EMDR is an efficacious and efficient treatment method for PTSD. This model posits that pathology results when distressing experiences are processed inadequately and hypothesizes that EMDR accelerates information processing, resulting in the adaptive resolution of traumatic memories (Shapiro & Maxfield, 2002).

Researchers S.A. Wilson et al. (1995) explored the effects of three, 90-min EMDR treatment sessions on traumatic memories of 80 participants. Participants were randomly assigned to treatment or delayed-treatment conditions and to one of five licensed therapists trained in EMDR. Participants receiving EMDR showed decreases in presenting complaints and in anxiety and increases in positive cognition (Wilson et al., 1995). Although some experiences may be retrained in the brain in a way that causes dysfunction, the primary message of EMDR is that the client is intrinsically healthy: once experiences are processed with EMDR, the client can quickly return to a state of equilibrium (Lovett, 1999). The choice of EMDR over trauma-focused CBT should therefore remain a matter of patient choice and clinician expertise; it is suggested, however, that Ems may be more effective at reducing distress and thereby allow other components of treatment to take place (Lovett, 1999). The only meaningful answers lie within an individual's mind, body, and spirit (Grand, 2001).

EMDR African-centered critique

A critique of EMDR from an African-centered perspective displays African-centered elements was an optimistic outlook in healing anxiety, depression, and other mental illnesses of African Americans. For instance, like SE, EMDR trusts the body's intuitive system in internal healing. EMDR utilizes the somatic processing through bilateral eye movements and light touch either by the client or therapist, that is, knees or hands. Regarding the communal aspect of African-centered practice, EMDR supports the dual attunement where the therapist acts as a conduit to internal calming of the amygdala and reduction in stress and anxiety. EMDR therapist allows the client to bring focus to spiritual or religious symbolism during treatment and thereby access to all religious traditions, rituals, and customs. EMDR can be conducted in individual, couples, family, and therapeutic group settings.

Brainspotting: where you look affects how you feel

Brainspotting is a psychotherapy based on the observation that the body activation experienced when describing a traumatic event has a resonating spot in the visual field (Corrigan & Grand, 2013). A Brainspot is seen as a physiological capsule holding emotional experience in memory form (Corrigan, Grand, & Raju, 2015). While the linkage of memory, emotion, and body sensation may require the parietal and frontal interconnections – and resolution in the prefrontal cortex – we suggest that the capacity for healing of the altered feeling about the self occurs in the midbrain at the level of the superior colliculi and the periaqueductal gray (Corrigan & Grand, 2013).

This relational attunement is seen as being both focused and deepened by the neurological attunement derived from observing and harnessing different aspects of the visual orienting reflexes of the client (Corrigan & Grand, 2013). In BSP this is called Focused Mindfulness as the mindfulness that ensues occurs in a state of Focused Activation. The Focused Mindfulness ensues, with the therapist closely and openly following along until the client comes to a state of resolution (Hildebrand, 2017).

Developed in 2003, David Grand's Neuro-experiential BSP model, is a revolutionary therapeutic intervention that exhibits many African-centered elements that could hold the long-awaited transformation for urban communities of color on a neurobiological level. BSP's neuro-experiential model is an integrative model that may be the optimal therapeutic intervention that enhances the healing of African and African Americans in urban communities.

Grand's BSP mantra says, "where you look affects how you feel." Unlike traditional therapies, Grand's BSP is an open and expansive model based on the uncertainty principle where only the client's intuition knows the meaning of thoughts, images, and reflective cues that emerge while their eyes are in a fixed position. With that in mind, BSP practitioners accompany clients on a neuro-experiential journey that is non-oppressive and expansive (Grand, 2013). In all BSP's phase one training, trainees learn the foundation of BSP with Grand's ice skater client who experienced performance anxiety while performing the triple loop. After integrating BSP in the client's therapy, the ice skater perfectly performed the triple loop. Curious about the correlation between the client's eye position, reflective cues, and somatic sensation, Grand's BSP neuro-experiential model has transformed lives by allowing clients to access trauma capsules in the subcortical region of the brain while locating the body's resource; calm, grounded or neutral in the body.

No larger than an almond and controlling 90% of the body's functions, the amygdala is responsible for detecting threats and ignites the flight, fight, and freeze response to danger. Grand's BSP appears to promote coherence between the sympathetic and parasympathetic activation (Corrigan & Grand, 2013). BSP can be done individually and in groups with all ages.

BSP from an African-Centered perspective

Grand's Gazespotting set-up is a natural inclination, most are unaware of to access intuition and body sensations through what we consider daydreaming. It is in this focused state or what Grand calls Advanced Gazespotting that individuals are encouraged to consider an issue that ultimately will induce somatic sensation in the body or reflexive eye movements (Grand, 2001). While individuals can consider traumatic events, Grand's BSP has been found beneficial for students and athletes wanting to excel in academic and sports performance.

There are noted similarities between the African-centered paradigm and BSP neuro-experiential model making Grand's BSP model not only culturally sensitive and relevant but also culturally attuned and responsible to African Americans' collective healing. BSP can be conducted in individual, family, or group sessions and utilizes a non-oppressive model while working with recovery, youth, and religious groups. BSP's dual attunement framework fosters a relationship between the client and the therapist that supports the client's intuitive knowing that healing is possible physically and subconsciously. BSP's newest training by Tracy Monroy –Loye, LPC, Mdiv– focuses on intersectionality and internal parts that open the way for more expansive access to infinite healing that is foundational to the African-centered paradigm. In African tradition, spirituality and communalism are the bases of the health and well-being of the collective. BSP is an inclusive and expansive model which nurtures communal healing that is infinite and begins between the client and the therapist. The BSP model opens individuals to internal and spiritual healing not otherwise welcomed or accessible in traditional therapies.

BSP is inclusive of the spirit and spirituality in its expansive model as a communal practice, typically discouraged in traditional therapy, in the healing process. Grand's model incorporates all parts, physical, mental, spiritual, and emotional, allowing for dialectical communication that opens the subcortical brain for continued healing through the creation of new neural pathways that occurred even after the therapy session. BSP therapists are open to clients' ancestral communication, use of traditions, languages, and rituals that previously would have been deemed psychotic or dissociative. BSP emphasizes the natural intuition of the client's system at every juncture of the therapeutic process.

Ann Dillard (2021) LMFT and director of the non-profit, Project Safety Nets, specializes in working with teens and mother–daughter relationships. For Dillard

(2021), BSP empowers Black teens and young adults to be brave in revealing their feelings and emotions about abuses they have experienced, lack of trust, and poor self-worth and confidence amongst their peers with deeper healing not observed with traditional therapies.

In Grand's initial experience with BSP's neuro-experiential model, it was not known that it would also be an integrative tool that enhances the healing of African and African clients seeking mental health treatment. BSP welcomes the entire person and utilizes the natural healing of the brain to address generational and complex trauma that has been ignored by traditional therapies. Grand's BSP continues to expand healing possibilities for African American children, families, and organizations with the introduction of BSP and intersectionality, BSP with children, and BSP for addiction.

Implications for further study and for therapy in African American communities

Utilizing BSP's neuro-experiential model with African American clients shows significant promise for further research to determine the level of effectiveness in accessing and healing generational trauma on the cellular and subconscious memory of Black people. Longitudinal studies by African American clinicians utilizing BSP in clinical and community-based settings are crucial in determining further effectiveness for African Americans across age, gender, socioeconomics, education, and health. Furthermore, research is needed to assess client satisfaction and treatment compliance utilizing BSP's therapeutic model for clients with mental and behavioral health issues, that is, addiction, depression, ADHD, and anxiety while destigmatizing mental illness in African American communities.

Currently, therapist John Edwards is the only Black, Caribbean BSP trainer in the world. Edwards, who openly raised concerns of Black practitioners navigate white fragility in white training spaces, had created the only Black Indigenous People of Color (BIPOC) BSP training. Edwards had forgone offering continuing education credits for his exclusive training as credentialing organizations have denied or thwarted his ability to offer CEUs. Nevertheless, Edwards has trained more than 700 BIPOC practitioners since 2019. Even with Edwards's effort, it remains necessary for Black clinicians to create safe spaces for healing and research by our own people. To accomplish any significant data collection and analysis, it is imperative that more BIPOC BSP therapists and researchers treating communities of color particularly in urban settings are trained.

Suggested readings, trainings, and other resources

I recommend readers explore expanding their knowledge and understanding of social work from an African-centered perspective through the Association of Black Social Workers Academy of African Centered Social Work. The Academy has been vital for many clinicians to learn African history and gain a better understanding of the African paradigm. This is available to Black professionals.

Shonte Javon Taylor's Optimind Institute's Neuroscience course is an excellent program that should be required for grasping neuroscience and brain basics. I believe this online course allows mental health clients access to basic brain science that enhances the therapeutic process by providing clients with psychoeducation about the brain's regulation. According to Taylor, "How you show up will determine how well you can lead, serve and empower others to reach their potential. But it's hard and sometimes tiring to find the daily mental inspiration, stamina and creative ideas to show up for others." https://shontejtaylor.lpages.co/optimind-program/.

The best way to understand BSP is to engage in consultation and or therapy with a BIPOC BSP therapist in a session. Organizations such as The Healing Institute in Maryland, The Clinician of Color in Private Practice (online), and John Edwards' West Coast Psychotherapy practice in California have access to BSP therapists. Brainspotting.com has a directory of BIPOC and non-BIPOC registered BSP practitioners.

If you are interested in learning BSP, John Edwards (2021) conducts BSP Phase 1–3 and some specialty courses: BSP with Children and Adolescents through www.westcoastpsychotherapy.com/brainspotting.

Grounding exercise

Here is a grounding exercise that uses natural Gazespotting BSP:

1. Think of an issue around a simple problem that you want an answer to.
2. Notice any feelings of activation in the body. Rate this feeling from 0 to 10.
3. Now, notice where you feel most calm, grounded, or neutral.
4. Allow your eyes to land on any spot in the room.
5. Focusing on the issue, bring your attention to the place in your body where you feel most calm, grounded, or neutral.
6. Notice any thoughts or images that come up. See how this relates to the original issues you selected.
7. Now, notice the place where you were feeling activated. Notice if your rating has decreased. If the rating has not decreased, spend a few minutes back on the area of your body that is the calmest until you feel a shift.

Websites

www.Blackpast.org/african-american-history/mental-illness-in-Black-community-1700-2019-a-short-history/

www.cdc.gov/violenceprevention/aces/about.html

www.cdc.gov/childrensmentalhealth/data.html

www.history.com/news/the-infamous-40-year-tuskegee-study
https://nami.org/Your-Journey/Identity-and-Cultural-Dimensions
https://nami.org/Your-Journey/Teens-Young Adults?gclid=CjwKCAjw_Ju
GBhBkEiwA1xmbRQRJrNNLfR8MwOQMzIT_NamPkOhnVzpfV9TG
K7TNL42JqOA7dWx2pxoCD8UQAvD_BwE
www.ncbi.nlm.nih.gov/pmc/articles/PMC4265215/#:~:text=Transportat
ion%20barriers%20lead%20to%20rescheduled,and%20thus%20poorer%20
health%20outcomes.
https://shontejtaylor.lpages.co/optimind-program/
www.westcoastpsychotherapy.com/brainspotting-clinicians-of-color
www.academy.cliniciansofcolor.org

References

Bernard, D. L., Calhoun, C. D., Banks, D. E., Halliday, C. A., Hughes-Halbert, C., & Danielson, C. K. (2021). Making the "C-ACE" for a culturally-informed adverse childhood experiences framework to understand the pervasive mental health impact of racism on Black youth. *Journal of Child & Adolescent Trauma, 14*(2), 233–247.

Buonagurio, N. (2020). The cycle continues: The effects of intergenerational trauma on the sense of self and the healing opportunities of dance/movement therapy: A literature review. *Expressive Therapies Capstone Theses.* 280. Retrieved from https://digitalcommons.lesley.edu/expressive_theses/280

Corrigan, F. M., & Grand, D. (2013). *Brainspotting: Recruiting the midbrain for accessing and healing sensorimotor memories of traumatic activation.* Oxford. https://doi.org/10.1016/j.mehy.2013.03.005

Corrigan, F. M., Grand, D., & Raju, R. (2015). Brainspotting: Sustained attention, spinothalamic tracts, thalamocortical processing, and the healing of adaptive orientation truncated by traumatic experience. *Medical Hypotheses, 84*(4), 384–394.

Degruy-Leary, J. (1994). *Post-traumatic slave syndrome: America's legacy of enduring injury.* Cape Coral, FL: Cabana Productions.

Dillard, A. (2021, June). Teen experience with Brainspotting, Interview.

Edwards, J. (2021). Brainspotting as a Neuro-experiential Model Interview with Dr. David Grand, Brainspotting Clinicians of Color, video.

Eyerman, R. (2001). *Cultural trauma: Slavery and the formation of African American identity.* Cambridge, MA: Cambridge University Press.

Gellhorn, E. (1967). *Principles of autonomic-somatic integrations: Physiological basis and psychological and clinical implications.* Minneapolis, MN: University of Minnesota Press.

Grand, D. (2001). *Emotional healing at warp speed: The power of EMDR.* New York, NY: Harmony Books.

Grand, D. (2013). *Brainspotting: The revolutionary new therapy for rapid and effective change.* Louisville, CO: Sounds True Publication.

Greeson, J. K., Briggs, E. C., Layne, C. M., Belcher, H. M., Ostrowski, S. A., Kim, S., . . . Fairbank, J. A. (2014). Traumatic childhood experiences in the 21st century: Broadening and building on the ACE studies with data from the National Child Traumatic Stress Network. *Journal of Interpersonal Violence, 29*(3), 536–556.

Gump, J. P. (2010). Reality matters: The shadow of trauma on African American subjectivity. *Psychoanalytic Psychology, 27*(1), 42.

Hildebrand, A., Grand, D., & Stemmler, M. (2017). Brainspotting – the efficacy of a new therapy approach for the treatment of Posttraumatic Stress Disorder in comparison to Eye Movement Desensitization and Reprocessing. *Mediterranean Journal of Clinical Psychology*, *5*(1).

Jefferies, F. W., & Davis, P. (2012, October). *What is the role of eye movements in eye movement desensitization and reprocessing (EMDR) for post-traumatic stress disorder (PTSD)? A review.* Published online by Cambridge University Press.

Jordan, T. (2020). *Combatting stigma and shame associated with professional mental health help-seeking attitudes in the African American community: An inquiry with African American pastors* (Doctoral dissertation). Nova Southeastern University.

King-Wagner, T. (2021, May 26). *Adult mental health disorders.* Child and Family Services Agency, Child Welfare Training Academy, Engage and Intervene Curriculum manual Washington, DC.

Lovett, J. (1999). *Small wonders: Healing childhood trauma with EMDR.* New York, NY: Simon and Schuster.

Merrick, M. T., Ports, K. A., Ford, D. C., Afifi, T. O., Gershoff, E. T., & Grogan-Kaylor, A. (2017). Unpacking the impact of adverse childhood experiences on adult mental health. *Child Abuse & Neglect*, *69*, 10–19.

Mims, S., Higginbottom, L., & Reid, O. (2008). *Post traumatic slavery disorder.* Dorchester, MA: Pyramid Builders Inc. Osiris Group.

National Center for Health Statistics (US), & National Center for Health Services Research. (1994). *Health, United States.* US Department of Health, Education, and Welfare, Public Health Service, Health Resources Administration, National Center for Health Statistics.

Payne, P., Levine, P., & Crane-G0dreau, M. (2015, February 4) Somatic experiencing: Using interoception and proprioception as core elements of trauma therapy. *Frontier Psychology.* https://doi.org/10.3389/fpsyg.2015.00093

Phillips, K. (2020). Mental illness is not anyone's fault: A review of NAMI, the National Alliance on Mental Illness. *Journal of Consumer Health on the Internet*, *24*(1), 75–81.

Shapiro, F. (2017). *Eye movement desensitization and reprocessing (EMDR): Basic principles, protocols and procedures* (2nd ed.). New York, NY: Guilford Press.

Shapiro, F., & Maxfield, L. (2002). Eye movement desensitization and reprocessing (EMDR): Information processing in the treatment of trauma. *Journal of Clinical Psychology*, *58*(8), 933–946.

Silva, S. M. G. (2014). *Engaging touch & movement in somatic experiencing® trauma resolution approach* (Doctoral dissertation, Doctoral thesis). IUGS.

Small, J., African. (2021, May 21). *Spirituality.* The Black Family Summit Advanced Meeting, lecture.

Umeh, U. (2019). Mental illness in Black community, 1700–2019: A short history. *BlackPast. Org.*

Van der Kolk, B. A. (2015). *The body keeps the score: Brain, mind, and body in the healing of trauma.* New York, NY: Penguin Books.

Wells-Wilbon, R., Porter, R., Geyton, T., & Estreet, A. (2021, April 26). Mental health disparities. In *Encyclopedia of social work.* New York, NY: Oxford University Press. https://doi.org/10.1093/acrefore/9780199975839.013.1253

Willis, W. W. (1998). *The adinkra dictionary.* Zenda, WI: The Pyramid Complex.

Wilson, S. A., Becker, L. A., & Tinker, R. H. (1995). Eye movement desensitization and reprocessing (EMDR) treatment for psychologically traumatized individuals. *Journal of Consulting and Clinical Psychology*, *63*(6), 928–937. https://doi.org/10.1037/0022-006X.63.6.928

Young, D. (2018). *Black therapists rock: A glimpse through the eyes of experts.* Books, Amazon, Black Therapist Rock.

5

CULTURALLY RELEVANT, TRAUMA-RESPONSIVE, AND HEALING-CENTERED SOCIAL WORK SUPERVISION

Paul Archibald, Nia Johnson

The need for culturally relevant, trauma-responsive, and healing-centered social work supervision has become more evident as we face the *super-pandemic* caused by the collision of the coronavirus disease 2019 (COVID-19) and structural racism. Consequently, supervision with Black supervisees cannot ignore the effects of the traumatic stress associated with COVID-19 and structural racism. The National Association of Social Workers (NASW) (2008) defined professional supervision as:

> the relationship between supervisor and supervisee in which the responsibility and accountability for the development of competence, demeanor, and ethical practice take place. The supervisor is responsible for providing direction to the supervisee, who applies social work theory, standardized knowledge, skills, competency, and applicable ethical content in the practice setting.
>
> *(p. 6)*

The NASW (2008) proposes that the supervision process includes interrelated functions and responsibilities that influence outcomes for clients. In addition, the NASW (2008) suggests that supervisors may choose any supervision model they deem most appropriate for their supervisees' professional development. This conceptualization lacks an understanding that supervision does not exist outside racialized social systems, especially for Black supervisees. Bonilla-Silva (1997) argued that racism should be viewed within the context of social systems that are hierarchically structured and based on socially constructed racial categories that benefit one group over another. This racialization framework considers the racial categories' initial or historical social formation and intent that inform the contemporary racial hierarchical structure. Racial phenomena such as stereotypes, prejudices, and discrimination become crystallized over the course of social systems' existence,

DOI: 10.4324/9780429276613-7

producing racial inequities that may ultimately affect the supervision process with Black people, if ignored.

Therefore, when working with Black supervisees, professional supervision should be considered as a relationship between supervisor, supervisee, client, and the racialized social system in which Black people are born, grow up, live, work and age in (Bonilla-Silva, 1997; WHO, 2019). This chapter will describe how to incorporate a trauma-responsive and healing-centered supervision process when working with Black supervisees. This supervision approach: *realizes* that trauma in the Black community is pervasive and healing is obtainable; *recognizes* the signs and symptoms in supervisees and clients; *responds* by fully integrating knowledge about historical and contemporary racial trauma into supervision policies, procedures, and practices; and *resists re-traumatizing* supervisees and clients.

Black adults and trauma

Realization of trauma prevalence in Black adults

Supervision with Black supervisees should be conducted with an understanding of the prevalence of trauma in Black adults and how it is experienced. Black adults experience higher rates of post-traumatic stress disorder (PTSD) in comparison to their white adult counterparts (Alegria et al., 2013; Roberts, Gilman, Breslau, Breslau, & Koenen, 2011). Alegria and colleagues (2013) also revealed that Black adults had a higher prevalence across six DSM-5 diagnostic criteria for PTSD than white adults. Roberts and colleagues (2011) found that Black adults (8.7%) had a lifetime prevalence of PTSD greater than whites (7.4%) and were less likely to seek treatment for their PTSD than whites. Williams, Metzger, Leins, and DeLapp (2018) proposed that the differential experiences of racism may provide some explanations for the etiology of PTSD among African Americans. Nobles and colleagues (2016) found that when the added impact of race and PTSD was considered, PTSD was associated with a greater risk of chronic health conditions among Black adults compared to white adults.

The trauma exposure that impacts PTSD symptoms occurs throughout the life course of Black adults (Pearlin, Schieman, Fazio, & Meersman, 2005). The seminal Adverse Childhood Experiences (ACEs) study found a direct link between childhood trauma and well-being through an individual's life span (Felitti et al., 1998). However, the unique historical and contemporary context of Black adults in the United States underscores the need to expand the ACEs to include traumatic community and cultural experiences (Cronholm et al., 2015; Dhaliwal, 2015; Degruy, 2005). Thus, when attempting to understand the PTSD disparity in the Black community, exposure to trauma in childhood (e.g., incarcerated family member), community (e.g., crime-ridden neighborhood), and culture (e.g., racism) has been shown to contribute to the higher prevalence and poor outcomes of PTSD among Black adults (Sibraya et al., 2019; Paradies et al., 2015; Cronholm et al., 2015; Dhaliwal, 2015; Degruy, 2005).

The prevalence of PTSD in the Black population extends beyond ACEs to include *adverse community experiences* and *adverse cultural experiences* linked to PTSD (Paradies et al., 2015; Berenz et al., 2017; Youssef et al., 2017). The adverse cultural experiences affect how Black people experience their childhood and community, ultimately influencing symptoms of PTSD. ACEs refer to adult memories of traumatic experiences in a person's life before age 18 (Felitti et al., 1998). They include exposure to physical, emotional, or sexual abuse, domestic violence toward a parent, behavioral health issues of a household member, incarceration of a household member, divorce or separation of a parent, and lack of necessities. Slopen and colleagues (2016) found that Black children were exposed to greater ACEs than their white counterparts. *Adverse community experiences* refer to the systemic inequities present in a person's community (Pinderhughes, Davis, & Williams, 2015). Examples include lack of affordable and safe housing, segregated neighborhoods, community violence, and an unkempt built environment. Black neighborhoods caused by residential racial segregation are plagued with increased poverty and higher community violence (Santilli et al., 2017; Logan & Oakley, 2017).

Adverse cultural experiences are defined as chronic exposures to historical and contemporary systemic racial injustices targeted to a specific ethnic group. The racial injustices are experienced through Ostrom's adapted socio-psychological ABC model of racism: **a**ffect (prejudice), **b**ehavior (discrimination, microaggressions), and **c**ognition (stereotype) and may elucidate the mediating role of discrimination (Ostrom, 1969). Stereotypes (cognition) are used to rationalize prejudice (beliefs), leading to discrimination (behavior) and creating a racialized social system that is socially structured based on racial categories to benefit one group over another (Dovidio & Gaertner, 1996; Bonilla-Silva, 1997). In this racialized social system, Black adults experience racism at disproportionate rates. Lee and colleagues (2019) replicated Boutwell and colleagues' (2017) study examining the prevalence of racism in the United States and found a more significant difference from their estimates. Boutwell and colleagues (2017) estimated that the racism prevalence rate was 31.88% for Blacks and 23.53% for whites. However, Lee and colleagues (2019) found a range of 69.45% to 73.62% for Blacks and 29.61% to 34.48% for whites which were more accurate estimates.

Since supervision is conducted in the context of employment and workplace relations, racial phenomena such as stereotypes, prejudices, and discrimination experienced by Black adult supervisees may be crystallized by the chronic racial inequities in the workplace. This ultimately influences PTSD, which is linked to perceived discrimination, racial micro-aggressions, and racial stigmatization (Williams et al., 2008). Paradies and colleagues (2015) evaluated data from 293 studies published between 1983 and 2013 and found an extensive association of self-reported racism with negative mental health outcomes. More than 20% of the studies reported an association with psychological distress and 4.8% with PTSD. Adverse mental health outcomes had the largest mean weighted effect size compared to positive mental health, physical health, and general health, with PTSD demonstrating the most significant effect size. This is important because, in the workplace, the negative racialized employment experiences of Black adults have remained constant since 1990 and are associated with PTSD (Quillan, Pager, Hexel, & Midtbøen, 2017; Brooks Holliday et al., 2020).

The differential experiences of racism among Black adults compared to other ethnic groups may explain the etiology of PTSD among Black adults. When comparing these differences, it was found that Black adults experienced significantly more episodes of discrimination associated with PTSD (Chou, Asnaani, & Hofmann, 2012). Several researchers have found similar results. Among a sample of 806 participants living in low-income, predominantly Black neighborhoods, any person who reported experiencing any discrimination was significantly more likely to meet the criteria for PTSD (Brooks Holliday et al., 2020). Sibraya and colleagues (2019) found that in their sample of Black adults, PTSD remission rates over five years of follow-up was 0.35 and significantly associated with a reported frequency of experiences with discrimination. The "triple-ACEs-effect" examines Black adults' exposure to childhood, community, and cultural adversities. It provides a foundation for supervisors to explore the deleterious effects of racialized social systems in the United States on Black supervisees and clients.

Recognizing the signs and symptoms of trauma in Black adults

Trauma in the Black community is expressed in many ways. Supervisors should become aware that their Black supervisees may also present with racial trauma symptoms caused by race-based stress (Comas-Díaz, Hall, & Neville, 2019). Due to its poor scientific understanding, the legitimacy of the clinical diagnosis of racial trauma is not widely accepted (Williams, Holloway, & Ross, 2019). People seem to be more ready to accept the effects of racial trauma based on work that originated in the 1960s to explain the collective distress described by some Jewish Holocaust survivors, termed "survivor syndrome" (Sadavoy, 1997). They identified that they presented with the following symptoms: denial, depersonalization, isolation, somatization, memory loss, agitation, anxiety, guilt, depression, intrusive thoughts, nightmares, psychic numbing, and survivor guilt.

Racial trauma is similar to PTSD described in the *Diagnostic and Statistical Manual of Mental Disorders*, 5th Edition (*DSM-5*) for PTSD (American Psychiatric Association, 2013), although it also has unique presentations. PTSD is a mental illness included as one of the trauma- and stressor-related disorders in the *DSM-5* and is characterized by symptoms of intrusion, avoidance, negative alterations in cognition and mood, and changes in arousal and reactivity after direct or indirect exposure to a traumatic event. Similar symptoms characterize racial trauma; however, it occurs after ongoing individual and collective exposure and re-exposure to real, perceived, or vicarious racial stereotypes, prejudices, discrimination, and violence (Comas-Díaz et al., 2019). Racial trauma is also cumulative and occurs in individuals who share a specific group identity and affiliation, such as nationality, religious affiliation, or ethnicity. It can affect those who have never experienced the traumatic event. The children and descendants exhibit signs and symptoms of trauma. In this context, racial trauma becomes an intergenerational or historical trauma that produces long-term distress among communities (Evans-Campbell, 2008).

Racial trauma may be expressed as follows:

1   The exposed individual may present with intrusion symptoms where the traumatic event is persistent re-experienced by unwanted upsetting memories, nightmares, flashbacks, emotional distress after exposure to traumatic reminders, physical reactivity after exposure to traumatic reminders. The exposed individual may experience avoidance symptoms where an individual avoids trauma-related thoughts or feelings or trauma-related external reminders. The exposed individual may experience negative thoughts or feelings that are exacerbated by the trauma, where an individual may not be able to recall key features of the trauma; has overly negative thoughts and assumptions about self or the world; engages in exaggerated blame of self or others for causing the trauma, presents with negative affect, decreased interest in activities, feelings of isolation and has difficulties experiencing positive affect. The exposed individual may experience alterations in arousal and reactivity where an individual is frequently irritable or aggressive, engages in risky or destructive behavior, is hyper vigilant, has a heightened startle reaction, has difficulty concentrating, and difficulty sleeping.

Williams and colleagues (2018) at the University of Connecticut have provided an argument for the inclusion of racial trauma in the Criterion A events of PTSD in the DSM-5. Currently, Criterion A limits a traumatic event to the following: direct exposure, witnessing exposure, indirect exposure by learning that a relative or close friend was exposed to trauma or vicarious trauma exposure during the course of work duties related to death, threatened death, actual or threatened serious injury, or actual or threatened sexual violence. However, Williams and her colleagues (2018) propose that one may use the *International Classification of Diseases* 10th Edition *(ICD-10)* criteria to generate a PTSD diagnosis for persons exposed to racial trauma since it is not as restrictive as the *DSM-5*. Williams and colleagues (2018) also developed the Uconn Racial/Ethnic Stress & Trauma Survey (UnRESTS); a semi-structured interview for clinicians to collect information about an individual's racial and ethnic group and ethnic identity and their experiences surrounding explicit racism, vicarious racism experienced by loved ones or by exposure through learning or watching using media, and experiences with microaggressions. This is a helpful tool because the symptoms generated are associated with the criteria of PTSD from the *DSM-5*.

Degruy (2005), in her theory of Post Traumatic Slave Syndrome (PTSS), identifies several ways that racial trauma manifests. One is *vacant esteem*, where an individual may experience insufficient development in multiple domains along with feelings of hopelessness, depression, and a general self-destructive outlook. Second is *marked propensity for anger and violence*, where an individual may experience extreme feelings of suspicion and perceived negative motivations of others. This is also where an individual engages in violence against self, property, and others. Third is *racist socialization and internalized racism*, where an individual engages in learned helplessness, literacy deprivation, distorted self-concept, and antipathy or aversion for the following: (1) members of one's own identified cultural/ethnic group; (2) mores and customs associated with one's own identified cultural/ethnic heritage; and (3) physical characteristics of one's own identified cultural/ethnic group.

Brief history of social work supervision

Tsui (1997) identified five historical stages of social work supervision, which reportedly started during the Charity Organization Societies (COS) movement. The first stage was the administrative function of supervision which was required for the untrained para-social workers known as *friendly visitors*. The initial supervision was focused on accountability for the middle- and working-class *friendly visitors* who received in-service training and orientation to their job responsibilities. The second stage moved supervision from the control of the agency to the university setting. Supervision became a learning process by which social workers learned the values, knowledge, and skills required to practice. Student supervision became a significant part of social work education, formal social work training programs that included fieldwork supervision. The third stage was influenced by social work practice theory and methods. During this therapeutic process, the supervisor was responsible for moving the supervisee through a helping process used to assist clients. It later moved toward being more psychodynamic, where social work supervision was regarded as a process that would be engaged through the professional life span of a social worker. The fourth stage was highly influenced by the development of the National Association of Social Workers in 1956. A debate ensued among social workers to determine if mature social workers required ongoing supervision or to become independent and engage in autonomous practice. The fifth stage saw a return to its administrative roots due to an increase in quality assurance and accountability for the treatment of clients by human service agencies.

Social work supervision models

Today, social work supervision seems rooted in administrative accountability influenced by politics and regulations (Kadushin, 1992). Next, we review prominent social work supervision models identified by Tsui (2004).

Practice theory as a model

Practice theory as a model of supervision includes a process parallel to the worker–client relationship. The same skills utilized during service delivery are displayed within supervision, including rapport building between the person of authority and the person requiring assistance (Kahn, 1979). This didactic form of supervision asserts a parallel hierarchical relationship between supervisor and supervisee and supervisee and client.

Structural–functional models

Structural–functional models of supervision focus on objectives in relation to their function within areas of supervision. While models may vary in their prioritization of supervisory domains, the functionality of the domains as a system of supervision is key. Examples of structural–functional models include the supervisory function model, the integrative model, and the models of authority. The supervisory function model compartmentalizes administrative, educational, and supportive domains that outline definitive tasks required for supervision. This delineation between domains and the focus on functionality creates clear boundaries within the supervisory relationship.

Agency models

Agency models of supervision illuminate a spectrum of agency control within the supervision process ranging from elevated administrative accountability within the casework model to autonomous practice models more fitting for experienced social workers. Other examples of these models include group and peer supervision models and team service delivery. Group supervision often serves as a supplemental form of supervision. This model saves the supervisor and agency time and resources. Processing shared professional experiences can foster team cohesiveness while overlooking less prevalent issues. Though peer supervision and team service delivery models extend more control to the worker due to shared decision-making, they also experience an increase in responsibilities and accountability (Brown & Bourne, 1996; Watson, 1973).

Interactional process

Interactional process models center the interactions occurring during supervision. Supervisee progress supplants the task orientation present in other models. Supervisors can adopt either a developmental or growth-oriented approach to the interactional process. The developmental approach focuses on supervisees' matriculation through the developmental stages of professional skill-building. Utilizing a growth-oriented approach shifts the focus from skill-building to personal and professional development.

Feminist partnership model

The feminist partnership model reconstructs the power dynamic within the supervisory relationship (Chernesky, 1986). This model relinquishes the significance of hierarchy and control, opting for a collegial partnership that assumes a supervisee's ability to self-direct and self-regulate.

Culturally relevant, trauma-response, and healing-centered supervision model

The current social work supervision models do not have an implicit trauma-informed framework that could help supervisors move to a culturally relevant, trauma-responsive, and healing-centered social work supervision model. We propose starting with integrating Substance Abuse and Mental Health Services Administration's (SAMHSA) (2014) six key principles of trauma-informed approach into the social work supervision process. The first principle, *safety*, requires that the supervisors collaborate with supervisees to co-design the supervision process. During this co-designing process, supervisees are empowered to define physical, psychological, social, and moral/spiritual safety and how it can be achieved and maintained. The second principle, *trustworthiness and transparency*, encourages supervisors to value highly an authentic character that recognizes the influences of their own background on responses to cultural differences. If achieved, the supervision becomes a process where the supervisor is comfortable with making all decisions and communications about supervisees in their presence. The third principle, *peer support*, promotes a way for supervisees who share common experiences, engage each other during the supervision process, build relationships, and share strengths and support. It must be noted here that the supervisor allows authentic relationships to be formed among supervisees with similar racial backgrounds, and shared experiences are explored and not assumed. The fourth principle, *collaboration and mutuality*, is the main ingredient of the co-design process for this trauma-informed social work supervision process. Having a collaborative process allows for supervisees to partner with supervisors to level out the power dynamics that often plague the supervision process. Trauma and hurt occur in relationships that do not allow for shared power and decision-making. Healing and resilience become possible in relationships that allow for meaningful shared power and decision-making. The fifth principle, *empowerment, voice, and choice*, creates an atmosphere where supervisees' strengths and individual experiences are recognized and used as a springboard for their professional success. The sixth principle, *cultural, historical, intergenerational, and gender issues*, focuses the supervisor on addressing any historical or contemporary cultural or gender stereotypes and biases. This is the area where the supervisor recognizes the multiple exposures of historical and contemporary racialized experiences in the lives of Black supervisees. A full integration of this principle creates for an easier transition to a culturally relevant, trauma-responsive, and healing-centered social work supervision approach.

To assist supervisors with implementing a culturally relevant, trauma-responsive, and healing-centered approach to their social work supervision model, we propose the use of the seven principles of *Nguzo Saba* (*Umoja, Kujichagulia, Ujima, Ujamaa, Nia, Kuumba, Imani*) (Karenga, 1988) and the seven healing-centered commitments

(*Relationships, Culture, Agency, Aspirations, Restoration of Identity, Assets, Meaning*) (Ginwright, 2018). These seven commitments and seven principles inform the activities and the grounding for interactions during the supervision process (see Table 5.1).

The uniqueness of this culturally relevant, trauma-responsive, and healing-centered approach is the crosswalk of the seven commitments and seven principles with the trauma-informed care principles presented in Table 5.1.

The culturally relevant, trauma-responsive, and healing-centered approach is developed based on characteristics of the African rites of passage. The African rites of passage identifies observances of change that can occur in place, state, or social

TABLE 5.1 Seven Principles of *Nguzo Saba* and Seven Healing-Centered Commitments

Nguzo Saba	*Healing-Centered*
Umoja (unity) To strive for and maintain unity in the family, community, nation, and race	**Relationships** The capacity to create, sustain, and grow healthy connections with others
Kujichagulia (self-determination) To define, name, create, and speak for oneself	**Agency** The individual and collective ability to act, create, and change the root causes of personal, social, and community challenges
Ujima (collective work & responsibility) To build and maintain our community together and make our brothers' and sisters' problems our problems and to solve them together	**Culture** Developing an awareness of one's own and others' racial and other social identities
Ujamaa (cooperative economics) To build and maintain our own stores, shops, and other businesses and to profit from them together	**Aspirations** The exploration of possibilities for our lives and the process of accomplishing goals for personal and collective well-being
Nia (purpose) To make our collective vocation the building and developing of our community to restore our people to their traditional greatness	**Restoration of identity** The healing process allows the space to be conducive for people to find their "who am I?" "why am I here?", and "what am I supposed to do?"
Kuumba (creativity) To do always as much as we can, in the way we can, in order to leave our community more beautiful and beneficial than we inherited it	**Assets** Identifying those things about self that are valuable for use by self and other community members
Imani (faith) To believe with all our heart in our people, our parents, our teachers, our leaders, and the righteousness and victory of our struggle	**Meaning** The profound discovery of who we are, where we are going, and what purpose we were born to serve

position (Gennep, 1960). For this social work supervision approach, the African rites of passage is being used to observe changes in the Black supervisees' professional growth while using trauma-responsive and healing-centered language and descriptions provided by the seven principles of *Nguzo Saba* and seven healing-centered commitments. This is being done based on the three phases identified by van Gennep in 1960. The first phase is the separation or preliminary phase. During this phase, Black supervisees with reported and recognized racial trauma exposure agree to engage in supervision that detaches them from a fixed view of social work supervision, trauma, community adversity, and healing. There is an exploration of the trauma-informed care principles with supervisees to determine the level of understanding. Black supervisees then help co-design a brave space that allows for the development of trust and risk-taking required to explore new attitudes and behaviors regarding trauma, community adversity, and healing (Ginwright, 2018; Yalom, 2005). The supervisor allows the supervisee to discuss how their racial trauma has impacted their social work practice. This is where the supervisee is encouraged to identify difficulties in any of the seven principles of *Nguzo Saba* and/ or the seven healing-centered commitments.

The second phase is the margin or liminal phase. It is through this phase that culturally relevant, trauma-responsive, and healing-centered social work supervision is fully encountered. The Black supervisee's state is often quite ambiguous during this phase as they maneuver through their past individual views of supervision and start to develop a collective state of healing-centered strategies that promote growth in their social work professional skills. During this phase supervisors may demonstrate how their interaction with racial trauma may interrupt their social work skills with clients. This can be done using the four-part – Safety, Emotions, Loss, and Future (SELF) – conversations to encourage supervisees to explore their strengths and opportunities for change (Bloom, Foderaro, & Ryan, 2010). During the SELF conversations, supervisors discuss how traumatic racial experiences can affect how they engage their cases with supervisees. In the first conversation, the different types of *safety* are identified (physical, psychological, social, moral/ spiritual) by allowing supervisees to draw examples from their community and life, listening nonjudgmentally, openly, and empathetically. In the second conversation, *emotional* responses are discussed and how they tie into engagement with clients and colleagues, validating struggles and successes. In the third conversation, personal, general, or community examples of different types of *losses* that occurred due to traumatic events are discussed, working toward solutions. The fourth conversation allows the supervisee to discuss *future* goals for their professional self, using humility and self-disclosure to encourage the supervisee to share.

The third phase is the aggregation or post-liminal phase. During this phase the supervisee-developed goals of the culturally relevant, trauma-responsive, and healing-centered social work supervision approach are consummated. The social work supervision process is now taking the Black supervisee on a journey toward healing from trauma and chronic adversity and a greater professional outcome. At this point, the social work supervision process is fully accepted. Supervisors and supervisees begin to think, speak, and behave according to culturally relevant, trauma-responsive, and healing-centered social work supervision expectations and standards (Turner, 1987).

Conclusion

This chapter highlights the necessity for a culturally relevant, trauma-responsive, and healing-centered approach within social work supervision. Social work supervision models have evolved from the didactic casework approach of practice theory models to the growth-oriented collaborative approaches of interactional and feminist models. However, the pervasiveness of racism requires that social work supervisors account for the implications of society's culture of inequity within their supervision practices. Including a culturally relevant, trauma-responsive, and healing-centered approach to social work supervision supports an integrated trauma-informed professional culture. Black social workers are not exempt from experiencing racial discrimination – and oppression based on any other intersectional identities – due to their professional status. To negate the impact of racial trauma leads to a disregard for the experiences of Black clients, perpetuates tokenism, and denies the full humanness of Black people. In this current racialized political climate coupled with the COVID-19 pandemic, it would be incumbent for the NASW to emphasize a culturally responsive trauma-informed approach within social work supervision. Black adults are disproportionately affected by both the racialized political system and the COVID-19 pandemic. A culturally responsive trauma-informed approach to social work supervision could assist Black social work supervisees with maneuvering through the intersection of race and education and personal and professional values that may conflict during this time of profound racial divide in the United States. In considering a culturally responsive trauma-informed approach within social work supervision, social work supervisors would acknowledge the challenges faced by many Black supervisees when navigating their authentic racial identity while also adapting to the values and ethics of the social work profession. This, in turn, reduces the re-traumatization of Black supervisees, moving them toward healing and resilience.

References

Alegria, M., Fortuna, L. R., Lin, J. Y., Norris, F. H., Gao, S., Takeuchi, D. T., . . ., Valentine, A. (2013). Prevalence, risk, and correlates of post-traumatic stress disorder across ethnic and racial minority groups in the United States. *Medical Care, 51*(12), 1114–1123.

American Psychiatric Association. (2013). *Diagnostic and statistical manual of mental disorders* (5th ed.). Washington, DC: Author.

Berenz, E. C., Roberson-Nay, R., Latendresse, S. J., Mezuk, B., Gardner, C. O., Amstadter, A. B., & York T. P. (2017). Post-traumatic stress disorder and alcohol dependence: Epidemiology and order of onset. *Psychological Trauma, 9*(4), 485–492.10.1037/tra0000185

Bloom, S. L., Foderaro, J. F., & Ryan, R. (2010). *SELF: A trauma-informed psychoeducational group curriculum.* Retrieved from http://sanctuaryweb.com/Products/SELFGroup Training.aspx

Bonilla-Silva, E. (1997). Rethinking racism: Toward a structural interpretation. *American Sociological Review, 62*(3), 465–480. https://doi.org/10.2307/2657316

Boutwell, B. B., Nedelec, J. L., Winegard, B., Shackelford, T., Beaver, K. M., Vaughn, M., . . . Wright, J. P. (2017). The prevalence of discrimination across racial groups in contemporary America: Results from a nationally representative sample of adults. *PloS One, 12*(8), e0183356. https://doi.org/10.1371/journal.pone.0183356

Brooks Holliday, S., Dubowitz, T., Haas, A., Ghosh-Dastidar, B., DeSantis, A., & Troxel, W. M. (2020). The association between discrimination and PTSD in African Americans: Exploring the role of gender. *Ethnicity & Health, 25*(5), 717–731. https://doi.org/10.10 80/13557858.2018.1444150

Brown, A., & Bourne, I. (1996). *The social work supervisor: Supervision in community, daycare, and residential settings*. Philadelphia: Open University Press.

Chernesky, R. H. (1986). A new model of supervision. *Feminist Visions for Social Work*, 128–148.

Chou, T., Asnaani, A., & Hofmann, S. G. (2012). Perception of racial discrimination and psychopathology across three US ethnic minority groups. *Cultural Diversity & Ethnic Minority Psychology, 18*(1), 74–81. https://doi.org/10.1037/a0025432

Comas-Díaz, L., Hall, G. N., & Neville, H. A. (2019). Racial trauma: Theory, research, and healing: Introduction to the special issue. *American Psychologist, 74*(1), 1–5. http://dx.doi.org/10.1037/amp0000442

Cronholm, P. F., Forke, C. M., Wade, R., Bair-Merritt, M. H., Davis, M., Harkins-Schwarz, M., . . . Fein, J. A. (2015). Adverse childhood experiences: Expanding the concept of adversity. *American Journal of Preventive Medicine, 49*(3), 354–361. https://doi.org/10.1016/j.amepre.2015.02.00

Dhaliwal, K. [Chart] (2015). *Trauma and social location*. RYSE Center Richmond, CA. [cited 2021 January 11]. Retrieved from www.acesconnection.com/blog/adding-layers- to-the-aces-pyramidwhat-do-you-think

DeGruy, J. (2005). *Post traumatic slave syndrome: America's legacy of enduring injury and healing*. Portland, OR: Joy DeGruy Publications Inc.

Dovidio, J. F., & Gaertner, S. L. (1996). Affirmative action, unintentional racial biases, and intergroup relations. *Journal of Social Issues, 52*(4), 51–75. https://doi.org/10.1111/j.1540-4560.1996.tb01848.x

Evans-Campbell, T. (2008). Historical trauma in American Indian/Native Alaska communities: A multilevel framework for exploring impacts on individuals, families, and communities. *Journal of Interpersonal Violence, 23*, 316–338.

Felitti, V. J., Anda, R. F., Nordenberg, D., Williamson, D. F., Spitz, A. M., Edwards, V., . . Marks, J. S. (1998). Relationship of childhood abuse and household dysfunction to many of the leading causes of death in adults. The Adverse Childhood Experiences (ACE) Study. *American Journal of Preventive Medicine, 14*(4), 245–258. https://doi.org/10.1016/s0749-3797 (98)00017–8

Gennep, A. v. (1960). *The rites of passage* (M. B. Vizedom & G. L. Caffee, Trans.). Chicago, IL: University of Chicago Press.

Ginwright, S. (2018, May 31). *The future of healing: Shifting from trauma informed care to healing centered engagement*. Retrieved from https://medium.com/@ginwright/the-future-of-healingshifting-from-trauma-informed-care-to-healing-centered-engagement-634f557ce69c

Kadushin, A. (1992). What's wrong, what's right with social work supervision. *The Clinical Supervisor, 10*(1), 3–19.

Kahn, E. M. (1979). The parallel process in social work treatment and supervision. *Social Casework, 60*(9), 520–528. https://doi.org/10.1177/104438947906000902

Karenga, M. (1988). *The African American holiday of Kwanzaa. A celebration of family, community and culture.* Timbuktu, Mali: University of Sankore.

Lee, R. T., Perez, A. D., Boykin, C. M., & Mendoza-Denton, R. (2019). On the prevalence of racial discrimination in the United States. *PloS One, 14*(1), e0210698. https://doi.org/10.1371/journal.pone.0210698

Logan, J. R., & Oakley, D. (2017). Black lives and policing: The larger context of ghettoization. *Journal of Urban Affairs, 39*(8), 1031–1046. https://doi.org/10.1080/07352166.2017.1328977

National Association of Social Workers. (2008). *Code of ethics of the National Association of Social Workers.* Washington, DC: Author.

Nobles, C. J., Valentine, S. E., Borba, C. P., Gerber, M. W., Shtasel, D. L., & Marques, L. (2016). Black-white disparities in the association between post-traumatic stress disorder and chronic illness. *Journal of Psychosomatic Research, 85*, 19–25.

Ostrom, T. M. (1969). The relationship between the affective, behavioral, and cognitive components of attitude. *Journal of Experimental Social Psychology, 5*(1), 12–30. https://doi.org/10.1016/0022-1031(69)90003-1

Paradies, Y., Ben, J., Denson, N., Elias, A., Priest, N., Pieterse, A., . . . Gee, G. (2015). Racism as a determinant of health: A systematic review and meta-analysis. *PloS One, 10*(9), e0138511. https://doi.org/10.1371/journal.pone.0138511

Pearlin, L. I., Schieman, S., Fazio, E. M., & Meersman, S. C. (2005). Stress, health, and the life course: Some conceptual perspectives. *Journal of Health and Social Behavior, 46*(2), 205–219. https://doi.org/10.1177/002214650504600206

Pinderhughes, H., Davis, R., & Williams, M. [Internet]. 2015 [cited 2021 January 7]. *Adverse community experiences and resilience: A framework for addressing and preventing community trauma.* Oakland, CA: Prevention Institute. Retrieved from www.preventioninstitute.org/sites/default/files/publications/Adverse%20Community%20Experiences%20and%20Resilience.pdf

Quillan, L., Pager, D., Hexel, O., & Midtbøen, A. H. (2017). Meta-analysis of field experiments shows no change in racial discrimination in hiring over time. *Proceedings of the National Academy of Sciences, 114*(41), 10870–10875. https://doi.org/10.1073/pnas.1706255114

Roberts, A. L., Gilman, S. E., Breslau, J., Breslau, N., & Koenen, K. C. (2011). Race/ethnic differences in exposure to traumatic events, development of post-traumatic stress disorder, and treatment-seeking for post-traumatic stress disorder in the United States. *Psychological Medicine, 41*(01), 71–83.

Sadavoy, J. (1997). Survivors. A review of the late-life effects of prior psychological trauma. *The American Journal of Geriatric, 5*(4), 287–301. https://doi.org/10.1097/00019442- 199700540-00004

Santilli, A., O'Connor Duffany, K., Carroll-Scott, A., Thomas, J., Greene, A., Arora, A., . . . Ickovics, J. (2017). Bridging the response to mass shootings and urban violence: Exposure to violence in New Haven, Connecticut. *American Journal of Public Health, 107*(3), 374–379. https://doi.org/10.2105/AJPH.2016.303613

Sibraya, N. J., Bjornsson, A. S., Pérez Benítez, A., Moitra, E., Weisberg, R. B., & Keller, M. B. (2019). Post-traumatic stress disorder in African American and Latinx adults: Clinical course and the role of racial and ethnic discrimination. *The American Psychologist, 74*(1), 101–116. https://doi.org/10.1037/amp0000339

Slopen, N., Shonkoff, J. P., Albert, M. A., Yoshikawa, H., Jacobs, A., Stoltz, R., & Williams, D. R. (2016). Racial disparities in child adversity in the U.S.: Interactions with family immigration history and income. *American Journal of Preventive Medicine, 50*(1), 47–56. https://doi.org/10.1016/j.amepre.2015.06.013

Substance Abuse and Mental Health Services Administration. (2014). *Concept of trauma and guidance for a trauma-informed care approach.* US Department of Health and Human Services. Retrieved from https://ncsacw.samhsa.gov/userfiles/files/SAMHSA _Trauma.pdf

Tsui, M. S. (1997). The roots of social work supervision. *The Clinical Supervisor, 15*(2), 191–198.

Tsui, M. S. (2004). *Social work supervision: Contexts and concepts.* Thousand Oaks, London, New Delhi: Sage.

Turner, V. (1987). Betwixt and between: The liminal period in rites of passage. In V. Turner (Ed.), *The forest of symbols* (pp. 93–111). Seattle, WA: University of Washington Press.

Watson, K. W. (1973). Differential supervision. *Social Work, 18*(6), 80–88.

Williams, D. R., Gonzalez, H. M., Williams, S., Mohammed, S. A., Moomal, H., & Stein, D. J. (2008). Perceived discrimination, race and health in South Africa. *Social Science & Medicine (1982), 67*(3), 441–452. https://doi.org/10.1016/j.socscimed.2008.03.02

Williams, J. C., Holloway, T. D., & Ross, D. A. (2019). Witnessing modern America: Violence and racial trauma. *Biological psychiatry, 86*(11), e41–e42. https://doi.org/10.1016/j.biopsych.2019.09.025

Williams, M. T., Metzger, I. W., Leins, C., & DeLapp, C. (2018). Assessing racial trauma within a DSM – 5 framework: The UConn racial/ethnic stress & trauma survey. *Practice Innovations, 3*(4), 242–260.

World Health Organization. (2019). *Social determinants of health: Key concepts.* Retrieved from http://www.who.int/social_determinants/thecommission/finalreport/key_concepts/en/index.html

Yalom, I. D. (2005). *Theory and practice of group psychopathology* (5th ed.). New York, NY: Basic Books.

Youssef, N. A., Belew, D., Hao, G., Wang, X., Treiber, F. A., Stefanek, M., . . . Su, S. (2017). Racial/ethnic differences in the association of childhood adversities with depression and the role of resilience. *Journal of Affective Disorders, 208*, 577–581. https://doi.org/10.1016/j.jad.2016.10.024

PART 3

Trauma and the legacy of the Black experience

6

ENCAPSULATING OUR TRUTHS

An Afrocentric approach to addressing trauma in African American culture

LaTanya N. Townsend, Tonya C. Phillips, Rhea C. Porter

Trauma is a response to an event, a series of events, or a set of circumstances experienced by an individual as physically or emotionally harmful or life-threatening with lasting adverse effects on the individual's functioning and mental, physical, social, emotional, and/or spiritual well-being (SAMHSA, 2019a). Traumatic events include historical trauma – inclusive of race-related stressors and microaggressions; adverse childhood experiences (ACEs) – inclusive of physical and sexual abuse, community, domestic, and intimate partner violence; natural disasters, post-traumatic stress disorder (PTSD), and more.

Violence data statistics summarize that 683,000 victims of child abuse and neglect were reported to child protective services in 2015 (U.S. Department of Health & Human Services, 2015); the Center for Disease Control and Prevention (2018) reports that more than ten million men and women experienced physical violence by an intimate partner annually; and one in five women and one in 71 men will be raped at some point in their lives (Black et al., 2011). Aside from the physical, mental, and emotional impact, financial repercussions indicate that annually more than US $671 billion is related to the cost of trauma – inclusive of physical/mental health treatment, rehabilitation, lodging, lost wages, protective endeavors and more (CDC, 2021).

ACEs are potentially traumatic events that can have negative, lasting effects on health and well-being (Felitti et al., 2019) – for example, experiencing violence, abuse, or neglect, witnessing violence in the home, and having a family member attempt or die by suicide (CDC, 2019a). A myriad of literature has identified African Americans as being at a higher risk for trauma exposure in comparison to their white counterparts with early associated childhood experiences (Davis, Ressler, Schwartz, Stephens, & Bradley, 2008; Merritt et al., 2013; Koenen et al., 2007). Several studies have identified ACEs in children and reported that major childhood adversities, including growing up in poverty, peer rejection, poor school

DOI: 10.4324/9780429276613-9

performance, property crime, and witnessing community violence, are associated with increased lifelong risk for negative life events and negative health outcomes (Oral et al., 2016). The identified adverse experiences included child abuse (emotional, physical, or sexual), child neglect (emotional or physical), and household dysfunction (domestic violence, substance abuse, mental illness, criminal activity, or parental absence (Dube et al., 2001; Felitti et al., 2019).

Types of trauma

Historical trauma, race-related stressors, and microaggressions

Mass trauma that is inflicted on a group of people based on their identity or ethnicity, religious background, and nationality affiliation is defined as historical trauma. The theoretical framework of historical trauma includes three major components: (1) the historical trauma experience, (2) historical trauma response, and (3) intergenerational transmission of historical trauma (Henderson, Acquaye-Doyle, Waites, & Howard, 2016; Brave Heart, 2003; Danieli, 1998).

Hampton, Gullotta, and Crowel (2010) described a specific definition of historical trauma for African Americans, which is "the collective spiritual, psychological, emotional, and cognitive distress perpetuated intergenerationally deriving from multiple denigrating experiences originating with slavery and continuing with patterned forms of racism and discrimination to the present day" (p. 32).

The contemporary events involving discrimination, racism, and daily hassles that are targeted at individuals from diverse racial and ethnic groups are known as racial microaggressions (Evans-Campbell, 2008). Racial microaggressions have led to feelings of powerlessness, invisibility, forced compliance and loss of integrity, and pressure to represent their race (Sue, Capodilupo, & Holder, 2008). Additionally, race-related stress has been associated with psychological problems, including negative self-esteem, concentration difficulties, anxiety, and depression (Reynolds, Sneva, & Beehler, 2010).

Family and intimate partner violence

Intimate partner violence (IPV) is any physical violence, sexual violence, stalking, and/or psychological aggression perpetrated by a current or former intimate partner (CDC, 2018). The CDC (2019c) defines four types of IPV behavior: (1) physical violence – attempts to hurt a partner by hitting, kicking, or using another type of physical force; (2) sexual violence – forcing or trying to force a partner to take part in a sex act, sexual touching, or a nonphysical sexual event (e.g., sexting) without consent; (3) stalking – repeated and/or unwanted attention by a partner resulting in fear or concern for one's own safety or the safety of someone close to the victim; and (4) psychological aggression – verbal and nonverbal communication with the intent to hurt another person mentally or emotionally to exert control over another person.

Childhood abuse

Child maltreatment is defined as

> [A]ny recent act or failure to act on the part of a parent or caregiver that results in death, serious physical or emotional harm, sexual abuse, or exploitation, or an act or failure to act that presents an imminent risk of serious harm.
>
> *(Child Abuse Prevention and Treatment Act, 2010)*

Seven types of child maltreatment have been defined by the United States Department of Health and Human Services:

- *Physical abuse* – is characterized by "any non-accidental physical injury to the child" including striking, kicking, burning, or biting or any action that results in a physical impairment of the child.
- *Child neglect* – is characterized by the failure of a parent or other person with responsibility for the child to provide needed food, clothing, shelter, medical care, or supervision to the degree that the child's health, safety, and well-being are threatened with harm.
- *Physical neglect* – refusal of, or delay in, seeking health care, food, clothing, or shelter; abandonment; expulsion from the home or refusal to allow a runaway to return home; and inadequate supervision.
- *Educational neglect* – the allowance of chronic truancy, failure to enroll a child of mandatory school age in school, and failure to attend to a special educational need.
- *Emotional neglect* – marked inattention to the child's needs for affection; refusal of or failure to provide needed psychological care; spouse abuse in the child's presence; and permission of drug or alcohol use by the child.
- *Sexual abuse* – includes fondling a child's genitals, intercourse, incest, rape, sodomy, exhibitionism, and commercial exploitation through prostitution or the production of pornographic materials.
- *Emotional abuse* – includes acts or omissions by the parents or other caregivers who have caused behavioral, cognitive, emotional, or mental injury.

Vicarious trauma

Community violence is defined as exposure to planned acts of interpersonal violence committed in public areas by persons who are not intimately related to the victim (The National Child Traumatic Stress Network [NCTSN], n.d.). The National Child Traumatic Stress Network (n.d.) identifies that the common types of community violence that affect youth involve individual and group conflicts, such as bullying, fights among gangs, shootings in public areas, civil wars in foreign countries or warlike environments in US cities. Other potentially traumatic experiences include police killings of unarmed African Americans, domestic and family violence, rape, drug addiction, murder, and poverty. Much of the trauma in African American communities can be related to high rates of crime and violence and police involved shootings or killings. The cumulative effect of these experiences can have a serious damaging impact on the mental and physical health of African Americans. Trauma-based reactions include fear, anger, disbelief, anxiety, extreme alertness, and of course avoidance.

Sudden and unexpected deaths also can contribute to trauma reactions. Natural disasters are large-scale geological or meteorological events that have the potential to cause loss of life or property (e.g., tornados, hurricanes, floods, wildfires, earthquakes, and drought) (SAMHSA, 2019b). The deaths related to natural disasters are frequently due to blunt trauma, crush-related injuries, or drowning (Watson, Gayer, & Connolly, 2007).

Current treatment interventions

There are a myriad of treatment modalities utilized to address mental health. Current treatment interventions utilized to address the mental health needs of those affected by trauma include cognitive behavioral therapy (CBT), trauma-informed care, eye movement desensitization reprocessing (EMDR), and trauma-focused cognitive behavioral treatment, to name a few.

Cognitive behavioral therapy

Several studies posit that CBT is one of the most effective means of treating individuals with trauma and stress-related disorders (Deacon & Abramowitz, 2004; Wolitzky-Taylor et al., 2019). CBT approaches are rooted in the fundamental principle that an individual's cognitions play a significant and primary role in the development and maintenance of emotional and behavioral responses to life situations (González-Prendes & Resko, 2012). Developed by Aaron Beck in the late 1960s, CBT alleges that restructuring of beliefs, meanings, expectations, and ideas play an important role in alleviating psychological responses. Beck purports that cognitive processes and content are accessible and can be known that thought processes mediate responses to environmental cues, and that such cognitions can be intentionally targeted, modified, and changed (González-Prendes & Resko, 2012).

CBT for PTSD

Specifically in the treatment of PTSD, CBT has demonstrated to be highly effective in promoting cognitive restructuring, which identifies the maladaptive thought patterns and then integrates more plausible and reasonable interpretations of the trauma into an autobiographical memory (Cahill, Rothbaum, Resick, & Follette, 2009). This allows the patient to correct distorted representations about the self, world, and trauma, thus they subsequently develop a more adaptive and realistic interpretation of the event and a reduction in overall distress. The elements of CBT for PTSD typically encompass the following:

- *Psychoeducation*: informing the patient about the disorder, the psychological basis of their symptoms to normalize their experience and a rational for treatment.
- *Anxiety management techniques*: training to manage physical manifestations which reduce arousal and facilitate engagement with the treatment components that follow.
- *Prolonged exposure*: the application of prolonged imaginal exposure guides the patient through the memory of the traumatic event for extended periods of time.
- *In vivo exposure:* exposure to real-life reminders of the traumatic event in a systematic manner.
- *Cognitive restructuring*: identifying and utilizing evidence to challenge maladaptive appraisals or interpretations of the trauma, the self, the world, or the future.
- *Relapse prevention*: identifying possible situations or stressors that may lead to setbacks and role-playing how to manage those situations.

Trauma-informed care

Trauma-informed care has become an important approach to serving those who have been exposed to trauma by focusing on treating the "whole" person rather than the individual symptoms or specific behaviors. A trauma-informed approach incorporates awareness of trauma and its impact across all aspects of functioning and is reflected in certain. Trauma-specific services are designed expressly for the purpose of treating the symptoms and syndromes related to current or past trauma, essentially recognizing the role that trauma has played in the client's life (Bryson et al., 2017).

Addressing trauma by utilizing trauma-informed care rests on the premises of an understanding of and responsiveness to the impact of trauma that emphasizes physical, psychological, and emotional safety for both providers and survivors and that creates opportunities for survivors to rebuild a sense of control and empowerment (Hopper, Bassuk, & Olivet, 2010, p. 82).

SAMHSA (2014) describes six key principles of a trauma-informed approach:

- Safety – ensuring the physical and emotional safety of the practitioner, agency, and the population that is being served.
- Trustworthiness and transparency – conducting interventions with transparency with the goal of building and maintaining trust amongst the practitioner and the client.
- Peer support – utilizing individuals with lived experiences to build trust, enhance motivation, and promote recovery and healing.

- Collaboration and mutuality – shared decision-making among all parties impacted.
- Empowerment, voice, and choice – recognizing and building upon individual strengths, incorporating shared decision-making, and self-advocacy.
- Cultural, historical, and gender issues – incorporating policies, protocols, and processes that are responsive.

Eye movement desensitization and reprocessing

Eye movement desensitization and reprocessing (EMDR) is a psychotherapy treatment originally designed to alleviate the distress associated with traumatic memories (Shapiro, 1989a, 1989b). After its inception, it was identified as an effective treatment for trauma and PTSD during a short period of therapy. The treatment seeks to restart the healing process of maladaptive responses which are stuck by using a three-pronged protocol where the past traumatic events are processed, the current circumstances that illicit distress are targeted and desensitized, and imaginal templates of future events are incorporated, thus acquiring new skills needed for adaptive functioning (Shapiro, 2007).

EMDR treatment modality aims to distance patients with PTSD from the negative self-conception that can develop following traumatic events, while affirming and installing positive self-assessments (Gainer, Alam, S., Alam, H. & Redding, 2020). These include obtaining a thorough client history, preparing the client for the EMDR therapy process (explaining each step), assessing the traumatic event(s), desensitizing and reprocessing the trauma (through eye movements or other bilateral stimulation), installing a positive cognition, conducting a body scan to determine if there is any residual trauma, providing session closure, and reevaluating the status of a trauma.

The integral component of this therapeutic process is the inclusion of the eye movements. According to Shapiro (2001), the therapist moves their fingers back and forth in front of the patient's face after instructing the patient to follow the movement with their eyes. This is done in conjunction with other stimulating events, including a series of sounds, taps, or alternating lights in a repeated manner until the patient is able to positively respond to the event (González-Prendes & Resko, 2012).

In contrast to cognitive behavioral approaches, which requires the patient to focus on anxiety provoking behaviors and irrational thoughts, treatment utilizing EMDR therapy access current resources and targets the experiences that caused the negative cognition which have become stuck in a patient's nervous system.

Trauma-focused cognitive behavioral therapy

Trauma-focused cognitive behavioral therapy (TF-CBT) is an evidence-based psychotherapy technique that was specifically designed to address children and adolescents aged 3–18 years of age following severe traumatic experiences. Developed by Cohen, Mannarino, and Deblinger (2006), TF-CBT is a relatively short-term, integrated approach aimed at reducing negative affective responses, distorted cognitions, and maladaptive behaviors that can arise from trauma exposure. TF-CBT utilizes gradual exposure to reminders of the traumatic experience and supports participants in constructing trauma narratives that focus on strengths and empowerment. Parents are an essential component of TF-CBT as parental engagement maximizes the level of support needed to manage the symptoms related to the traumatic experience; this family therapy component is integral to the success of treatment (Phipps, R., & Thorne, S., 2019).

The core components of TF-CBT are **P**sychoeducation and Parenting Skills, **R**elaxation, **A**ffect Regulation, **C**ognitive Restructuring, **T**rauma Narrative, **I**n Vivo Exposure, **C**onjoint Parent – Child Sessions and **E**nhancing Safety Planning. Although a great deal of research has been conducted studying the use of TF-CBT with child and adolescent survivors of sexual abuse, TF-CBT has been also shown to be effective with clients who have been exposed to community violence, traumatic grief and loss, as well as natural disasters (Phipps & Thorne, 2019).

The Afrocentric paradigm

Understanding trauma from a cultural lens is critical in tailoring practice interventions and treatment outcomes for persons with trauma in urban environments. The Afrocentric perspective employs humanistic values, which are fundamental to the development of healthy families and communities. Its perspective is predicated on traditional African philosophical postulations that emphasize the interconnectedness and interdependency of natural phenomena. From this perspective, all modalities and realities are viewed as one, and there is no delineation between the spiritual and material (Asante, 1980). Asante further states that Afrocentricity is a frame of reference wherein phenomena are viewed from the perspective of the African person . . . centering on placing people in control of their lives and attitudes about the world and making them key players rather than victims. This aligns with Schiele's (1994) view that an Afrocentric view holds fast to the idea that an "individual cannot be understood separate from other people" (p. 154).

Spirituality is another essential component of the Afrocentric paradigm, as the recognition of the connectedness of the mind, body, and soul undergird the delivery of interventions addressed in clinical practice. The historical experiences of African Americans specifically lend credence to the inclusion of this component as the belief of a higher power connecting all human beings to each other and the creator (Schiele, 1997). Chipungu et al. (2000) note that such values as communalism and spirituality increase resiliency and other protective factors while decreasing or mediating risk factors. This overall acknowledgment of the spiritual nature of individuals posits the legitimacy of the delivery of services to address systemic oppression, structural racism, and marginalization, and loss of culture will yield substantive changes within the urban community as a whole.

The Afrocentric paradigm in social work is an important professional development toward rendering social work practices and draws heavily on the shared cultural values and practices of traditional Africa (Schiele, 2017). The values of African culture, all-encompassing of spirituality, wholeness, collectivity, and oneness with nature are critical to the building and reinforcement of individuals within the urban environment. Gilbert, Harvey, and Belgrave (2009) continue to state that "when individuals lack cultural knowledge, self-appreciation and positive racial identification but internalize negative views, myths and stereotypes they become engaged in a constellation of coping responses that are not self-enhancing" (p. 245). This could be no truer than for those within the urban population who have been stigmatized, oppressed, and discriminated against specifically in relation to traumatic experiences. Thus, centrality of Africa as a starting point for analysis and synthesis of trauma survivors is a prerequisite for effective clinical practice.

Clinical interventions in urban settings utilizing an African-centered approach

Eurocentric theories have not provided effective models to address trauma within the urban community. Many of the current treatment methodologies concentrate on the behavioral factors affecting brain development or behavioral responses to the trauma exposure. The African worldview supports the use of Afrocentric interventions with trauma survivors as it emphasizes groupness, commonalities, collective responsibility, interdependence, and survival of the tribe – a staunch contrast to the European worldview. The African-centered perspective employs humanistic principles which are fundamental to the development of healthy families and communities (King, 2019). The literature supporting this view highlights the following components as essential to integrating African-centered interventions: (a) all human beings have inherent rights and dignity; (b) environmental conditions that support human development and growth; (c) community well-being and survival is paramount; (d) protection for the most vulnerable; and (e) individual commitment to peace with other human beings, with nature, and with the Spirit (Harvell, 2010).

There are numerous risk factors that impact the daily survival of individuals within urban populations, inclusive of poverty, poor education, access to health care, exposure to substance use, exposure to community violence, and so forth. The development of therapeutic techniques to address the particular needs of this vulnerable and distressed population who are often victimized is critical to strengthening and uplifting not only the individuals impacted directly but the community as a whole. In contrast to the cognitive behavioral interventions which focus on the intersection of thoughts, feelings, behaviors, and maladaptive patterns which influence those behaviors, African-centered interventions would value and understand the historical experiences and utilize cultural influences as protective factors (Byrdsong, Mitchelle, & Yamatani, 2013). Modifying interventions to incorporate culture, traditions, values, and spiritual influences demonstrate an understanding of the urban population and seek to ensure clinical outcomes that are effective and efficient. Negating these influences may cause more harm than good to the client, which in turn impacts the community. However, the inclusion of culturally specific metaphors, rituals, proverbs, and the *Nguzu Saba* may promote self-esteem and self-efficacy, thus influencing changes in thoughts and behaviors as well as the restoration of individual and collective identity.

Adaptations to current psychotherapy interventions

CBT techniques for trauma- and stress-related disorders seek to change thinking and behavioral patterns following exposure to traumatic events. However, this process is not inclusive of the feelings and emotions of the survivors as a whole. In fact, the inclusion of cognitive behavioral approaches specifically mandates a structured, short-term approach which negates the need for empathetic interaction between the practitioner and the client. This necessary component of the African-centered perspective recognizes the need for empathy and a sense of shared experiences as critical to overall healing. The efficacy of incorporating the practitioner's feelings and life experiences contribute to the need for equality and oneness, providing an opportunity for the client to feel safe in the expression of their feelings and creating positive change.

EMDR therapy solicits a change in perceptions and attitudes, as well as changing the way a person thinks, believes, and feels by targeting negative cognitions that are "stuck" in a client's nervous system. This practice relies on sounds, taps, and other stimulating factors to create positive changes and behavioral responses. In contrast, the Afrocentric approach incorporates rituals and practices to connect one to their experiences, not to detach them from their experiences. The significance of the inclusion of the principles of the *Nguzu Saba* and the *Ma'at* in tailoring behavioral changes, in addition to EMDR treatment approaches, would infuse themes that would transform thoughts, feelings, and behavior, as well as develop protective factors essential to individual and collective growth.

The delivery of trauma-informed care postulates trauma as an individual experience and does not take into consideration the collective harm caused by urban exposure. In addition, root causes of trauma are not addressed in a collective manner. The inclusion of the environmental impact on an individual's response and recovery from trauma must be addressed, taking into consideration those environmental influences that create the harm in the first place. Afrocentric social work practice promotes the holistic approach which views trauma not only as an individually isolated experience but a collective experience that must be addressed to promote strength, empowerment, and healing of the community. Connecting these two approaches would bring forth a humanistic framework centering on restorative practices impacting well-being and transformation.

Implications

Clinicians must consider the unique experiences of individuals in urban environments when completing assessments so that they can help them access resources and appropriate treatment interventions. Clinicians must also advocate for more policies supporting collaborative relationships with legal, primary care settings treatment, church, and community. Bridging the gap between mental health and spiritual care to facilitate "healing" and provide culturally competent care is also essential. Additionally, empowering the community to recognize and understand adverse experiences and the long-term effects of these traumatic experiences is critical.

Research on the programmatic outcomes associated with the inclusion of African-centered interventions or the overall usage of the African-centered approach is paramount to validating evidence-based interventions and furthermore expounding on the overall paradigm.

Many programs have demonstrated the inclusion of African-centered interventions into their service delivery model, however, many of them do not focus specifically on trauma approaches. Replicating these interventions and documenting outcomes will further expand the use of the paradigm and contribute to the development of a formalized, evidence-based African-centered theory.

With regard to education, the adverse impact of traumatic exposure and the high rate of service use among trauma-exposed individuals have urged many social work schools to incorporate trauma content into their curriculum (Vasquez & Boel-studt, 2017). Many schools offer trauma certificate programs or electives; however, it may be beneficial for social work programs to include required trauma-related courses. Furthermore, incorporating the Afrocentric perspective in social work education can further assist with working with trauma-informed clients, specifically in urban communities.

Conclusion

There are several factors that may influence responses to trauma and the treatment of trauma, inclusive of the type of trauma, the number of traumatic experiences, and the time elapsed since the trauma exposure or experience. Nonetheless, there are significant implications which impact overall outcomes and efficacy when working with various populations, but even more significant in urban populations. Developing new practice models inclusive of Afrocentric approaches to address the underlying issues inclusive of systemic oppression, structural racism, marginalization, and loss of culture and identity will contribute to the overall effectiveness consistent with the commitment to social justice and transformation of vulnerable communities. An emphasis on feelings, spirituality, and interconnectedness targets growth and promotes the well-being of the community as a whole. The collective impact on treating individuals who have experienced trauma is critical to the enhancement of the urban population and the emergence of a healthy, flourishing society.

Case of "Michelle"

- Parents divorced at age 11
- Brother murdered (unsolved)

- Chronic parental alcohol and cocaine abuse
- Father had multiple incarcerations
- Mother had multiple boyfriends
- Raped at 14 years old
- Somatic issues including reoccurring headaches, GI problems
- Poor concentration

Review questions

1) Reflect on your own personal experiences growing up. What messages did you receive about trauma? How have these messages been confirmed in your lived experiences? How have these messages been refuted in your lived experiences?
2) Identify each adverse experience noted in the case vignette. Based on the research mentioned in this chapter, how many adverse experiences are mentioned? How have relationships and social interactions been impacted? Are there co-occurring problems?
3) What treatment approach would you use to address the case vignette?
4) What are some techniques for raising awareness of the prevalence of trauma in African American communities?

References

Asante, M. K. (1980). International/intercultural relations. In M. K. Asante & A. S. Vandi (Eds.), *Contemporary Black thought: Alternative analyses in social and behavioral science*. Beverly Hills: Sage Publications.

Black, M. C., Basile, K. C., Breiding, M. J., Smith, S. G., Walters, M. L., Merrick, M. T., . . . Stevens, M. R. (2011). *The National Intimate Partner and Sexual Violence Survey (NISVS): 2010 Summary report*. National Center for Injury Prevention and Control, Centers for Disease Control and Prevention. Retrieved from https://www.cdc.gov/violenceprevention/pdf/nisvs_executive_summary-a.pdf

Black, M. C., & Breiding, M. J. (2008). Adverse health conditions and health risk behaviors associated with intimate partner violence – United States. *Morbidity and Mortality Weekly Report, 57*(5), 113–117.

Brave Heart, M. Y. H. (2003). The historical trauma response among Natives and its relationship with substance abuse: A Lakota illustration. *Journal of Psychoactive Drugs, 35*(1), 7–13. https://doi.org/10.1080/02791072.2003.10399988

Bryson, S., Gauvin, E., Jamieson, A., Rathgeber, M., Faulkner Gibson, L., Bell, S., & Burke, S. (2017). What are effective strategies for implementing trauma-informed care in youth inpatient psychiatric and residential treatment settings? A realist systematic review. *International Journal of Mental Health Systems, 11*(36), 1–16. https://doi.org/10.1186/s13033-017-0137-3

Byrdsong, T. R., Mitchell, A., & Yamatani, H. (2013). Afrocentric intervention and paradigm: An overview of successful application by a grassroots organization. *Journal of Human Behavior in the Social Environment, 23*(8), 931–937. https://doi.org/10.1080/10911359.2013.831298

Cahill, S. P., Rothbaum, B. O., Resick, P. A., & Follette, V. M. (2009). Cognitive behavioral therapy for adults. In E. B. Foa, T. M. Keane, M. J. Friedman, & J. A. Cohen (Eds.),

Effective treatments for PTSD: Practice guidelines from the International Society for Traumatic Stress Studies (pp. 139–222). New York: Guilford Press.

Centers for Disease Control and Prevention. (2018). *Intimate partner violence*. Retrieved from www.cdc.gov/violenceprevention/intimatepartnerviolence/index.html

Centers for Disease Control and Prevention. (2019a). *About adverse childhood experiences*. Retrieved from www.cdc.gov/violenceprevention/aces/index.html

Centers for Disease Control and Prevention. (2019b). *National violent death reporting system (NVDRS)*. Retrieved from www.cdc.gov/violenceprevention/datasources/nvdrs/index.html

Centers for Disease Control and Prevention. (2019c). *Preventing intimate partner violence*. Retrieved from www.cdc.gov/violenceprevention/intimatepartnerviolence/fastfact.html

Centers for Disease Control and Prevention. (2021). *Cost of injury data*. Retrieved from https://www.cdc.gov/injury/wisqars/cost/index.html

Child Abuse Prevention and Treatment Act. (2010). CAPTA Reauthorization Act of 2010 (P.L. 111–320), 42 U.S.C. § 5101, Note (§ 3)

Child Welfare Information Gateway. (2019). *Definitions of child abuse and neglect*. Retrieved from www.childwelfare.gov/pubpdfs/define.pdf

Chipungu, S. S., Hermann, J., Sambrano, S., Nistler, M., Sale, E., & Springer, J. F. (2000). Prevention programming for African American youth. A review of strategies in CSAP's National cross-site evaluation of high-risk youth programs. *Journal of Black Psychology*. *24*(4), 360–385. https://doi.org/10.1177%2F0095798400026004002

Cohen, J. A., Mannarino, A. P., & Deblinger, E. (2006). *Treating trauma and traumatic grief in children and adolescents*. New York: Guilford Press.

Danieli, Y. (Ed.). (1998). *International handbook of multigenerational legacies of trauma*. New York: Plenum.

Davis, R. G., Ressler, K. J., Schwartz, A. C., Stephens, K. J., & Bradley, R. G. (2008). Treatment barriers for low-income, urban African Americans with undiagnosed post-traumatic stress disorder. *Journal of Traumatic Stress: Official Publication of the International Society for Traumatic Stress Studies*, *21*(2), 218–222. https://doi.org/10.1002/jts.20313

Deacon, B. J., & Abramowitz, J. S. (2004). Cognitive and behavioral treatments for anxiety disorders: A review of meta-analytic findings. *Journal of Clinical Psychology*, *60*(4), 429–441. https://doi.org/10.1002/jclp.10255

Dube, S. R., Anda, R. F., Felitti, V. J., Chapman, D. P., Williamson, D. F., & Giles, W. H. (2001). Childhood abuse, household dysfunction, and the risk of attempted suicide throughout the life span: Findings from the Adverse Childhood Experiences Study. *JAMA*, *286*(24), 3089–3096. https://doi.org/10.1001/jama.286.24.3089

Evans-Campbell, T. (2008). Historical trauma in American Indian/Native Alaska communities: A multilevel framework for exploring impacts on individuals, families, and communities. *Journal of Interpersonal Violence*, *23*(3), 316–338. https://doi.org/10.1177/0886260507312290

Felitti, V. J., Anda, R. F., Nordenberg, D., Williamson, D. F., Spitz, A. M., Edwards, V., . . . Marks, J. S. (2019). Relationship of childhood abuse and household dysfunction to many of the leading causes of death in adults: The Adverse Childhood Experiences (ACE) study. *American Journal of Preventive Medicine*, *56*(6), 774–786. https://doi.org/10.1016/j.amepre.2019.04.001

Gainer, D., Alam, S., Alam, H., & Redding, H. (2020). A flash of hope: Eye movement desensitization and reprocessing (EMDR) therapy. *Innovations in Clinical Neuroscience*, *17*(7–9), 12–20.

Gilbert, D. J., Harvey, A. R., & Belgrave, F. Z. (2009). Advancing the Africentric paradigm shift discourse: Building toward evidence-based Africentric interventions in social work practice with African Americans. *Social Work, 54*(3), 243–252. https://doi.org/10.1093/sw/54.3.243

González-Prendes, A., & Resko, S. (2012). Cognitive-behavioral theory. In S. Ringel & J. Brandell (Eds.), *Trauma: Contemporary directions in theory, practice, and research* (pp. 14–40). Thousand Oaks, CA: Sage Publications. https://doi.org/10.4135/9781452230597.n2

Hampton, R. L., Gullotta, T. P., & Crowel, R. L. (Eds.). (2010). *Handbook of African American health.* New York: Guilford Press.

Harvell, V. G. (2010). Afrocentric humanism and African American women's humanizing activism. *Journal of Black Studies, 40*(6), 1052–1074. https://doi.org/10.1177/0021934708325380

Henderson, Z., Acquaye-Doyle, L. A., Waites, S., & Howard, T. (2016). Putting principles into practice: Addressing historical trauma, mistrust, and apprehension in research Methods Courses. *Journal of Social Work Education, 52*(1), 69–78. https://doi.org/10.1080/10437797.2016.1112631

Hopper, E. K., Bassuk, E. L., & Olivet, J. (2010). Shelter from the storm: Trauma-informed care in homelessness service settings. *The Open Health Services and Policy Journal, 3*(1), 80–100. https://doi.org/10.2174/1874924001003010080

King, I. R. (2019). DIASPORA model: Teaching the Afrocentric perspective to social work students. *Urban Social Work, 3*(S1), S70–S85.

Koenen, K. C., Stellman, S. D., Dohrenwend, B. P., Sommer, J. F., Jr., & Stellman, J. M. (2007). The consistency of combat exposure reporting and course of PTSD in Vietnam War veterans. *Journal of Traumatic Stress, 20*(1), 3–13. https://doi.org/10.1002/jts.20191

Merritt, M. B., Cronholm, P., Davis, M., Dempsey, S., Fein, J., Kuykendall, S. A., . . . Wade, R. (2013). *Findings from the Philadelphia urban ACE survey.* Institute for Safe Families. Retrieved from www.rwjf.org/en/library/research/2013/09/findings-from-the-philadelphia-urban- ace-survey.html

Oral, R., Ramirez, M., Coohey, C., Nakada, S., Walz, A., Kuntz, A., & Peek-Asa, C. (2016). Adverse childhood experiences and trauma informed care: The future of health care. *Pediatric Research, 79*(1), 227–233. https://doi.org/10.1038/pr.2015.197

Phipps, R., & Thorne, S. (2019). Utilizing trauma-focused cognitive behavioral therapy as a framework for addressing cultural trauma in African American children and adolescents: A proposal. *Professional Counselor, 9*(1), 35–50.

Reynolds, A. L., Sneva, J. N., & Beehler, G. P. (2010). The influence of racism-related stress on the academic motivation of Black and Latino/a students. *Journal of College Student Development, 51*(2), 135–149. https://doi.org/10.1353/csd.0.0120

Schiele, J. H. (1994). Afrocentricity: Implications for higher education. *Journal of Black Studies, 25*(2), 150–169. https://doi.org/10.1177/002193479402500202

Schiele, J. H. (1997). The contour and meaning of afrocentric social work. *Journal of Black Studies, 27*(6), 800–819. https://doi.org/10.1177/002193479702700605

Schiele, J. H. (2017). The Afrocentric paradigm in social work: A historical perspective and future outlook. *Journal of Human Behavior in the Social Environment, 27*(1–2), 15–26. https://doi.org/10.1080/10911359.2016.1252601

Shapiro, F. (1989a). Efficacy of the eye movement desensitization procedure in the treatment of traumatic memories. *Journal of Traumatic Stress, 2*(2), 199–223. https://doi.org/10.1002/jts.2490020207

Shapiro, F. (1989b). Eye movement desensitization: A new treatment for post-traumatic stress disorder. *Journal of Behavior Therapy and Experimental Psychiatry, 20*(3), 211–217. https://doi.org/10.1016/0005-7916(89)90025-6

Shapiro, F. (2001). *Eye movement desensitization and reprocessing: Basic principles, protocols, and procedures* (2nd ed.). New York: Guilford Press.

Shapiro, F. (2007). EMDR, adaptive information processing, and case conceptualization. *Journal of EMDR Practice and Research, 1*(2), 68–87. https://doi.org/10.1891/1933-3196.1.2.68

Substance Abuse and Mental Health Services Administration. (2014). *SAMHSA's concept of trauma and guidance for a trauma-informed approach.* Retrieved from https://ncsacw.samhsa.gov/userfiles/files/SAMHSA_Trauma.pdf

Substance Abuse and Mental Health Services Administration. (2019a). *Trauma and violence.* U.S. Department of Health and Services. Retrieved from www.samhsa.gov/trauma-violence

Substance Abuse and Mental Health Services Administration. (2019b). *Types of disasters.* U.S. Department of Health and Services. Retrieved from www.samhsa.gov/find-help/disaster-distress-helpline/disaster-types

Sue, D. W., Capodilupo, C. M., & Holder, A. M. B. (2008). Racial microaggressions in the life experience of Black Americans. *Professional Psychology, Research and Practice, 39*(3), 329–336. https://doi.org/10.1037/0735-7028.39.3.329

The National Child Traumatic Stress Network (n.d.). *Community violence.* Retrieved from www.nctsn.org/what-is-child-trauma/trauma-types/community-violence

U.S. Department of Health & Human Services, Administration for Children and Families, Administration on Children, Youth and Families, Children's Bureau. (2017). *Child maltreatment 2015.* Retrieved from www.acf.hhs.gov/sites/default/files/documents/cb/cm2015.pdf

Vasquez, M. L., & Boel-Studt, S. (2017). Integrating a trauma-informed care perspective in baccalaureate social work education: Guiding principles. *Advances in Social Work, 18*(1), 1–24. https://doi.org/10.18060/21243

Watson, J. T., Gayer, M., & Connolly, M. A. (2007). Epidemics after natural disasters. *Emerging Infectious Diseases, 13*(1), 1–5. https://doi.org/10.3201/eid1301.060779

Wolitzky-Taylor, K., Chung, B., Bearman, S. K., Arch, J., Grossman, J., Fenwick, K., . . . Miranda, J. (2019). Stakeholder perceptions of the barriers to receiving and delivering exposure-based cognitive behavioral therapy for anxiety disorders in adult community mental health settings. *Community Mental Health Journal, 55*(1), 83–99. https://doi.org/10.1007/s10597-018-0250-z

7

INTIMATE PARTNER VIOLENCE, TRAUMA, AND MENTAL HEALTH

Tricia Bent-Goodley, Noelle St. Vil, Aaliah Zonicle, Lennon Jackson, Sakima Romero-Chandler

Domestic violence is a pattern of coercive behaviors that are used when one partner attempts to gain power and control over the other and can be physical, sexual, emotional, financial, and spiritual (Bent-Goodley, 2011). In the United States, one out of four women and one out of ten men have reported experiencing violence by an intimate partner (Breiding et al., 2014). Communities of African ancestry are not immune from domestic violence. In fact, 40–45% of Black women have reported experiencing domestic violence (Breiding et al., 2014). The need for culturally based interventions is profoundly important in responding to and preventing domestic violence from occurring in communities of African ancestry. The focus of this chapter is on identifying and critiquing clinical practice models on domestic violence and how they connect to communities of African ancestry in the United States with a focus on trauma and mental health implications.

Barriers to help-seeking

In communities of African ancestry, domestic violence continues to be reported at higher levels compared to other communities (Breiding et al., 2014). There are reasons for the large numbers of reported violence within communities of African ancestry. Structural barriers and within group challenges are enormously impactful. There is a resistance to seek help from resources outside of the community due largely to a historical context and contemporary experiences related to structural racism and discrimination. Because of the limitations and challenges within and outside of communities of African ancestry, domestic violence is often unaddressed, or help-seeking is so delayed that the problem is further exacerbated. Thus, these barriers impact help-seeking behaviors and can lead to greater risks of more lethal violence.

DOI: 10.4324/9780429276613-10

Some of the barriers that prevent help-seeking among victims of African ancestry include mistrust in law enforcement, challenges with the criminal justice response, lack of culturally competent services, and intracommunity dynamics. This mistrust is a result of generations of over-policing in the Black community and police brutality beginning with the enslavement of African people in the United States (Rodgers, 2020). African Americans are more likely to receive harsher penalties and longer sentences for the same crimes committed by white people (Richie, 2012). The consequence of this discriminatory treatment in the criminal justice system is the perception that there is no justice for the Black community within these systems (Deutsch et al., 2017). Therefore, many victims of African ancestry do all they can to avoid the criminal justice process even if such systemic responses, such as protection orders, are needed.

With law enforcement and criminal justice systems often not being viewed as options, the social service and domestic violence system is sometimes viewed as not much better (Bent-Goodley, 2013; Deutsch et al., 2017; Satyen, 2019). Too often, providers operate from a lack of understanding of community context, stereotypes of the Black community and awareness of how these problematic responses impact the helping relationship (Bent-Goodley, 2005; Gillum, 2008). Because of discriminatory treatment or treatment that lacks awareness of cultural context, there is a lack of understanding of the lived experiences of victims, and thus programs and services designed to help them often do not (Bent-Goodley, 2017). This results in an increasing alienation between formal provider systems and communities of African ancestry.

Messages of keeping family business closed and within the family also impact help-seeking (Bent-Goodley, 2011). One place where it is relatively acceptable to share one's troubles in the family is within communities of faith. However, often faith-based communities still encourage victims to stay in abusive relationships, ignore the signs of abuse and violence, and suggest or engage in couples counseling which puts the safety of the survivor at risk (Bent-Goodley, St. Vil, & Hubbert, 2012; Gillum, 2009). This reality results in many survivors suffering in silence which further complicates issues associated with mental health and trauma.

Trauma, mental health, and domestic violence connection

Much of the research on the topic of trauma and mental health, as connected to domestic violence, has been written from the perspective of the female as the victim and the male as the perpetrator. It is important that more research be conducted to better understand the dynamics associated with men as victims of domestic violence. However, the connection between mental health, trauma, and domestic violence has been found in prior research. Survivors of domestic violence have been more likely to experience mental health conditions, such as anxiety disorder, substance use disorder, and suicidal ideation compared to non-domestic violence survivors (Afifi et al., 2009). Black women, who are at increased risks of domestic violence, already have a high prevalence of mental health conditions with 39.9% having a mental illness, 16.7% having a mood disorder, 14.6% having a major depressive episode, and 23.7% having anxiety disorder (Lacey et al., 2015).

Specifically, Black women who experience severe domestic violence are in some cases as much as three times as likely to experience anxiety disorders, mood disorders, substance use disorder, eating disorders, and suicidal ideation compared to Black women who have not experienced domestic violence (Lacey et al., 2015).

Post-traumatic stress disorder (PTSD) is one of the most significant mental health outcomes of domestic violence with research suggesting anywhere between 31% and 84% of domestic violence survivors meet the criteria for a PTSD diagnosis (Jones, Hughes, & Unterstaller, 2001; Pill, Day, & Mildred, 2017). PTSD refers to a normal reaction to an abnormal event characterized by physiological arousal to include the feeling that one is still experiencing the traumatic event, changes in sleep patterns, being hyper vigilant, having difficulty concentrating, and an overall constant fearfulness and worry (Jones et al., 2001; Pill et al., 2017). Approximately 12% of Black women experience PTSD (Lacey et al., 2015), however, the likelihood of experiencing PTSD increases with experiences of domestic violence, and the likelihood of experiencing co-occurring PTSD and depression increases as severity of domestic violence increases (Sabri et al., 2013).

The connection, then, between domestic violence, mental health, and trauma is incredibly important to consider as survivors often struggle with domestic violence without the necessary supports. These issues are critical to address for survivors (Sabri & Gielen, 2019). The need for interventions at the intersection of these complex issues for survivors of African ancestry could not be more necessary. For many Black women who are survivors of domestic violence, one must execute a trauma-informed approach that can address the intimate partner violence, as well as community violence, sexual abuse, historical trauma, and the cumulative effects of each of these on the lived experiences of the survivor (Anyikwa, 2016). Also, such interventions necessitate an intersectional approach that emphasizes cultural context, shared power, building authentic relationships, advocating for support and equity, and honoring the lived experiences of the individual and ancestorial values (Bent-Goodley, 2005; Kulkarni, 2019).

Clinical interventions for domestic violence

The need for clinical interventions that address domestic violence is profoundly important. Given the high psychological toll of domestic violence, the implementation of effective clinical interventions to strategically respond to the unique circumstances of survivors of African ancestry is timely and needed. Domestic violence interventions should always focus first on maintaining the physical and psychological safety of survivors (Goodman, Fauci, Sullivan, DiGiovanni, & Wilson, 2016). In addition, clinical interventions targeting domestic violence survivors must also acknowledge the importance of environmental factors that can impact the violence, the role that historical and community trauma play in mental health, and the accessibility and implications of receiving treatment which can also trigger re-victimization (Condino, Tanzilli, Speranza, & Lingiardi, 2016). Clinical interventions for survivors can be inclusive of extensive counseling as well as therapeutic and advocacy programs. Moreover, the implementation of cognitive–behavioral strategies in clinical interventions has been regarded as effective in addressing the trauma endured by domestic violence survivors (Anyikwa, 2016; Sorrentino et al., 2020). Clinical interventions, therefore, should encourage hope, responsive engagement, and have a positive impact on the well-being of the survivor (Hackett, McWhirter, & Lesher, 2016). There are clinical or direct-level interventions that have been utilized to support survivors of domestic violence that are identified in the following approaches.

Duluth model

The Duluth model was created in the early 1980s in Northern Minnesota. The model is centered on the idea that domestic violence is gender-based and a result of men feeling that they are structurally and morally positioned to dominate women (Bohall, Bautista, & Musson, 2016). It places power and control at the center of domestic violence; specifically, men's power to control women. The Duluth model, while not necessarily considered clinical, uses a feminist lens as its primary framework and largely assumes that the perpetrator is male and that the victim is female (Snead, Bennett, & Babcock, 2018). Feminism puts women's lived experiences at the center of the issue; however, it is often white women's experiences at the center and is often not inclusive of the experiences of women of color which results in a model that ultimately neglects some of the lived experiences of diverse groups of women.

Safety planning

Safety planning is another critical intervention used to address domestic violence. The model is largely centered on providing a thoughtful crisis response and helping a survivor plan to navigate leaving a domestic violence situation that recognizes particular risks with an intentional response. While there are aspects of safety planning that are not centered on the idea of leaving, this tool is often used to help women consider their risk and help them identify their options given the abusive situation (Logan & Walker, 2018a). Many women do not try to leave their relationship as much as they try to make the violence stop. In some ways, safety planning takes this into account by addressing plans for what to do at the time of an abusive incident. Hence, part of the challenge of this intervention is that there are no widely used protocols for safety plans and no evidence for when one approach should be used versus another approach (Heron, 2017). In addition, there are no distinctions on how to address high-risk situations (Logan & Walker, 2018b). It also does not differentiate how diverse communities identify safety risks (Bent-Goodley, 2013; Sabri et al., 2018). These issues create significant challenges for use of this intervention.

Danger Assessment

The Danger Assessment, while not a clinical tool, is also used to work directly with victims of domestic violence and has been proven to be effective (Messing,

Campbell, & Snider, 2017). The Danger Assessment identifies risk areas that could potentially lead to domestic violence fatality (Campbell, Webster, & Glass, 2009). Once this information is obtained, it is shared with the survivor with the hopes that the person seeing their high risk will leave the relationship. Unfortunately, this intervention does not take into account the cultural context experienced by communities of African ancestry that may have other risk factors or that may not view the identified risks as actual danger (Bent-Goodley, 2013; Sabri et al., 2018). While the Danger Assessment development did include African American participants in its research (Campbell et al., 2009), the tool was not designed to address the nuances of cultural context for diverse populations. For example, the Danger Assessment was used to inform the development of the Lethality Assessment Plan (LAP) and the Domestic Violence High Risk Team (DVHRT) Danger Assessment Law Enforcement (DA-LE). While there have been some encouraging findings (Maxwell, Sullivan, Backes, & Kaufman, 2020), both models require reaching out to law enforcement to make use of the assessment (Messing, Campbell, Dunne, & Dubus, 2020). For many communities of African ancestry, they are resistant and mistrust law enforcement systems, thus creating a barrier for the community. In addition, the language of the Danger Assessment itself may not connect with the language used in diverse communities to describe high-risk situations (Bent-Goodley, 2013). Work has been done to explore how to create a culturally competent version of the Danger Assessment (Sabri et al., 2019). Thus, while still an important lethality risk assessment tool, there are still real challenges posed by use of this model.

Relapse prevention and relationship safety

The Relapse Prevention and Relationship Safety (RPRS) intervention has been strategically designed to reduce drug use and the occurrence of intimate partner violence (IPV) among women on methadone (Gilbert et al., 2006). In addition to drug use and IPV, RPRS also aims to decrease depression, PTSD, as well as risky sexual behaviors amongst this significantly vulnerable population. RPRS does not require that the survivor stay or leave the relationship; instead, the focus is on creating a space for relationships that are free from violence and abuse (Gilbert et al., 2006). To effectively reduce drug use and promote relationship safety, RPRS comprises 11 two-hour group sessions and one individual session. RPRS meticulously implements exercises centered on building social cognitive skills and group cohesion. Driven by empowerment and social cognitive theories, the RPRS intervention is noted as culturally specific to low-income African American and Latina women as it seeks to enhance the self-esteem and cultural pride as part of a risk-reduction strategy (Gilbert et al., 2006).

Cognitive Trauma Therapy for Battered Women

Cognitive Trauma Therapy for Battered Women (CTT-BW) is a multifaceted intervention designed specifically to treat survivors of IPV suffering from PTSD

(Kubany, Hill, & Owens, 2003). Developed in collaboration with researchers, survivors, and advocates, CTT-BW strategically incorporates stress management strategies, the ability to identify and respond to negative thoughts, and addressing issues of trauma through psychoeducation and completion of homework assignments (Kubany et al., 2004). An essential feature of CTT-BW is its inclusion of specialized techniques that aim to evaluate and simultaneously reduce guilt-related beliefs and negative self-talk. Moreover, CTT-BW comprises modules that are centered on participants becoming more empowered and able to identify unhealthy relationship patterns and manage negative interactions with former partners (Kubany et al., 2003). This intervention provides 8–11 sessions of individual treatment delivered in 90 minutes. Research asserts that CTT-BW significantly reduces PTSD, depression, anxiety, negative post-trauma cognitions, guilt, and shame (Beck et al., 2016) and enhances the neuropsychological functioning as one mentally prepares for upcoming interactions (Aupperle et al., 2013).

HOPE: Helping to Overcome PTSD through Empowerment

Helping to Overcome PTSD through Empowerment (HOPE) is a 9–12 session cognitive behavioral treatment (CBT) that has been strategically designed to provide PTSD treatment to survivors of IPV residing in shelters (Johnson, Zlotnick, & Perez, 2011). HOPE is based heavily on Herman's (1992) multistage model that emphasizes three stages of recovery: (1) establishing safety and self-care, (2) remembering and mourning, and (3) reconnection. Recognizing that survivors of IPV seek refuge in shelters and the need to establish safety and access resources, HOPE significantly emphasizes Herman's first stage of recovery. Therefore, HOPE meticulously addresses the cognitive, behavioral, and interpersonal issues linked to PTSD, which subsequently inhibits survivors' ability to effectively establish safety and utilize shelter resources. As such a unique clinical intervention, HOPE promotes collaborative efforts with shelter personnel, integrates personal goals, prioritizes prevalent safety needs, and emphasizes empowerment in treatment within shelter settings (Johnson, Johnson, Perez, Palmieri, & Zlotnick, 2016). For instance, early sessions of HOPE highlight psychoeducation as well as empowerment strategies that assist survivors in establishing their independence and decision-making, while later sessions focus on developing cognitive behavioral skills that manage PTSD and other co-occurring issues frequently experienced by survivors (Johnson & Zlotnick, 2006).

Moving to an African-centered perspective

Each of these interventions is important and can be integrated into a culturally specific approach. However, at their base, they are not fundamentally culturally centered and thus, miss important cues and opportunities to address the lived experiences of persons of African ancestry which could, in turn, impact changes related to domestic violence in the community. The principles of *Ma'at* and the *Nguzo*

Saba present African-centered value systems. They offer a worldview that builds on the cultural experience, strengths, and way of life within the community. The principles of *Ma'at* identify the following important values in the African experience: truth, justice, harmony, balance, order, reciprocity, and righteousness (Browder, 1989). The *Nguzo Saba*, often aligned with the celebration of *Kwanzaa*, has principles noted as unity, self-determination, collective work and responsibility, purpose, creativity, faith, and economic cooperation (Karenga, 1994). They are guiding posts for how present-day persons of African ancestry continue to pass down these worldviews even today (Bent-Goodley, 2005). These principles have been found to be present even as Africans were enslaved in America. They are ways of living and values that have transcended the historical experience of persons of African ancestry in the United States (Martin & Martin, 2003). These values continue to be a part of the experience of communities of African ancestry today and can be valuable in designing and framing interventions within the community. There are interventions that have been developed and anchored in these Afrocentric principles that can help support survivors of domestic violence.

In Circle

The In Circle intervention is a theory-based African-centered intervention that targeted Black couples in the prevention of domestic violence, increase of healthy relationship strategies, and increase in safer sex practices (Bent-Goodley, 2017). In Circle is a seven-week intervention undergird by the Principles of *Ma'at*. The intervention focuses on providing a holistic approach to domestic violence, attention to improve help-seeking behaviors, growing social support networks, and building on the cultural strengths of the community. In addition to utilizing creativity – such as music and dance – the intervention incorporates spirituality through meditations and use of storytelling as a part of recognizing cultural use of language and the oral tradition in the African American community (Bent-Goodley, 2005). The intervention decreased isolation by emphasizing interconnectedness and addressed stereotypes of Black male and womanhood along with community discussion of secrecy and the stigma associated with domestic violence in communities of African ancestry. The intervention demonstrates positive findings and was replicated for males and females incorporating a gender-based approach.

Project Eban

Project Eban is one of the largest HIV randomized clinical trials for African American couples funded as an HIV/AIDS Risk Reduction model through the National Institute of Mental Health (El-Bassel et al., 2008). This multisite intervention was administered among 535 African American couples in four cities. It was adapted from an evidence-based model, but the principles of the *Nguzo Saba* served as the organizing principles from the conception to the content to the implementation of the intervention. This comprehensive approach focused on building on the resilience of the African American experience, emphasizing relationship building and equity, and recognizing the use of spirituality as critical components. Project Eban was found to be effective among the couples as an Afrocentric intervention for couples (El-Bassel et al., 2010).

The SISTA intervention

The Sisters Informing Sisters About Topics on AIDS (SISTA) Intervention is a five-session intervention with booster sessions that focus on using a cultural- and gender-related approach to addressing HIV risk reduction among Black women (DiClemente & Wingood, 1995). The intervention utilizes the principles of the *Nguzo Saba* as an organizing framework and is anchored in the cultural beliefs and norms of the community. A major focus of the intervention is to enhance ethnic pride and is spiritual-based, acknowledging the importance of this factor for communities of African ancestry. The intervention was found to be effective among African American females (DiClemente & Wingood, 1995; Prather et al., 2006).

Implications

Placing the African-centered perspective at the center of crafting interventions can be extremely impactful in addressing the needs of communities of African ancestry. This impact can be seen in the identified interventions developed to address domestic violence, HIV risk reduction, and healthy relationship education. There is a need to develop more interventions that center the experience of communities of African ancestry as opposed to adapting models that are not designed or built to work within that community. While adaptation is sometimes more convenient, there can still be substantive losses inherent in not framing an intervention from within the worldview of a people (Williams, Wyatt, & Wingood, 2010). It can miss important nuances and perceptions of the lived experience and dull or limit the potential of the intervention. More time and resources are needed to invest in growing the number of tested interventions with African-centered perspectives at the core. More investment in such approaches could help to address the existing structural barriers and honor the resilience of the African experiences still alive in this country. More should be done to uplift the approaches currently being utilized in the community already found to be productive but lack the evaluative data. More time and investment should be given to highlighting and assessing these approaches so that they can be recognized for their contributions without diminishing or diluting their effectiveness in the scientific process.

Conclusion

The need to continue to grow domestic violence interventions rooted in and shaped by African-centered worldviews is timely and important to developing programs that are effective within communities of African ancestry. While the current models are positive, more research is needed to further test these models and add to the empirical base for culturally responsive practices that are engrained and rooted in the values of the community. More research is also needed in developing clinical interventions that incorporate the role of historical trauma in the lives of survivors of African ancestry. It would also be helpful to create more measures that are specific to both the domestic violence and mental health needs and thinking of communities of African ancestry so that we could do a better job of capturing research data that is really connected to the language and perspectives of the community. In addition, more models are needed that target specific generations, such as teens and young adults, as well as intergenerational models that help build connectedness within communities of African ancestry around these issues. With models of how this can be done and knowledge of its importance, the community is ready to receive such programs and more should be done to offer clinical interventions that honor the deep legacy and culture that continues to exist within communities of African ancestry.

References

Afifi, T. O., MacMillan, H., Cox, B. J., Asmundson, G. J. G., Stein, M. B., & Sareen, J. (2009). Mental health correlates of intimate partner violence in marital relationships in a nationally representative sample of males and females. *Journal of Interpersonal Violence, 24*(8), 1398–1417. https://doi.org/10.1177/0886260508322192

Anyikwa, V. A. (2016). Trauma-informed approach to survivors of intimate partner violence. *Journal of Evidence-informed Social Work, 13*(5), 484–491. https://doi.org/10.1080/23761407.2016.1166824

Aupperle, R. L., Allard, C. B., Simmons, A. N., Flagan, T., Thorp, S. R., Norman, S. B., . . . Stein, M. B. (2013). Neural responses during emotional processing before and after cognitive trauma therapy for battered women. *Psychiatry Research: Neuroimaging, 214*(1), 48–55. https://doi.org/10.1016/j.pscychresns.2013.05.001

Beck, J., Tran, H., Dodson, T., Henschel, A., Woodward, M., & Eddinger, J. (2016). Cognitive trauma therapy for battered women: Replication and extension. *Psychology of Violence, 6*(3), 368–377. https://doi.org/10.1037/vio0000024

Bent-Goodley, T. B. (2005). An African-centered approach to domestic violence. *Families in Society, 86*(2), 197–206. https://doi.org/10.1606/1044-3894.2455

Bent-Goodley, T. B. (2011). *The ultimate betrayal: A renewed look at intimate partner violence.* Washington, DC: NASW Press.

Bent-Goodley, T. B. (2013). Domestic violence fatality reviews and the African American community. *Homicide Studies, 17*(4), 375–390. https://doi.org/10.1177/1088767913497949

Bent-Goodley, T. (2017). In circle: A healthy relationship, domestic violence, and HIV intervention for African American couples. *Journal of Human Behavior in the Social Environment, 27*(1–2), 132–140. https://doi.org/10.1080/10911359.2016.1273686

Bent-Goodley, T., St. Vil, N. M., & Hubbert, P. (2012). A spirit unbroken: The black church's evolving response to domestic violence. *Social Work and Christianity, 39*(1), 52–65.

Bohall, G., Bautista, M.-J., & Musson, S. (2016). Intimate partner violence and the Duluth model: An examination of the model and recommendations for future research and Practice. *Journal of Family Violence, 31*(8), 1029–1033. https://doi.org/10.1007/s10896-016-9888-x

Breiding, M. J., Smith, S. G., Basile, K. C., Walters, M. L., Chen, J., & Merrick, M. T. (2014). Prevalence and characteristics of sexual violence, stalking, and intimate partner violence victimization – National Intimate Partner and Sexual Violence Survey, United States, 2011. *Morbidity and Mortality Weekly Report, 63*, 1–18. https://doi.org/10.2105/AJPH.2015.302634

Browder, A. T. (1989). *From the Browder file: 22 essays on the African American experience.* Washington, DC: Institute of Kamic Guidance.

Campbell, J. C., Webster, D. W., & Glass, N. (2009). The danger assessment: Validation of a lethality risk assessment instrument for intimate partner femicide. *Journal of Interpersonal Violence, 24*(4), 653–674. https://doi.org/10.1177/0886260508317180

Condino, V., Tanzilli, A., Speranza, A. M., & Lingiardi, V. (2016). Therapeutic interventions in intimate partner violence: An overview. *Research in Psychotherapy, 19*(2), 79–88. https://doi.org/10.4081/ripppo.2016.241

Deutsch, L. S., Resch, K., Barber, T., Zuckerman, Y., Stone, J. T., & Cerulli, C. (2017). Bruise documentation, race and barriers to seeking legal relief for intimate partner violence survivors: A retrospective qualitative study. *Journal of Family Violence, 32*(8), 767–773. https://doi.org/10.1007/s10896-017-9917-4

DiClemente, R. J., & Wingood, G. M. (1995). A randomized controlled trial of an HIV sexual risk-reduction intervention for young African-American women. *JAMA, 274*(16), 1271–1276.

El-Bassel, N., Jemmott, J. B., Landis, J. R., Peguegnat, W., Wingood, G. M., Wyatt, G. E., Bellamy, S. L., & NIMH Multistate HIV/STD Prevention Trial for African American Couples Group. (2008). Eban HIV/STD risk reduction intervention: Conceptual basis and procedures. *Journal of Acquired Immune Deficiency Syndromes, 49*(Suppl1), S15–S27. https://doi.org/10.1097/QAI.0b013e318184255d

El-Bassel, N., Jemmott, J. B., Landis, J. R., Pequegnat, W., Wingood, G. M., Wyatt, G. E., Bellamy, S. L., & NIMH Multisite HIV/STD Prevention Trial for African American Couples Group. (2010). National institute of mental health multisite Eban HIV/STD prevention intervention for African American HIV serodiscordant couples: A cluster randomized trial. *Archives of Internal Medicine, 170*(17), 1594–1601. https://doi.org/10.1001/archinternmed.2010.261

Gilbert, L., El-Bassel, N., Manuel, J., Wu, E., Go, H., Golder, S., . . . Sanders, G. (2006). An integrated relapse prevention and relationship safety intervention for women on methadone: Testing short-term effects on intimate partner violence and substance use. *Violence and Victims, 21*(5), 657–672. https://doi.org/10.1891/0886-6708.21.5.657

Gillum, T. L. (2008). Community response and needs of African American female survivors of domestic violence. *Journal of Interpersonal Violence, 23*, 39–57. https://doi.org/10.1177%2F0886260507307650

Gillum, T. L. (2009). *The intersection of spirituality, religion and intimate partner violence in the African American Community.* Institute on Domestic Violence in The African American Community. Retrieved from www.communitysolutionsva.org/files/TheIntersectionofSpirituality%281%29.pdf

Goodman, L. A., Fauci, J. E., Sullivan, C. M., DiGiovanni, C. D., & Wilson, J. M. (2016). Domestic violence survivors' empowerment and mental health: Exploring the role of the alliance with advocates. *American journal of orthopsychiatry, 86*(3), 286–296. https://doi.org/10.1037/ort0000137

Hackett, S., McWhirter, P. T., & Lesher, S. (2016). The therapeutic efficacy of domestic violence victim interventions. *Trauma, Violence & Abuse, 17*(2), 123–132. https://doi.org/10.1177/1524838014566720

Herman, J. L. (1992). *Trauma and recovery*. New York: Basic Books.

Heron, C. A. (2017). *Exploring the differences between domestic homicide and homicide – suicide: Implications for risk assessment and safety planning* (Publication No. 4473) (Master's thesis). University of Western Ontario. Electronic Thesis and Dissertation Repository.

Johnson, D. M., Johnson, N. L., Perez, S. K., Palmieri, P. A., & Zlotnick, C. (2016). Comparison of adding treatment of PTSD during and after shelter stay to standard care in residents of battered women's shelters: Results of a randomized clinical trial. *Journal of Traumatic Stress, 29*(4), 365–373. https://doi.org/10.1002/jts.22117

Johnson, D. M., & Zlotnick, C. (2006). A cognitive-behavioral treatment for battered women with PTSD in shelters: Findings from a pilot study. *Journal of Traumatic Stress, 19*(4), 559–564. https://doi.org/10.1002/jts.20148

Johnson, D. M., Zlotnick, C., & Perez, S. (2011). Cognitive behavioral treatment of PTSD in residents of battered women's shelters: Results of a randomized clinical trial. *Journal of Consulting and Clinical Psychology, 79*(4), 542–551. https://doi.org/10.1037/a0023822

Jones, L., Hughes, M., & Unterstaller, U. (2001). Post-traumatic stress disorder (PTSD) in victims of domestic violence: A review of the research. *Trauma, Violence, & Abuse, 2*(2), 99–119. http://doi.org/10.1177/1524838001002002001

Karenga, M. (1994). *The moral idea in Ancient Egypt: A study in classical African ethics*. Los Angeles, CA: University of Southern California.

Kubany, E. S., Hill, E. E., & Owens, J. A. (2003). Cognitive trauma therapy for battered women with PTSD: Preliminary findings. *Journal of traumatic stress, 16*(1), 81–91. https://doi.org/10.1023/A:1022019629803

Kubany, E. S., Hill, E. E., Owens, J. A., Iannce-Spencer, C., McCaig, M. A., Tremayne, K. J., & Williams, P. L. (2004). Cognitive trauma therapy for battered women with PTSD (CTT-BW). *Journal of Consulting and Clinical Psychology, 72*(1), 3–18. https://doi.org/10.1037/0022-006X.72.1.3

Kulkarni, S. (2019). Intersectional trauma-informed intimate partner violence (IPV) services: Narrowing the gap between intimate partner violence service delivery and survivor needs. *Journal of Family Violence, 34*(4), 55–64. https://doi.org/10.1007/s10896-018-0001-5

Lacey, K. K., Parnell, R., Mouzon, D. M., Matusko, N., Head, D., Abelson, J. M., & Jackson, J. S. (2015). The mental health of US Black women: The roles of social context and severe intimate partner violence. *BMJ Open, 5*(10), e008415. http://doi.org/10.1136/bmjopen-2015-008415

Logan, T. K., & Walker, R. (2018a). Advocate safety planning training, feedback, and personal challenges. *Journal of Family Violence, 33*(3), 213–225. https://doi.org/10.1007/s10896-017-9949-9

Logan, T. K., & Walker, R. (2018b). Looking into the day-to-day process of victim safety planning. *Journal of Family Violence, 33*(3), 197–211. https://doi.org/10.1007/s10896-018-9951-x

Martin, E. P., & Martin, J. M. (2003). *Spirituality and the Black helping tradition in social work*. Washington, DC: NASW Press.

Maxwell, C. D., Sullivan, T. P., Backes, B. L., & Kaufman, J. S. (2020, June 22). *New approaches to policing high-risk intimate partner victims and offenders*. National Institute of Justice. Retrieved from https://nij.ojp.gov/topics/articles/new-approaches-policing-high-risk-intimate-partner-victims-and-offenders

Messing, J. T., Campbell, J., Dunne, K., & Dubus, S. (2020). Development and testing of the danger assessment for law enforcement (DA-LE). *Social Work Research, 44*(3), 143–156. https://doi.org/10.1093/swr/svaa005

Messing, J. T., Campbell, J. C., & Snider, C. (2017). Validation and adaptation of the danger assessment-5: A brief intimate partner violence risk assessment. *Journal of Advanced Nursing, 73*(12), 3220–3230. https://doi.org/10.1111/jan.13459

Pill, N., Day, A., & Mildred, H. (2017). Trauma responses to intimate partner violence: A review of current knowledge. *Aggression and Violent Behavior, 34*, 178–184. http://doi.org/10.1016/j.avb.2017.01.014

Prather, C., Fuller, T. R., King, W., Brown, M., Moering, M., Little, S., & Phillips, K. (2006). Diffusing an HIV prevention intervention for African American women: Integrating Afrocentric components into the SISTA diffusion strategy. *AIDS Education and Prevention, 18*, 149–160. https://doi.org/10.1521/aeap.2006.18.supp.149

Richie, B. E. (2012). *Arrested justice: Black women, violence, and America's prison nation*. New York: New York University Press.

Rodgers, S. T. (2020, May 29). Womanism and domestic violence. *Encyclopedia of Social Work*. Oxford Research Encyclopedias. https://doi.org/10.1093/acrefore/9780199975839.013.1073

Sabri, B., Bolyard, R., McFadgion, A. L., Stockman, J. K., Lucea, M. B., Callwood, G. B., . . . Campbell, J. C. (2013). Intimate partner violence, depression, PTSD, and use of mental health resources among ethnically diverse Black women. *Social Work in Health Care, 52*(4), 351–369. https://doi.org/10.1080/00981389.2012.745461

Sabri, B., & Gielen, A. (2019). Integrated multicomponent interventions for safety and health risks among black female survivors of violence: A systematic review. *Trauma, Violence & Abuse, 20*(5), 720–731. https://doi.org/10.1177/1524838017730647

Sabri, B., Njie-Carr, V., Messing, J. T., Glass, N., Brockie, T., Hanson, G., . . . Campbell, J. C. (2019). The weWomen and ourCircle randomized controlled trial protocol: A web-based intervention for immigrant, refugee and indigenous women with intimate partner violence experiences. *Contemporary Clinical Trials, 76*, 79–84. https://doi.org/10.1016/j.cct.2018.11.013

Sabri, B., Nnawulezi, N., Njie-Carr, V. P. S., Messing, J., Ward-Lasher, A., Alvarez, C., & Campbell, J. C. (2018). Multilevel risk and protective factors for intimate partner violence among African, Asian and Latina immigrant and refugee women: Perceptions of effective safety planning interventions. *Race and Social Problems, 10*(4), 348–365. https://doi.org/10.1007/s12552-018-9247-z

Satyen, L., Rogic, A. C., & Supol, M. (2019). Intimate partner violence and help-seeking behaviour: A systematic review of cross-cultural differences. *Journal of Immigrant and Minority Health, 21*(4), 879–892. https://doi.org/10.1007/s10903-018-0803-9

Snead, A. L., Bennett, V. E., & Babcock, J. C. (2018). Treatments that work for intimate partner violence: Beyond the Duluth model. In E. Jelic & C. Calkins (Eds.), *New Frontiers in Offender Treatment* (pp. 269–285). Cham: Springer. https://doi.org/10.1007/978-3-030-01030-0_14

Sorrentino, A. E., Iverson, K. M., Tuepker, A., True, G., Cusack, M., Newell, S., & Dichter, M. E. (2020). Mental health care in the context of intimate partner violence: Survivor perspectives. *Psychological Services*. https://doi.org/10.1037/ser0000427

Williams, J. K., Wyatt, G. E., & Wingood, G. (2010). The four C's of HIV prevention with African Americans: Crisis, condoms, culture and community. *Current HIV/AIDS Report, 7*, 185–193. https://doi.org/10.1007/s11904-010-0058-0

8

SEXUAL ASSAULT INTERVENTIONS

Inclusion of African-centered intervention strategies for sexual assault survivors

Yolanda Bogan, Rhea C. Porter, Chelsey Henderson, Rhonda Wells-Wilbon

Sexual violence is a term used to capture various sexual acts that are considered crimes; although the legal definition for a crime varies from state to state, there are common behaviors that are considered sexually violent. The Rape, Abuse & Incest National Network (RAINN) identifies the following as sexual violence: sexual harassment, sexual assault, child sexual abuse, incest, rape, drug-facilitated sexual assault, human trafficking, stalking, use of technology to hurt others, sexual exploitation by helping professionals, and sexual abuse by medical professionals (RAINN, 2021). Women and men of all ages and from all racial, ethnic, and socioeconomic backgrounds can be sexually violated. In the United States, every 68 seconds someone is sexually assaulted; one out of every six women has been the victim of an attempted or completed rape in her lifetime; one in 33 men have experienced an attempted or completed rape in their lifetime; From 2009 to 2013, Child Protective Services agencies substantiated or found strong evidence to indicate that, 63,000 children a year were victims of sexual abuse; 66% of these child victims of sexual assault and rape were aged 12–17 (RAINN, 2021). While this is a broad issue with many diverse populations at higher risk for being victimized, the focus of this chapter is African-Americans, as they have the highest rate of violent victimization of any racial group (31.2 per 1000) (US Department of Justice), and Black women are particularly vulnerable. Most sexual assault committed against African-American women goes unreported and for every African-American woman who reports her rape, at least 15 African-American women do not report theirs (Bureau of Justice Statistics, US Department of Justice). In this chapter, the authors examine the ethical relevance of engaging in competent practice; review common treatment strategies; and finally, critically examine the alignments of

DOI: 10.4324/9780429276613-11

current treatment strategies with African-centered principles to offer a framework for culturally focused intervention strategies for sexual assault survivors.

What we know

When seeking information on "sexual assault interventions," there is a dearth of information available to mental health professionals (MHP) who seek to provide culturally focused interventions for African-American sexual assault survivors. This chapter helps to provide greatly needed information for a range of mental health professionals including social workers, psychologists, licensed mental health therapists, psychiatric nurse practitioners, and other engage professionals who may engage with a Black woman who has experienced sexual violence.

The *Diagnostic and Statistical Manual (DSM)* (2013) *of Mental Disorders*, Fifth Edition includes sexual violence as an example of trauma in its definition of post-traumatic sexual disorder (PTSD). Also, in this edition (2013), PTSD was moved from anxiety disorders to trauma- and stressor-related disorders. This re-categorization is the result of expanding knowledge of the trauma victim's experiences, evidencing reactions that are more closely defined by moods characterized by anhedonia and dysphoria, anger and aggression, and dissociation.

In addition to the reclassification of PTSD and the inclusion of sexual trauma, the most recent PTSD criteria includes four additional symptom areas of at least a month duration that cause clinically significant impairment or distress (2013). These symptom areas refer to subsequent intrusive symptoms related to the trauma, persistent avoidance of trauma-related stimuli, negative change in mood and cognitions associated with the trauma, and markedly heightened arousal and reactivity associated with the trauma (2013).

Responsibility for ethical practice

Counseling services are a standard part of the response protocol for sexual assault (Schrag & Edmond, 2018). MHP ground their work in the agreed-upon standards of practice for their profession. Ethics represent the personal and professional standards of behavior that members of a profession are expected to follow in their identity, administration, teaching, supervision, consultation, and practice of the profession. Competent and well-credentialed MHP follow their respective ethical guidelines as a basic requirement of their professional identity (APA, 2017a). The respective ethics codes for MHP include the importance of practicing within one's area of competence as well as respecting how matters of diversity impact the effectiveness of one's professional services. The gap between African Americans who could benefit from therapy and MHP who are trained in African-centered principles aligned with the ethos of African-American people is vast. Both African-American and non-African-American MHP must seek culturally competent knowledge and experiences beyond the Eurocentric principles emphasized in most academic programs.

Wholistic therapeutic relationships

Psychotherapy can offer a nonjudgmental and supportive environment in which to process the assault. High-quality psychotherapy services have several commonalities: the ability for the client to emotionally connect with the MHP through acceptance, genuine empathy, and positive regard of the client. The therapist's job in assisting the client includes being adept at using techniques that have been shown to be effective for the presenting problem. Thus, it is necessary to publish culturally competent and culturally adapted techniques for use with diverse populations, as it is incumbent on the MHP to have a repertoire of strategies that address the psychological needs of the survivor.

Kimerling and Calhoun (1994) found in their largely African-American sample that sexual assault survivors primarily used medical assistance for follow-up services instead of seeking psychological care. Victims' underutilization of psychological support services was inconsistent with the results of self-report measures which revealed that victims had symptoms consistent with the moderate-to-severe range of depression, indicating the need for psychological treatment. There are several well-known barriers to psychological care in the African-American community including cultural stigma, availability of and access to culturally competent therapists, and cost (Ayalon & Alvidrez, 2007). In addition to these barriers, victims of sexual assault may feel that others will blame them for their victimization (Zinzow & Thompson, 2011). African-American victims' concerns about help-seeking (Black & Weisz, 2003) may be compounded by negative cultural and racial stereotypes of African-American women as sexual objects or sexually immoral, even when access is not an issue (Alvidrez, Shumway, Morazes, & Boccellari, 2011).

Sexual assault recovery continues to be a relevant topic. Self-care is recognized as an important aspect of mental health (Dale, Pierre-Louis, Bogart, O'Cleirigh, & Safren, 2018; Leach & Schoenberg, 2008). The enduring stigma of mental health requires multiple messages to increase social support for federal services and policies (McGinty, Pescosolido, Kennedy-Hendricks, & Barry, 2018); however, when icons/role models such as Michelle Obama discuss mental health in social media (Goodman, Wennerstrom, & Springgate, 2011), African-American women are more likely to increase their use of psychotherapy.

Recommended treatments for sexual assault

Evidence-based treatments for PTSD

In 2017, the Veterans Health Administration and the Department of Defense (VA/DoD) and the American Psychological Association (APA) each published guidelines for the treatment of PTSD. Watkins, Sprang, and Rothbaum (2018) provide a brief review of evidence-based treatments for PTSD that were strongly recommended by each of these treatment guidelines. Both guidelines strongly recommended Prolonged Exposure (PE), Cognitive Processing Therapy (CPT), and trauma-focused Cognitive Behavioral Therapy (CBT). There are several commonalities to these treatment modalities. Each is evidence-based and focuses specifically on trauma by addressing memories, thoughts, and feelings related to the traumatic event.

Prolonged exposure

Emotional processing theory is the basis for PE. This theory suggests that the emotional processing associated with a traumatic event is not processed at the time of the trauma. Moreover, emotional processing theory posits that fear is represented in memory as a cognitive structure that includes representations of the stimuli associated with the trauma, the fear responses, and the meaning associated with the trauma-related stimuli. In normal situations, fear structures are an adaptive response to a realistic threat. In PTSD, fear structures contribute to dysfunction when the responses are associated with stimuli that do not accurately reflect real threats. When physiological and avoidant responses are associated with nonthreatening stimuli, and excessive responses are associated with harmless stimuli, individuals are more likely to have problems with adaptive functioning. The goal of PE is to alter the fear structures so that new information and associations may be incorporated in the fear structure (Watkins et al., 2018).

PE is an effective form of treatment for trauma for African-Americans (Ghafoor & Khoo, 2020). A meta-analysis found that at the end of treatment, the PE-treated patients report significant reductions in symptoms such that they often no longer meet criteria for PTSD, ranging from 41% to 95% (Jonas et al., 2013). Regarding efficacy, a 2010 meta-analysis found that the average patient treatment with PE was better than 86% of those in the control group with regard to PTSD symptoms at the end of treatment (Powers, Halpern, Ferenschak, Gillihan, & Foa, 2010).

PE allows for sustained engagement with feelings of guilt and shame through confronted trauma-related triggers, bringing related thoughts to one's mental awareness, and disclosing these thoughts within a safe, nonjudgmental environment (Kubany & Watson, 2003). The therapeutic environment in which the patient's anticipated ridicule of guilt and shame are absent allows for reconditioning/new learning to take place for reducing guilt and shame.

Cognitive processing therapy

Originally developed to treat rape victims, social cognitive theory and informed emotional processing are the theoretical foundations for CPT (Resick & Schnicke, 1992). CPT focuses on how the victim integrates the traumatic experience through assimilation, accommodation, or over-accommodation that may lead to distorted cognitions about self, the world, or others. Assimilation is when new information is altered to confirm a preexisting belief, such as the world is dangerous.

Accommodation happens when one alters beliefs to accommodate new learning such as "I can't control other people's actions." Over-accommodation is a type of prophylactic way of thinking in that it alters beliefs in an attempt to prevent future trauma such as "No one is trustworthy." The effectiveness of CPT is aimed at shifting beliefs toward accommodation by eliciting cognitions about the trauma to identify and address assimilated and over-accommodated cognitions resulting from that traumatic event (Resick & Schnicke, 1992).

Cognitive behavioral therapy

The final strongly recommended therapy listed in the guidelines by APA and the VA/DoD is CBT for PTSD. Trauma-focused CBT is based on cognitive and behavioral models such as PE and CPT. Therapists may elicit exposure to the traumatic memories of the event through imaginal exposure, narrative writing, or reading the memory out loud (Watkins et al., 2018). Exposure to trauma-related stimuli may be done in vivo or through teaching patients to identify triggers of re-experiencing and practice discrimination of "then vs now" such as while visiting the site of the trauma and identifying differences between time periods (Ehlers, Clark, Hackmann, McManus, & Fennell, 2005). Ehlers and Clark (2000) theorize that individuals with PTSD may re-experience the trauma due to excessive negative appraisals, destructive self-attributions, and behavioral and cognitive coping skills that PTSD victims use that may prevent them from altering their negative cognitions related to the trauma. Thus, the goal of CBT is to eliminate the cognitive and behavioral barriers that interfere with the ability to alter autobiographical information and the negative associations of the trauma for more adaptive thinking and functioning (Watkins et al., 2018). Cognitive restructuring teaches patients how to identify and challenge maladaptive and dysfunctional thoughts through rational thought processes to allow reappraisal of their thinking about themselves, the world, and others.

Rape crisis centers

Rape crisis centers (RCCs) have been integral in the treatment of sexual assault survivors since the early 1970s, and research indicates they benefit those who utilize the services (Campbell et al., 1998). RCCs began in response to the growing discontentment of feminists around the inadequate treatment of sexual assault survivors when seeking professional help (Collins & Whalen, 1989; Decker & Naugle, 2009). RCCs filled a gap in immediate support, validation, and service linkage which could not be found elsewhere. RCCs are available in all 50 states, with at least 1,300 locations nationwide (Bein, 2010). Most manage a 24-hour crisis hotline and provide services such as crisis intervention, support groups, medical and legal advocacy, counseling/therapy, and support groups. RCCs often provide advocacy and outreach including accompaniment to the hospital, resource referrals, and legal support to pursue charges against the attacker if the survivor chooses (Bein, 2010).

Rape, Abuse, and Incest National Network (RAINN)

RAINN began as an effort to provide a nationalized service for survivors of sexual assault (RAINN, 2019). Started in 1994, the organization was developed as a telephone hotline for sexual assault survivors to call from anywhere in the United States. RAINN has since emerged to include an online chat service, education and training, and a focus on public policy. The primary focus of RAINN is providing crisis intervention services, as well as referrals and additional resources (Finn & Hughes, 2008). RAINN is the "nation's largest anti-sexual violence organization" (RAINN, 2019). Serving approximately 16,000 people monthly, more than 2.5 million people have received services since its inception (RAINN, 2021).

Modalities critiqued utilizing the Afrocentric framework

Afracentric theory is a practice framework that speaks of the unique experiences of African Americans. The theory explores a worldview which accounts for the "historical trauma and collective disenfranchisement" of enslaved Africans and its subsequent effects (Estreet, 2016). At the heart of the African worldview is strong beliefs and values centered in spirituality and oneness with the universe and a superior energy force which most believe is God. The Afracentric theoretical framework utilizes guiding principles and virtues including *Ma'at* and the *Nguzo Saba*. The virtues of *Ma'at* include truth, justice, righteousness, harmony, balance, reciprocity, and order (Wells-Wilbon & Simpson, 2009; The Afrocentric Eye, 2021). The principles of the *Nguzo Saba* include *Umoja* (unity), *Kujichagulia* (self-determination), *Ujima* (collective work and responsibility), *Ujamaa* (cooperative economics), *Nia* (purpose), *Kuumba* (creativity), and *Imani* (faith) (Us Organization, 1999-2004). The virtues and principles of *Ma'at* and the *Nguzo Saba* are described as representing "wholeness" and necessary for African Americans' survival and ability to flourish (Wells-Wilbon & Simpson, 2009; Kalonji, 2014). The following is a critique of PE, CPT, CBT, and RCCs utilizing the aforementioned virtues and principles. The modalities will be critiqued through the lens of working with African-American female sexual assault survivors.

Prolonged exposure therapy critique

Congruent with African core values

This approach utilizes individualized sessions between the client and the therapist (American Psychological Association [APA], 2017d). As with any therapy modality, the therapeutic alliance is integral to the success of the intervention. For African-American sexual assault survivors, this therapeutic alliance encompasses the principles of reciprocity and harmony, which emphasize the importance of being aligned with doing that which is proper and what is good for oneself and others (The Afrocentric Eye, 2021). The therapist's role of providing a safe space before addressing trauma-related cognitions and memories allows for reciprocity and harmony for the survivor (APA, 2017d). The principle of self-determination is highlighted in the patient's comfort level and direction in dictating the pace of the exposures (Us Organization, 1999–2004). The principle's core emphasis is on the importance of speaking for oneself and defining one's own experience, which aligns with the patient's ability to explore their traumatic experiences in a way that feels safe for them (Us Organization, 1999–2004). Balance within the principles is defined by the necessity of not conflicting with oneself, others, and community (The Afrocentric Eye, 2021). This principle of balance is represented in the concise focus of PE on reducing or eliminating trauma-related symptoms such as anxiety. Addressing these trauma-related symptoms eliminates internal conflict with oneself.

Incongruent with African core values

The individualistic nature of PE, with the therapist working individually with a client, eliminates the opportunity for collective work and responsibility. A group format with other sexual assault survivors would allow for collectivity in sharing and healing after an assault. Conducting group-based exposure therapy has the potential to fill this gap (Castillo et al., 2016).

Cognitive processing therapy critique

Congruent with African core values

CPT aligns with the Afracentric framework regarding the importance of client readiness for intervention. The principle of self-determination, which explores one's capacity to self-define, allows the client to engage when it is appropriate for her (APA, 2017b). The virtue order is demonstrated in the organized and methodical duration of sessions, with each session having a set agenda and focal points (Resick, Monson, & Chard, 2017). Order is defined within the *Ma'at* principles as a respect for divine government and connection with what brings order to the world (The Afrocentric Eye, 2021). Organized sessions speak of the order, and in turn, healing, that can be brought to the survivor and the larger community. The purpose of each session, which embodies the principle of purpose (restoration of community), provides space for the patient to heal. This leads to restoration of self and consequently, restoration of the community.

Incongruent with African core values

CPT is not in congruence with the principles in regard to lack of creativity and the inessential component of developing a therapeutic alliance (Resick et al., 2017). CPT is a highly structured and manualized therapy modality. Each week contains modules with a set agenda and homework assignments (Resick et al., 2017). The modality also involves identifying an index trauma and stuck points. This may present challenges to the sexual assault survivor who may be better assisted through a combination of therapeutic interventions such as creative expression (drawing, guided imagery, etc.). Balance between order and creativity is important. Also, CPT does not emphasize the necessity of developing a therapeutic alliance before sessions begin (Resick et al., 2017). Rather, it is recommended that survivors begin treatment as soon as possible. For sexual assault survivors who prefer an opportunity to get a "feel" for the therapist before addressing their trauma history, this modality may be problematic.

Cognitive behavioral therapy critique

Congruent with African core values

CBT is a treatment modality with a high level of efficacy (APA, 2017c). CBT identifies and challenges negative thinking patterns that inhibit the client's ability to cope with challenging situations. The principle of justice is represented in the identification of negative automatic thoughts in CBT. The principle of justice presents the challenge to be fair and not cheat oneself or others (The Afrocentric Eye, 2021). Negative, unhelpful thinking patterns distort one's processing of events (APA, 2017c). CBT challenges these thoughts and provides space for the survivor to be "fair" to oneself by presenting more accurate information for one's life. CBT also focuses on behavioral patterns such as learning to confront fears and practicing strategies to promote relaxation (APA, 2017c). This focus is congruent with the principles of truth and righteousness, which seek to know what is right and to be correct in one's actions (The Afrocentric Eye, 2021). Confronting fears and learning coping strategies honor one's mental and physical health which is "right" for the mind and body and promotes healing. Also, CBT emphasizes collective work and responsibility, defined as taking on the problems of brothers and sisters in the community and assisting with solving dilemmas as they arise (Us Organization, 1999–2004). This collective work is essential in the collaborative relationship between the therapist and the survivor.

Incongruent with African core values

CBT is incongruent with the core values because of its primary focus on the present. While CBT minimally addresses trauma history, it is much more concerned with the impact of traumatic experiences on present functioning. Its attention to current unhelpful thinking and exploring current relational challenges highlights CBT's focus on what is current (APA, 2017c). This defies the principles of truth and balance. Truth, an understanding of what is correct, and balance, not being in conflict with self or the community, may be compromised as the survivor's desire to deeply explore trauma history may be inhibited by the therapist (The Afrocentric Eye, 2021).

RCCs and RAINN critique

Congruent with African core values

RCCs are unique in their focus on survivors of sexual violence. This includes survivors of sexual assault and child/adolescent sexual abuse (Bein, 2010). Their unique focus centers the needs and voices of this population. The principle of purpose (developing community greatness) is met in RCC's emphasis on advocating and creating a safe space for survivors (Bein, 2010; Us Organization, 1999–2004). The principle of self-determination is evident in survivors having the space to define for themselves what healing will look like and to share that work with other survivors. Additionally, survivors who have worked through much of their own trauma often serve as volunteers and paid staff in RCCs, this honors reciprocity. The DC RCC (2019a), for example, emphasizes the necessity of survivors telling their story and being an expert on their own lives. Collective work and responsibility emphasize the necessity of collectivity and community (Us Organization, 1999–2004). RCCs are community oriented as illustrated in one of their core services – support groups (Bein, 2010). Cooperative economics is represented in rape RCC's exclusivity to survivors and the collective call of these 1,300 agencies throughout the United States to address the needs of survivors (Bein, 2010). RAINN's crisis, education, online chat, and public policy focus have made the organization a central entity in the fight against sexual violence. Creativity is represented when survivors have opportunities to explore their own healing journey. "No Straight Path" on the DC RCC (2019b) website encourages survivors to learn and grow in their healing, learning new tools, using those that work, and discarding and moving beyond those that no longer benefit their healing process. This creativity allows survivors to take an active role in their own healing.

Incongruent with African core values

It could be argued that there is a lack of harmony with the goal of RCCs to center the needs of and advocate for survivors. The principle of harmony suggests that one will not oppose one's family or race. For survivors of sexual assault and sexual abuse, telling one's story could potentially bring shame to the social circle or family of the survivor. Additionally, within the Black family, fear of potentially being involved with the criminal justice system or seeking help outside the Black community could be considered taboo. Research shows that, at times, families are not supportive of a survivor sharing their story of assault or abuse (Anderson & Overby, 2019; Scoglio, Marine, & Molnar, 2021; Singh, Garnett, & Williams, 2012; Wimbrow, 2002). Bringing shame to one's family, however, should not discourage a survivor to seek out services that will bring necessary healing. Potential challenges that cause additional imbalance for survivors and their families and/or their race as a result of sharing their story should always be considered (i.e. Anita Hill, Megan the Stallion) (Crenshaw, 2019; Zaru, 2020).

Newer alternative models

Somatic, EMDR, and Brainspotting

Somatic psychotherapy is a modality grounded in the mind–body connection (Mallorquí-Bagué, Bulbena, Pailhez, Garfinkel, & Critchley, 2016). It is believed that viewing the mind and body as one entity is essential to the therapeutic process, and that sensations associated with past trauma get trapped within the body, reflected in facial expressions, posture, muscular pain, or other forms of body language (Mallorquí-Bagué et al., 2016).

Brainspotting (BSP) is designed to help people access, process, and overcome trauma, negative emotions, and pain, including psychologically induced physical pain (Hildebrand, Grand, & Stemmler, 2017). It was developed through work with survivors of trauma, and mental health professionals have found it to be an effective form of treatment for a variety of mental health concerns (Hildebrand et al., 2017). During BSP, therapists help people position their eyes in ways that enable them to target sources of negative emotion caused by stored trauma, which activates the body's innate ability to heal itself from trauma (Hildebrand et al., 2017).

Eye Movement Desensitization and Reprocessing (EMDR) therapy is an interactive psychotherapy technique used to relieve psychological stress. Over time, this technique is believed to lessen the impact of the memories or thoughts (Hildebrand et al., 2017). It is an effective treatment for trauma and PTSD (Hildebrand et al., 2017). During EMDR therapy, you relive traumatic or triggering experiences in brief doses while the therapist directs your eye movements (Hildebrand et al., 2017). Recalling distressing events when your attention is diverted can allow exposure to the memories or thoughts without having a strong psychological response (Hildebrand et al., 2017).

Usefulness from an African-centered perspective

There is a metaphysical and creative component to these techniques that may be in line with some core African spiritual values. To achieve harmony, balance, and order, one has to be in tune with self and an internal life force. An African-centered journey is not always a collective journey, but it is sometimes an individual journey to wellness that ultimately benefits the collective. More collective and group opportunities to participate in these techniques would make them even more congruent with African core values. Unfortunately, there are not many Black professionals who are trained in these techniques. Additionally, Blacks are reluctant to participate in anything that is perceived as being mind control or altering.

Conclusion

In conclusion, the modalities discussed undoubtedly benefit sexual assault survivors. For African-American women who have survived sexual assault, practitioners should be mindful of how they can creatively incorporate spirituality and the principles of *Ma'at* and *Nguzo Saba* into their work. The Afracentric framework holds important value not only for African-Americans but for all races of people seeking to strengthen their communities. Approaches may include holistic goal planning by including objectives that address physical, spiritual, and physical health as part of overall mental health wellness (Howard, 2003). Such approaches may also incorporate strength-based strategies that support the client's cultural heritage, identity, and resiliency. White feminists are also challenged to be more inclusive and not create additional layers and barriers to power for African-American women and other women of color.

References

Alvidrez, J., Shumway, M., Morazes, J., & Boccellari, A. (2011). Ethnic disparities in men Bogantal health treatment engagement among female sexual assault victims. *Journal of Aggression, Maltreatment & Trauma, 20*(4), 415–425. https://doi.org/10.1080/10926771.2011.568997.

American Psychiatric Association. (2013). *Diagnostic and statistical manual of mental disorders* (5th ed.). Washington, DC: Author.

American Psychological Association. (2017a). *Ethical principles of psychologists and code of conduct*. Washington, DC: Author.

American Psychological Association. (2017b). *Cognitive behavioral therapy*. Retrieved from www.apa.org/ptsd-guideline/treatments/cognitive-behavioral-therapy.

American Psychological Association. (2017c). *What is cognitive behavioral therapy?* Retrieved from www.apa.org/ptsd-guideline/patients-and-families/cognitive-behavioral

American Psychological Association. (2017d). *Prolonged exposure*. Retrieved from www.apa.org/ptsd-guideline/treatments/prolonged-exposure.

Anderson, G. D., & Overby, R. (2019). Barriers in seeking support: Perspectives of service providers who are survivors of sexual violence. *Journal of Community Psychology, 48*(5), 1564–1582.

Ayalon, L., & Alvidrez, J. (2007). The experience of black consumers in the mental health system-Identifying barriers to and facilitators of mental health treatment using the consumers' perspective. *Issues in Mental Health Nursing, 28*(12), 1323–1340. https://doi.org/10.1080/01612840701651454.

Bein, K. (2010). *Core services and characteristics of rape crisis centers*. National Sexual Assault Coalition Resource Sharing Project. Retrieved from https://resourcesharingproject.org/sites/default/files/Core_Services_and_Characteristics_ of_RCCs_0.pdf.

Black, B. M., & Weisz, A. N. (2003). Dating violence: Help-seeking behaviors of African American middle schoolers. *Violence Against Women, 9*(2), 187–206. https://doi.org/10.1177/1077801202239005.

Campbell, R., Baker, C. K., & Mazurek, T. L. (1998). Remaining radical? Organizational predictors of rape crisis centers' social change initiatives. *American Journal of Community Psychology, 26*(3), 457–483.

Castillo, D. T., Chee, C. L., Nason, E., Keller, J., Baca, J. C., Qualls, C., . . . Keane, T. M. (2016). Group-delivered cognitive/exposure therapy for PTSD in women veterans: A randomized controlled trial. *Psychological Trauma: Theory, Research, Practice, and Policy, 8*(3), 404–412.

Collins, B. G., & Whalen, B. M. (1989). The rape crisis movement: Radical or reformist? *Social Work, 34*(1), 61–63.

Crenshaw, K. W. (2019). We still have not learned from Anita Hill's testimony. *UCLA Women's Law Journal, 26*(1), 1–5.

Dale, S. K., Pierre-Louis, C., Bogart, L. M., O'Cleirigh, C., & Safren, S. A. (2018). Still I rise: The need for self-validation and self-care in the midst of adversities faced by Black women with HIV. *Cultural Diversity and Ethnic Minority Psychology, 24*(1), 15–25. https://doi.org/10.1037/cdp0000165.

DC Rape Crisis Center. (2019a). *Counseling philosophy.* Retrieved from https://dcrcc.org/counseling/counseling-philosophy/

DC Rape Crisis Center. (2019b). *No straight path.* Retrieved from https://dcrcc.org/counseling/no-straight- path/

Decker, S. E., & Naugle, A. E. (2009). Immediate intervention for sexual assault: A review with recommendations and implications for practitioners. *Journal of Aggression, Maltreatment, & Trauma, 18*(4), 419–441.

Ehlers, A., & Clark, D. M. (2000). A cognitive model of posttraumatic stress disorder. *Behaviour Research and Therapy, 38*, 319–345. https://doi.org/10.1016/S0005-7967(99)00123-0

Ehlers, A., Clark, D. M., Hackmann, A., McManus, F., & Fennell, M. (2005). Cognitive therapy for post-traumatic stress disorder: Development and evaluation. *Behaviour Research and Therapy, 43*, 413–431. https://doi.org/10.1016/j.brat.2004.03.006.

Estreet, A. (2016). Substance use prevention in the urban environment. In R. Wells-Wilbon, A. R. McPhatter, & H. F. Vakalahi (Eds.), *Social work practice with African Americans in urban environments.* New York, NY: Springer Publishing Company.

Finn, J., & Hughes, P. (2008). Evaluation of the RAINN national sexual assault online hotline. *Journal of Technology in Human Services, 26*(2/4), 203–222.

Ghafoor, B., & Khoo, S. F. (2020). A pilot study of racial and ethnic differences in mental health outcomes during the first 6 weeks of trauma-focused treatment. *Community Mental Health Journal.* Advance online publication. Retrieved from https://link.springer.com/article/10.1007%2Fs10597-020-00620-9.

Goodman, J., Wennerstrom, A., & Springgate, B. F. (2011). Participatory and social media to engage youth: From the Obama campaign to public health practice. *Ethnicity & Disease, 21*(3 Suppl 1), S1–99.

Hildebrand, A., Grand, D., & Stemmler, M. (2017). Brainspotting – the efficacy of a new therapy approach for the treatment of Posttraumatic Stress Disorder in comparison to Eye Movement Desensitization and Reprocessing. *Mediterranean Journal of Clinical Psychology, 5*(1).

Howard, D. L. (2003). Are the treatment goals of culturally competent outpatient substance abuse treatment units congruent with their client profile? *Journal of Substance Abuse Treatment, 24*(2), 103–113.

Jonas, D. E., Cusack, K., Forneris, C. A., Watkins, T. M., Sonis, J., Middleton, J. C. et al. (2013). *Psychological and pharmacological treatments of adults with post-traumatic stress disorder (PTSD): Comparative effectiveness review no. 92.* (Prepared by the RTI International-University of North Carolina Evidence-based Practice Center, Under Contract No. 290–2007–10056-I) AHRQ Publication No 13-EHC011-EF. Rockville, MD: Agency for Healthcare Research and Quality.

Kalonji, T. (2014). The Nguzo Saba and Ma'at, a path for self-reconstruction and recoverdness: Exploring a Kawaida Paradigm for healing addiction in the Black community. *Journal of Pan African Studies, 7*(4), 195–210.

Kimerling, R., & Calhoun, K. (1994). Somatic symptoms, social support, and treatment seeking among sexual assault victims. *Journal of Consulting and Clinical Psychology, 62*(2), 333–340.

Kubany, E., & Watson, S. (2003). Guilt: Elaboration of a multidimensional model. *The Psychological Record, 53*, 51–90.

Leach, C. R., & Schoenberg, N. E. (2008). Striving for control: Cognitive, self-care, and faith strategies employed by vulnerable black and white older adults with multiple chronic conditions. *Journal of Cross-Cultural Gerontology, 23*, 377–399. https://doi.org/10.1007/s10823-008-9086-2.

Mallorquí-Bagué, N., Bulbena, A., Pailhez, G., Garfinkel, S. N., & Critchley, H. D. (2016). Mind-body interactions in anxiety and somatic symptoms. *Harvard Review of Psychiatry, 24*(1), 53–60.

McGinty, E., Pescosolido, B., Kennedy-Hendricks, A., & Barry, C. (2018). Communication strategies to counter stigma and improve mental illness and substance abuse disorder policy. *Psychiatric Services, 69*(2), 136–146. https://doi.org/10.1176/appi.ps.201700076.

Powers, M. B., Halpern, J. M., Ferenschak, M. P., Gillihan, S. J., & Foa, E. B. (2010). A meta-analytic review of prolonged exposure for posttraumatic stress disorder. *Clinical Psychology Review, 30*, 635–641. http://dx.doi.org/10.1016/j.cpr.2010.04.007.

Rape, Abuse, and Incest National Network. (2019). *RAINN's president and founder reflects on 25 years*. Retrieved from www.rainn.org/news/rainns-president-and-founder-reflects-25-years

Rape, Abuse, and Incest National Network. (2021). *National sexual assault hotline: Statistics*. Retrieved from www.rainn.org/statistics/people-helped-through-national-sexual-assault-hotline

Resick, P. A., Monson, M. C., & Chard, K. M. (2017). *Cognitive processing therapy*. New York: Guilford Press.

Resick, P. A., & Schnicke, M. A. (1992). Cognitive processing therapy for sexual assault victims. *Journal of Consulting and Clinical Psychology, 60*, 748–756. https://doi.org/10.1037/0022-006x.60.5.748.

Schrag, R. V., & Edmond, T. E. (2018). Treatment goals, assessment, and evaluation practices in rape crisis centers. *Violence and Victims, 33*(6), 1055–1071.

Scoglio, A. A. J., Marine, S. B., & Molnar, B. E. (2021). Responder perspectives on justice and healing for sexual violence survivors. *Psychology of Violence, 11*(1), 1–10.

Singh, A. A., Garnett, A., & Williams, D. (2012). Resilience strategies of African-American women survivors of child sexual abuse: A qualitative inquiry. *The Counseling Psychologist, 41*(8), 1093–1124.

The Afrocentric Eye. (2021). *The principles of Ma'at*. Retrieved from http://theace.me/maat- principles.html.

Us Organization. (1999–2004). *Nguzo saba (the seven principles)*. Retrieved from www.us-organization.org/nguzosaba/NguzoSaba.html.

Watkins, L. E., Sprang, K. R., & Rothbaum, B. O. (2018). Treating PTSD: A review of evidence- based psychotherapy interventions. *Frontiers in Behavioral Neuroscience, 12*. https://doi.org/10.3389/fnbeh.2018.00258.

Wells-Wilbon, R., & Simpson, G. M. (2009). Transitioning the caregiving role for the next generation: An African-Centered womanist perspective. *Black Women, Gender, and Families, 3*(2), 87–105.

Wimbrow, M. (2002). The problem with rape crisis centers. *Off Our Backs, 32*(9/10), 1.

Zaru, W. (2020, October 31). 'Protect Black women': How Megan Thee Stallion's story became part of a movement. *ABC News*. Retrieved from https://abcnews.go.com/US/protect-black- women-megan-thee-stallions-story-part/story?id=73630195.

Zinzow, H., & Thompson, M. (2011). Barriers to reporting sexual victimization: Prevalence and correlates among undergraduate women. *Journal of Aggression, Maltreatment & Trauma, 20*(7), 711–725. https://doi.org/10.1080/10926771.2011.613447.

9

THE FINGERPRINT OF TRAUMA ON BLACK YOUTH

A critical analysis of Eurocentric social work models with African American adolescents and the shift toward the Afrocentric paradigm

Cashmere O'Neal, Loren Henderson

Post-traumatic stress disorder (PTSD) is often associated with returning war veterans; however, many low-income African American adolescents find themselves living in urban war-like settings and at an increased risk of developing PTSD. Systemic racism, oppressive practices, and the bilateral parallel of trauma stemming from slavery in the United States to racial disparities in contemporary America undergirds the intergenerational experience of mental health symptomatology consistent with PTSD criterion. The severity of the symptoms is often correlated with the type and length of exposure to the trauma (Shalev, Tuval-Mashiach, & Hadar, 2004). While debilitating for adults, these symptoms can be onerous and manifest differently among adolescents, who tend to display many of these symptoms alongside impulsive and aggressive behaviors (Hamblen & Barnet, 2018). In addition, adolescence is a stage of vulnerability due to the significant neurological and social development changes occurring during puberty (Larsen & Luna, 2018). Thus, Black youth experiencing PTSD often suffer from severe mental health effects, neurological impairments (Herring, Phillips, Fournier, Kronhaus, & Germain, 2013), social and economic disruptions (Guessoum et al., 2020), as well as debilitating disruption to their quality of life, and at worst morbidity (Carr et al., 2013).

Interestingly, PTSD does not manifest equally among adolescents. For example, according to Merikangas et al. (2010) using data from The National Comorbidity Survey Adolescent Supplement, the data determined that girls are more likely than boys (8.0% vs 2.3%) to suffer from PTSD, and as age increases so does the rate of PTSD. Disturbingly, 33% of women have experienced sexual abuse before reaching 18 years old (Wyatt, Axelrod, Chin, Carmona, & Loeb, 2000). With such large numbers of women reporting sexual abuse before age 18, which we can be sure is much higher due to underreporting, adolescent girls are clearly at risk for PTSD.

DOI: 10.4324/9780429276613-12

African Americans are also more likely to suffer from multiple traumatic events. These multiple experiences create an increased risk of delinquency compared with their White peers, but there are mixed results on the rates of racial differences in PTSD among adolescents (López et al., 2017). Unfortunately, low-income African American adolescents are more likely to live in residentially segregated communities with high levels of crime and parental incarceration (Morsy & Rothstein, 2019). Living in violent neighborhoods with exposure to trauma increases the risk for developing PTSD (Gillikin et al., 2016).

Living in urban neighborhoods also increases the risk of experiencing a traumatic event (Breslau & Davis, 1992). Given the vast differences in the lived experiences between African American and White adolescents that may lead to PTSD, this chapter will explore Eurocentric modalities of choice for clinical interventions for trauma Black adolescents face, which often result in some form of the Freudian talk therapy paradigm inclusive of psychotherapy, cognitive behavioral therapy (CBT), self-centered therapy, group and family therapy. We posit that CBT models are limited in their use due to cultural limitations and their partial effectiveness among Black youth. Effectiveness may increase if an Afrocentric perspective is used alone or in conjunction with the CBT model. It is imperative that race and culture be considered in selecting therapeutic modalities as shifting toward a more holistic approach using African-centered intervention models that are culturally and spiritually grounded may prove to be more successful.

Trauma exposure in Black youth

PTSD is defined in the *Diagnostic Statistical Manual of Mental Disorders*, or *DSM-5*, as a trauma- and stressor-related disorder developed in relation to an event that causes psychological trauma in response to one's perceived mortality due to a threat of or actual death, serious injury or sexual violence (American Psychiatric Association, 2013). The diagnostic criteria for trauma in general, is inundated with the terminology related to PTSD. The development of the PTSD diagnosis can be tracked from *DSM-III* through *DSM-5*. In the *DSM-III*, trauma was generally associated with one's experience with combat or an extreme natural disaster but was later expanded in the *DSM-IV TR* (Text Revision) to include direct or indirect exposure to life threatening events (American Psychiatric Association, 2013). Diagnostic criteria accounts for the actual or perceived threat of death or serious injury. The event itself can be sudden or unpredictable and destabilizing causing shock, fear, or helplessness (American Psychiatric Association, 2000).

Trauma may be experienced singularly, simultaneously, or in recurrent successions. Because of the complex nature of trauma, it is categorized as acute (single episode), chronic (recurrent episodes), or complex (multiple simultaneous co-occurring episodes) (American Psychiatric Association, 2000). The *DSM- 5* frames the diagnostic criteria for PTSD into clusters of individual and co-occurring symptoms unrelated to substance use or other underlying medical condition: *stressor exposure, intrusion of thoughts* or re-experiencing the event, *avoidance, negative alterations in cognitions, alterations in arousal and reactivity* (American Psychiatric Association, 2013). Intrusions of thoughts often manifest as fear and hypervigilance. An example of this uncontrolled response is the feeling African Americans feel when driving in any community where the predominant race is not Black (Bell, Hopson, Craig, & Robinson, 2014). Negative alterations in cognitions refer to the persistent negative beliefs, distorted blame, or trauma-related emotions stemming from a traumatic event (American Psychiatric Association, 2013). Alterations in arousal and reactivity manifest in heightened aggressive response and reckless or self-destructive behavior (American Psychiatric Association, 2013).

The *DSM-5* does not include alternative definitions of trauma in real time. Eagle and Kaminer (2013) attempted to provide that definition through the conceptualization of *continuous traumatic stress* as a supplemental construct to PTSD. Continuous traumatic stress, coined by Eagle and Kaminer (2013), conceptualizes trauma beyond the boundaries of PTSD criterion, giving space for current and future trauma of lived experiences, and weighs the absence of protection the same as a real or perceived threat of violence. Clinically, PTSD is not accepted as a primary diagnosis which presents limitations with trauma theory and PTSD diagnostic criteria because they do not account for cultural, historical, or environmental factors. PTSD is often observed in tandem with other psychiatric diagnoses such as depression, anxiety, and drug addiction (Hamblen & Barnett, 2018).

According to Graves, Kaslow, and Frabutt (2010) Black males present increased rates of aggression and suicide even though research on the impact of trauma on African American adolescents is scarce, presenting significant gaps in the literature. Black boys are, by and large, socialized to internalize or displace emotional vulnerability and often face several challenges with deconstructing perceived pillars of masculinity which have created barriers in their social and intimate relationships. This behavior may stem from the formulation of unspoken cultural norms shaped around the silent suffering of young boys as a rite of passage toward manhood and Black male identity development. The rate of substance abuse has increased indicating that self-medication to numb the pain away (or numbing the numbness of trauma desensitization) is a collective coping strategy of choice for those bearing the burden of trauma and other PTSD symptoms (King, Mrug, & Windle, 2020).

A section of the Black adolescent population has voiced disdain for the current climate of Black America. This has resulted in attempts to disconnect from America in its entirety. With the recent uprisings taking place in most major cities across the United States stemming from police involved murders of young Black men and women like Oscar Grant, Freddie Gray, Trayvon Martin, Philando Castille, and Sandra Bland, there has been a radical and defiant shift back toward the collective African center to reclaim voice, vision, purpose, and power. African American youth have single-handedly seized public focus on police brutality, exposed the system of white supremacy, baited major media outlets to provide coverage, and changed the narrative once media arrived so that the unbiased truth is publicized without tampering.

Mainstream interventions and Black youth

Although, African American adolescents suffer from high levels of exposure to community-based and interpersonal violence, structural barriers such as poverty and lack of access to high-quality mental health care, and a general distrust of the mental health community, they continue to function and survive using culturally appropriate Afrocentric models and spiritual coping mechanisms learned within the Black community (Novacek et al., 2020; Utsey, Bolden, Lanier, & Williams, 2007). However, once exposed to trauma the National Institutes of Mental Health suggests that individuals be screened for emergent or persistent symptoms of mental distress (National Institute of Mental Health, 2017). Unfortunately, urban youth have severe difficulty accessing culturally competent mental health care (Rich & Grey, 2005).

For Black youth who can access mental health treatment, it is imperative that practitioners consider not only the type of trauma experienced and the symptoms that are manifesting but also the cultural context in which these youth live to provide the best possible treatment for PTSD (Shalev et al., 2004). Gregory (2019) performed a meta-analysis examining research studies focused on the use of CBT with African American males finding high efficacy for anxiety symptoms not the diagnosis itself. Gregory (2019) concludes that CBT is an effective model to use in the treatment of depression and anxiety with Black youth, but the key factor of effectiveness is unknown.

We infer that in using CBT, the key factor for effectiveness in its use with anxiety-related symptoms is the methods used to address the anxiety symptoms as these symptoms create universal physiological responses (e.g., panic, fear, uneasiness, rumination, obsession, and worry). But what happens after the anxiety is managed? This question positions itself on the limitations of CBT as an effective model to use with African Americans whilst offering expansion to an Afrocentric perspective. Simply put, CBT is limited in its ability to reorient the Black youth to the community while supporting their strengths and spiritual connectedness.

The African-centered perspective (Afrocentricity)

Afrocentricity bridges the history and culture and philosophical teachings of Africans, with social and psychological interpretations of social phenomena to create relevant approaches toward social change for personal, family, and community healing (Bent-Goodley, Fairfax, & Carlton-LaNey, 2017). The conceptual framework and ideals of Afrocentricity predates modern civilization, rooted in antiquities' paradigms which provided a theoretical foundation before it was named and identified by contemporary scholars. Afrocentricity – the African-centered perspective – is, in a sense, a way of living which preexisted the so-called *enlightened* Western knowledge and civilization (Bent-Goodley et al., 2017). Afrocentricity encompasses much more than practice principles or ideas, it provides a manifesto, a spiritual ethos of thinking, behaving, and living to advance social justice, social welfare, and human rights specific to those apart of the diaspora but inclusive to all (Bent-Goodley et al., 2017). Martin and Martin (2002) state,

> The caregiver personality in the Black helping tradition, then, is a spiritualized, socialized, and racialized personality seeking psychic stability and wholeness and promoting a sense of "we-ness" among the people. Spirituality, racial identity and worth, and communal action go together as the pillars of the Black helping tradition. The spiritual attached Black people to their place and role in the world and determined the extent to which they felt a sense of commitment to the well-being and uplift of Black people.
>
> *(p. 7)*

The clash between individualism and collectivism

From a clinical perspective, Gregory (2019) suggests that CBT and traditional talk therapy (inclusive of self-centered therapy, group therapy, and family therapy) are overwhelmingly chosen as the primary mode of therapeutic intervention amongst African American adolescents. What is also evident is that beyond a specific point in the therapeutic engagement, CBT plateaus in effectiveness, confirming what Yung (2016) implicates, the "initial treatments are more 'benign' and non-specific, such as supportive psychotherapy, while treatments for later stages are more 'toxic' but specific, such as antidepressants for depression and antipsychotics for psychotic disorders" (Yung, 2016, p. 328). It is no secret that the social work profession is rooted in psychology which set the stage for intra-practicum conflict between spirituality and psychotherapy (Martin & Martin, 2002; Mendes, 1982). Martin and Martin (2002) referenced Mendes (1982) when discussing the relationship between the philosophical approach of spirituality and psychology,

> Psychotherapy has come to explain physical and social phenomena in the empirical world solely in terms of natural causation and remedies and to view "humanity, not God or some other supraempirical reality" as "the center of life" (p. 206). Black people, of course, operated from a religious and spiritual perspective that saw "God-determination, rather than self-determination" as "the highest value" (p. 206).
>
> *(p. 10)*

Simply put, much of the Black community internalizes and disseminates the belief that one is not just human but a spiritual being subjected to human experiences. To be disconnected from one's spiritual thrust is akin to existing without purpose or the power of inspiration. Makeda Graham (2005) infers that the relationship between psychotherapy and psychiatry "highlight power relationships that can marginalize and negate the interpretative frameworks of Black communities to explain human behavior" (p. 212).

Traditional trauma models did not include people of color in their inception or initial application, does not consider a spiritual component, and negates the root of maladaptive behavior that stems from being disconnected from one's spiritual center. Martin and Martin (2002) discuss the Caregiving Personality conceptualizing the theoretical approach around the traditional African foundation where the individual is no longer compartmentalized but perceived in a holistic viewpoint of mind, body, and spirit. Martin and Martin (2002) chart this dynamic in a clear depiction where the *racial self* (the development of racial identity based on the cumulative experiences rooted in race and culture) and *communal self* (the family/community centered identity developed in relationship with the external experiences) revolve around the *spiritual center* in search for balance and homeostasis.

People of the African diaspora, traditionally, fundamentally, and socio-collectively, are tribal or communal. This feature of Africanism has maintained its truth well beyond the Middle Passage of the trans-Atlantic slave trade, the Black Codes, segregation and Jim Crow, and the recent shift toward mass incarceration. Researchers have for decades attempted to explain Black phenomenon centered around maladaptive and often deviant behavior inclusive of intragroup violence, failure to obtain or pursue higher education, overrepresentation in special education, gang affiliation and activity but failed to see the communal nature of both the positive and negative behaviors. While Black gangs are often the subject of scrutiny, it reflects the gravitational pull of Black youth toward a community – deviant or otherwise – to meet a need often unaddressed in the Eurocentric affirmed helping profession. Black adolescents gravitate toward what speaks to their spirit, the core of who they are, and ascribe to become. The question is, are we listening or are we attempting to treat them out of inherent biases and stereotypical assumptions?

What is suggested is a shift from the psychodynamic paradigm which birthed psychosocial theory, CBT, and other talk therapy approaches toward a more holistic approach. For this to occur, it would require a complete paradigm shift as Eurocentric models are conceptually linear and are limited in their capacity to perform deep work along a continuum. It is vital that the proposed paradigm shift even follows the cyclical nature of the African-centered perspective. This shift must allow for the exploration of transmuted trauma and allow for its explanation through a cellular or genetic scope.

The epigenetic transmission of middle passage trauma

Kellerman (2013) critically analyzed the intergenerational impact of Holocaust trauma on the offspring of Holocaust survivors. Kellerman provides an example of Transgenerational Transmission of Trauma (TTT):

> Many children of Holocaust survivors have had such terrible nightmares in which they are chased, persecuted, tortured or annihilated, as if they were re-living the Second World War over and over again. At these times, they suffer from debilitating anxiety and depression which reduce their ability to cope with

stress and adversely impact their occupational and social function. It seems that these individuals, who are now adults, somehow have absorbed the repressed and insufficiently worked-through Holocaust trauma of their parents; as if they have actually inherited the unconscious minds of their parents. Apparently, not only children of Holocaust survivors, but offspring of other PTSD parents are also vulnerable to such a burdensome legacy, including descendants of war veterans (Dekel & Goldblatt, 2008), survivors of war trauma and childhood sexual abuse, refugees, torture victims and many others (Danieli, 1998). Moreover, the transmission may continue beyond the second generation and include the grandchildren, great grandchildren and perhaps others as well.

(p. 1)

If we collectively accept the Holocaust experience of the Jewish experience, then the experience of the African in America surely must be one of intergenerational, psychosocial, and spiritual torment.

Jablonka and Raz (2009) argue from a biological perspective through their research on host organisms where stress exposure, adverse conditional effects, and emotional trauma were found to be in direct association with altered genetic expression in subsequent generations of bacterium, plant species, and animals resulting in genetic inheritance of trauma markers. Jablonka and Raz (2009) posit that from a cellular level, trauma inheritance is a short-term effect on subsequent generations of cells but "For more persistent memory and cell heredity, autocatalysis is necessary, and all the EISs [Epigenetic Inheritance Systems] we describe depend on mechanisms that enable self-perpetuation" (pg. 133). Kellerman (2013) effectively articulated the use of this argument to provide a foundation for understanding trauma transmission which can be applied to other racial groups inclusive of African Americans and indigenous people/Native Americans.

The Trans-Atlantic trauma experience has been, without a doubt, genetically reproduced and transmitted through intergenerational DNA and permeated by the various systems of racial oppression of which the descendants of slaves remain subject (Leary, 2005). Black youth, carrying these DNA markers, also carry genetic memory of rage, frustration, and an overwhelming sense of urgency to treat the resulting conditions of racial oppression and despair. We can deduce that such trauma exposure can and may have resulted in a communicable transmission of communal PTSD symptomatology. Eagle and Kaminer (2013) highlight this phenomenon as *collective trauma* – the traumatization of entire groups of people due to their identity. Their research suggests that collective trauma may be transmitted intergenerationally and indirectly carried by descendants with little to no experience of the traumatic events themselves (Eagle & Kaminer, 2013; Gone, 2007; Danieli, 1998).

Presentation of African-centered concepts

The determinants of depression, rage, and racial oppression support that African American youth who are socialized around racial oppression and indoctrinated in their own cultural strengths show positive development of ego-strengths and social outcomes (Jackson-Gliffort, Liddle, Tejeda, & Dakof, 2001; Stevenson, Reed, Bodison, & Bishop, 1997). Congruent research purports that African American youth who are socialized to embrace Afrocentric values, subsequently forming a strong racial identity, report less favorable attitudes toward substance use (Jackson-Gliffort et al., 2001). In a more concise explanation, one who is rooted in their cultural existence is more likely to reject maladaptive coping strategies to numb the physical experience while seeking to escape the recurring exposure and psycho-emotional strain of the interpretation of those experiences. Here, we present the *Maafa* and the *Nguzo Saba* as the foundation for culturally appropriate therapeutic interventions.

Mainstream therapeutic models do not consider the components of the historical trauma markers which resulted from the African diaspora experience. *Maafa* (Mourning) is a term coined by Marimba Ani (1994) depicting not only the tragedies of Middle Passage and chattel slavery in the Americas but the resounding effects that can be overtly observed through the fingerprint of Eurocentric domination and colonialization. African American communities share a collective grieving or a spiritual moaning that can be felt iNTUitively throughout the collective. The systemic effects of racial oppression are complex as they can be seen in everything in our society today from racial tension and division recently hyper-emotionalized with the election of President Donald Trump, health disparities exacerbated by the COVID-19 pandemic, overrepresentation of incarcerated African Americans in the U.S. penal system, to oppressive housing policies and practices. Gilbert, Harvey, and Belgrave (2009) argue that the etiology of African American disparities and rates of premature mortality stem from systemic barriers inclusive of institutionalized racism and discrimination. Gilbert et al. (2009) further argue that internalizing racial stereotypes and negative depictions of one's race serves to diminish self-appreciation, cultural knowledge, and racial identity resulting in the development of maladaptive coping strategies.

The *Nguzo Saba* promotes the seven principles of *Kawaidi* philosophy which has been explained in the African American celebration of the *Kwanzaa* tradition (Johnson, 2001; Karenga, 1965). These principles are *Umoja*, *Kujichagulia*, *Ujima*, *Ujamma*, *Nia*, *Kuumba*, and *Imani*. *Umoja* is to seek and promote unity in race, family, community, and nation. *Kujichagulia* promotes self-determination in the process of naming, speaking, and creating for ourselves rather than having our destiny being determined for us. *Ujima* refers to the collective work and responsibility where we collectively take on the responsibility of each individual problem as if it were our own, with the intention to solve the problem collectively. *Ujamma* refers to cooperative economics focused with the goal to build, serve, profit, and redistribute the wealth amongst our own people. *Nia* is an individual's purpose or the drive by which we have answered the call of collective action to rebuild our community to the heights of traditional greatness. *Kuumba* speaks to our internal creativity used with intentionality to beautify our community leaving it more beneficial than previously inherited. *Imani* is a spiritual faith resonating in and with

God, the ancestors, the elders and leaders, and a level of propriety because of our victory in struggle.

What should be noted for practicum purposes is that the pillars of the *Nguzo Saba* fundamentally parallel the National Association of Social Workers's (NASW) ethical doctrine making it an ethical responsibility to utilize as it adheres to culturally relevant best practices. The NASW Code of Ethics specifies six principles which must be promoted and upheld in social work practice which are *service, social justice, dignity and worth of the person, the importance of human relationships, integrity,* and *competence* (National Association of Social Workers, 2008). Gilbert et al. (2009) support the use of African-centered interventions to address the psychosocial problems caused by psychological distress and racial oppression along a continuum. Furthermore, Black resilience, cultural identity development, and racial liberation are dependent on the survival of African heritage as it provides healing for people of African descent.

The Afrocentric paradigm and current African-centered models

Models that can be used in conjunction with Martin and Martin (2002) Caregiver Personality Model that have been presented in a conceptual framework of the Afrocentric paradigm are The African NTU Therapeutic Model and the Black Identity Development Model. The Afrocentric paradigm upholds the fundamental ideal of the human identity as a *collective identity*, unabridged by racial lines or influenced by socioeconomic position. This paradigm presents the *spiritual* or nonmaterial component as the centralizing attribute for its capacity to be used universally, rather than race or sex as they are limiting and neglect some section of the population. The *affective domain* – the simultaneous working of the spiritual realm in tandem to the natural world while maintaining and manifesting physiological influence in the natural world – is comprehensively woven through the fibers of the various models and teachings on Afrocentrism (Martin & Martin, 2002).

Black Racial Identity Development Model

The way in which trauma is experienced, perceived, internalized, and rationalized has a direct relationship with that individual's culture (Henderson, 2019). Consequently, the healing process is also dependent on one's culture and should be considered in the therapeutic process of trauma work. Henderson's (2019) research in Black youth trauma expression suggests that trauma work should be undergirded with intervention models specific to cultural identity development. The Black Racial Identity Model was developed by W. E. Cross in the 1970s focusing on the challenges of Eurocentric acculturation. Cross's model intended to shift the trauma experience away from the central focus and place the experiencer into the center where they then have the capacity to draw from cultural strengths to mediate their interpretation of the traumatic event (Ritchey, 2014). There are five pillars of the Black Racial Identity Model as discussed by Ritchey (2014): pre-encounter, encounter, immersion–emersion, internalization, and internalization–commitment.

The *pre-encounter* refers to experiencing inferiority due to the internalization of Eurocentric beliefs and values that Blacks are inherently inferior to whites, racial stereotypes are true, and racism is non-existent. An *encounter* refers to how racism is acknowledged through a specific event where the individual will seek to cultivate their identity in the African American group. *Immersion–Emersion* refers to the development and refinement of Black identity while mediating feelings of hatred toward European American community which results in the formulation of a positive, strong, affirmed sense of self through racial history and culture indoctrination. *Internalization* supports Black racial identity development as the individual becomes more accepting of European Americans, often partnering with them and other groups to work toward social change. *Internalization–Commitment* requires self-acceptance as one is transformed into a commitment to societal change and the individual becomes an advocate for African Americans and other minority racial groups (Ritchey, 2014).

African NTU therapeutic model

NTU was developed from Afrocentric psychology and the humanistic approach by Phillips (1990), who sought to address trauma from an African-centered, spiritual-oriented, family focused, culturally competent, holistic value-driven therapeutic framework. NTU (BaNTU terminology meaning *essence*) refers to the healing force of the universe or the essence of all life. The characteristics of NTU are steeped in Afrocentric elements which aid in the reduction of anxiety inducing symptoms, promotes oneness with self, the collective and the universe, and promotes one's ability to sync with spirit to achieve homeostasis (Gregory & Phillips, 1996; Phillips, 1990). The values of balance, harmony, interconnectedness, and authenticity are primary characteristics which undergird NTU pillars of harmony, awareness, alignment, actualization, and synthesis (Phillips, 1990).

Phillips (1990) defines *harmony* as one's state of being in union with mind, body, and spirit, the universe, and in life. Adaptation is a key function of harmony. *Awareness* is the state of incubation and contemplation where new African-centered beliefs and values are processed and considered for internalization. *Alignment* is the state of breakthrough and insight where one develops equilibrium among self, opposing forces, and the universe. *Actualization* refers to the normalization of processing balance in thoughts, practice, and encourages metaphysical re-creation for the self-determination of one's destiny and their capacity to affect change. *Synthesis* then is focused reintegration of self, purpose, and one's creativity to achieve a desired outcome.

Conclusion

The necessity of the African-centered approach is applicable to and inclusive of the African American experience as well as other groups across the racial spectrum. As emphasized in this chapter, there is a dearth of research that exists on the African-centered intervention models that are culturally and spiritually grounded for the treatment of depression and PTSD among African American adolescents. The Afrocentric paradigm has been sought to expand and include a more diverse orientation toward mental health interventions among African Americans in general. The literature suggests that it is imperative that mental health treatment modalities aimed at African American adolescents incorporate African-centered intervention models that are culturally and spiritually grounded. An Afrocentric perspective counters the notions that Eurocentric therapies are adequate to fully address the robust systemic racism and spiritual connections that undergird the lived experiences of African American adolescents, particularly those living in low-income communities due to its exclusive influence in the marginalization of African Americans.

Practitioners should consider the possibilities of enhanced connection and therapy success when incorporating the Black Racial Identity Model and the African NTU Model as compared to more traditional Eurocentric models that tend to have a lower success rate among African Americans than whites (Bent-Goodley et al., 2017). Such activities are inclusive of rite of passage programs, intergenerational talks, gap bridging workshops between elders and youth, and circle welcoming activities for youth to be reengaged by the collective from a socio-spiritual perspective. Clinicians strive to assist clients in reducing symptoms and enhancing quality of life. When engaging African American adolescents in a therapeutic relationship, clinicians should consider opportunities to address issues of racial oppression while assisting clients to develop ego-strengths to cope with and heal from trauma. By infusing the core tenets of the Black Racial Identity and the NTU models, clinicians have a practical path to aid Black youth in recovering from trauma-related symptoms while reducing the likelihood of future physical, social, and economic consequences related to their previous trauma. In consideration of cultural perceptions, be it direct or indirect exposure, intergenerational transmission of trauma occurs comprehensively and should consider cultural oral traditions as effective interventions. The tradition of the spoken word allows for the passing of either healing or residual trauma from historical events (Somé, 1999). Poetry, spoken word, rap, and Hip-Hop therapy can all be considered as therapeutic outlets.

Considering that Black youth equate to 15% of the population and account for 37% of all suicides, Black male adolescents reporting the highest percentage among all racial groups, it is pertinent that alternative culturally supportive intervention models be considered (Merikangas et al., 2010). Examples of alternative interventions should include healing rituals, ancestral libation rituals outlined by Somé (1999). Critical analysis and assessment of case studies using the Black Racial Identity Model and NTU concepts as an overlay in the school of social work curriculum may be necessary for knowledge and skill development with youth in urban communities.

Harvey and Hill (2004) focused their research on programs that were developed using the Afrocentric approach with special emphasis on the *Nguzo Saba* which yielded data suggesting that African American youth who are culturally connected through rituals and rites of passage ceremonies report higher rates of self-esteem, individual and family empowerment, and resilience. Rites of passage activities should include the formulation of unity circles, ancestral drum rituals, the pouring of libations and connecting to the spirit world, and the reorientation to peers as communal family members. In terms of school of social work educational resources, suggested readings should include Michelle Alexander's (2020) *The New Jim Crow* and Somé's (1999) *The Healing Wisdom of Africa* for an overview of community trauma and a blueprint for developing healing interventions that can be used on a wide scale. It is also worthy to note that these activities and interventions can be considered for further research in other racial groups inclusive of the various Hispanic and LatinX communities.

Clay (2019) critiques the Black Resilience Neoliberalism (BRN) perspective stating:

> Notions of "fairness" and "progressive" are discursively leveraged to justify divestment in Black public schools, while the language of "resilience" is employed to encourage Black youth to withstand structural poverty in order to achieve academic success.
>
> *(p. 90)*

It is in this way that despite systemic racism, oppression, and discriminatory practices and policies, we see the true resilience and strength of Black youth. Even in a game tilted in favor of the majority group, Black youth have been expected to achieve at higher rates with more restrictive parameters in every psychosocial life domain. The critical component of discussion is what if there were a level playing field even in the resources that were meant to stabilize an individual or the community? What if one's Blackness, and the communal experience attached to it, was valued and qualified as a strength to be matched with services that assessed and supported Black resilience? Statistical data quantifying disparities amongst Black youth may drastically shift and highlight a real closing of gaps.

References

Alexander, M. (2020). *The New Jim Crow: Mass incarceration in the age of colorblindness*. New York: The New Press.

American Psychiatric Association. (2000). *Diagnostic and statistical manual of mental disorders* (4th ed., text rev.). Washington, DC: Author.

American Psychiatric Association. (2013). *Diagnostic and statistical manual of mental disorders* (5th ed.). Washington, DC: Author.

Ani, M. (1994). *Yurugu: An African-centered critique of European cultural thought and behavior*. Trenton, NJ: Africa World Press.

Bell, G. C., Hopson, M. C., Craig, R., & Robinson, N. W. (2014). Exploring black and white accounts of 21st-ceNTUry racial profiling: Riding and driving while black. *Qualitative Research Reports in Communication*, *15*(1), 33–42.

Bent-Goodley, T., Fairfax, C. N., & Carlton-LaNey, I. (2017). The significance of African-centered social work for social work practice. *Journal of Human Behavior in the Social Environment, 27*(1/2), 1–6.

Breslau, N., & Davis, G. C. (1992). Posttraumatic stress disorder in an urban population of young adults: Risk factors for chronicity. *The American Journal of Psychiatry, 149*(5), 671–675.

Carr, E. R., Woods, A. M., Vahabzadeh, A., Sutton, C., Wittenauer, J., & Kaslow, N. J. (2013). PTSD, depressive symptoms, and suicidal ideation in African American women: A mediated model. *Journal of Clinical Psychology in Medical Settings, 20*(1), 37–45.

Center for Substance Abuse Treatment. (2014). *Trauma-informed care in behavioral health services*. Retrieved from www.ncbi.nlm.nih.gov/books/NBK207191/box/part1_ch3. box16/?report=objecton ly

Clay, K. L. (2019). "Despite the odds": Unpacking the politics of Black resilience neoliberalism. *American Educational Research Journal, 56*(1), 75–110.

Danieli, Y. (Ed.). (1998). *International handbook of multigenerational legacies of trauma*. New York: Plenum. https://doi.org/10.1007/978-1-4757-5567-1

Dekel, R., & Goldblatt, H. (2008). Is there intergenerational transmission of trauma? The case of combat veterans' children. *American Journal of Orthopsychiatry, 78*(3), 281–289.

Eagle, G., & Kaminer, D. (2013). Continuous traumatic stress: Expanding the lexicon of traumatic stress. *Peace and Conflict: Journal of Peace Psychology, 19*(2), 85–99.

Gilbert, D. J., Harvey, A. R., & Belgrave, F. Z. (2009). Advancing the Africentric paradigm shift discourse: Building toward evidence based Africentric interventions in social work practice with African Americans. *Social Work, 54*(3), 243–252

Gillikin, C., Habib, L., Evces, M., Bradley, B., Ressler, K. J., & Sanders, J. (2016). Trauma exposure and PTSD symptoms associated with violence in inner city civilians. *Journal of Psychiatric Research, 83*, 1–7. https://doi.org/10.1016/j.jpsychires.2016.07.027

Gone, J. P. (2007). "We never was happy living like a White man": Mental health disparities and the postcolonial predicament in American Indian communities. *American Journal of Community Psychology, 40*, 290–300. https://doi.org/10.1007/s10464-007-9136-x

Graham, M. (2005). An African-centered paradigm for psychological and spiritual healing. *Integrating Traditional Healing Practices into Counseling and Psychotherapy*, 210–233.

Graves, K. N., Kaslow, N. J., & Frabutt, J. M. (2010). A culturally informed approach to trauma, suicidal behavior, and overt aggression in African American adolescents. *Aggression and Violent Behavior, 15*(1), 36–41.

Gregory, S. D., & Phillips, F. B. (1996). NTU: Progressive Life Center's Afrocentric approach to therapeutic foster care. *Model Programs in Child and Family Mental Health*, 333–350.

Gregory Jr., V. L. (2019). Cognitive-behavioral therapy for anxious symptoms in persons of African descent: A meta-analysis. *Journal of Social Service Research, 45*(1), 87–101.

Guessoum, S. B., Lachal, J., Radjack, R., Carretier, E., Minassian, S., Benoit, L., & Moro, M. R. (2020). Adolescent psychiatric disorders during the COVID-19 pandemic and lockdown. *Psychiatry Research, 291*, 113264. https://doi.org/10.1016/j. psychres.2020.113264

Hamblen, J., & Barnett, E. (2018). *PTSD: National center for PTSD*. Retrieved from www.ptsd. va.gov/professional/treatment/children/ptsd_in_children_and_adolescents_overview_ for_professionals.asp.

Harvey, A. R., & Hill, R. B. (2004). Afrocentric youth and family rites of passage program: Promoting resilience among at-risk African American youths. *Social Work, 49*(1), 65–74.

Henderson, Z. (2019). In their own words: How Black teens define trauma. *Journal of Child & Adolescent Trauma, 12*(1), 141–151.

Herring, R. J., Phillips, M. L., Fournier, J. C., Kronhaus, D. M., & Germain, A. (2013). Childhood and adult trauma both correlate with dorsal anterior cingulate activation to threat in combat veterans. *Psychological Medicine*, *43*(7), 1533–1542. https://doi.org/10.1017/S0033291712002310

Jablonka, E., & Raz, G. (2009). Transgenerational epigenetic inheritance: Prevalence, mechanisms, and implications for the study of heredity and evolution. *The Quarterly Review of Biology*, *84*(2), 131–176.

Jackson-Gliffort, A., Liddle, H. A., Tejeda, M. J., & Dakof, G. A. (2001). Facilitating engagement of African American male adolescents in family therapy: A culture theme process study. *Journal of Black Psychology*, *27*(3), 321–340.

Johnson, V. D. (2001). The Nguzo Saba as a foundation for African American college student development theory. *Journal of Black Studies*, *31*(4), 406–422.

Karenga, M. (1965). *Kwanzaa: Origin, concepts, and practice*. Los Angeles, CA: Kawaida Publications.

Kellerman, N. P. (2013). Epigenetic transmission of holocaust trauma: Can nightmares be inherited. *Israel Journal of Psychiatry and Related Sciences*, *50*(1), 33–39.

King, V. L., Mrug, S., & Windle, M. (2020). Predictors of motives for marijuana use in African American adolescents and emerging adults. *Journal of Ethnicity in Substance Abuse*, 1–19.

Larsen, B., & Luna, B. (2018). Adolescence as a neurobiological critical period for the development of higher-order cognition. *Neuroscience and Biobehavioral Reviews*, *94*, 179–195. https://doi.org/10.1016/j.neubiorev.2018.09.005

Leary, J. D. (2005). *Post traumatic slave syndrome: America's legacy of enduring injury & healing*. Milwaukie, OR: Uptone Press.

López, C. M., Andrews, A. R., Chisholm, A. M., de Arellano, M. A., Saunders, B., & Kilpatrick, D. G. (2017). Racial/ethnic differences in trauma exposure and mental health disorders in adolescents. *Cultural Diversity & Ethnic Minority Psychology*, *23*(3), 382–387. https://doi.org/10.1037/cdp0000126

Martin, E. P., & Martin, J. M. (2002). *Spirituality and the Black helping tradition in social work*. Washington, DC: NASW Press.

Mendes, H. A. (1982). The role of religion in psychotherapy with Afro-Americans. In B. A. Bass, G. E. Wyatt, & G. J. Powell (Eds.), *The Afro-American family: Assessment, treatment, and research issues* (pp. 203–210). New York: Grune & Stratton.

Merikangas, K. R., He, J. P., Burstein, M., Swanson, S. A., Avenevoli, S., Cui, L., . . . Swendsen, J. (2010). Lifetime prevalence of mental disorders in U.S. adolescents: Results from the National Comorbidity Survey Replication – Adolescent Supplement (NCS-A). *Journal of the American Academy of Child and Adolescent Psychiatry*, *49*(10), 980–989. https://doi.org/10.1016/j.jaac.2010.05.017

Morsy, L., & Rothstein, R. (2019). *Toxic stress and children's outcomes: African American children growing up poor are at greater risk of disrupted physiological functioning and depressed academic achievement*. Washington, DC: Economic Policy Institute.

National Institute of Mental Health. (2017). *Coping with traumatic events*. Retrieved from www.nimh.nih.gov/ health/topics/coping-with-traumatic-events/index.shtml.

Novacek, D. M., Hampton-Anderson, J. N., Ebor, M. T., Loeb, T. B., & Wyatt, G. E. (2020). Mental health ramifications of the COVID-19 pandemic for Black Americans: Clinical and research recommendations. *Psychological Trauma: Theory, Research, Practice, and Policy*, *12*(5), 449.

Phillips, F. B. (1990). NTU psychotherapy: An Afrocentric approach. *Journal of Black Psychology*, *17*(1), 55–74.

Rich, J. A., & Grey, C. M. (2005). Pathways to recurrent trauma among young black men: traumatic stress, substance use, and the "code of the street". *American Journal of Public Health, 95*(5), 816–824.

Ritchey, K. (2014). Black identity development. *The Vermont Connection, 35*(12), 98–105.

Shalev, A. Y, Tuval-Mashiach, R., & Hadar, H. (2004). Posttraumatic stress disorder as a result of mass trauma. *Journal of Clinical Psychiatry, 65*(Suppl 1), 4–10. PMID: 14728091.

Somé, M. P. (1999). *The healing wisdom of Africa: Finding life purpose through nature, ritual, and community.* London: Thorsons.

Stevenson, H. C., Reed, J., Bodison, P., & Bishop, A. (1997). Youth & society. In E. Anderson (Ed.), *Streetwise: Race, class, and change in an urban community* (pp. 197–222). Chicago, IL: University of Chicago Press

Utsey, S. O., Bolden, M. A., Lanier, Y., & Williams III, O. (2007). Examining the role of culture-specific coping as a predictor of resilient outcomes in African Americans from high-risk urban communities. *Journal of Black Psychology, 33*(1), 75–93.

Workers, N. A. (2008). *NASW code of ethics: Guide to the everyday professional conduct of social workers.* Washington, DC: NASW.

Wyatt, G. E., Axelrod, J., Chin, D., Carmona, J. V., & Loeb, T. B. (2000). Examining patterns of vulnerability to domestic violence among African American women. *Violence Against Women, 65*, 495–514.

Yung, A. R. (2016). Youth services: The need to integrate mental health, physical health and social care: Commentary on Malla et al: From early intervention in psychosis to youth mental health reform: A review of the evolution and transformation of mental health services for young people. Social Psychiatry and Psychiatric Epidemiology: *The International Journal for Research in Social and Genetic Epidemiology and Mental Health Services, 51*(3), 327–329. https://doi-org.proxy-ms.researchport.umd.edu/10.1007/s00127-016-1195-6

10

COCOA BUTTER

How Black mothers prevent, protect, and heal their daughters from racialized gender trauma

S. Rasheem

Conversations about trauma often position Black people as somehow the creators and perpetrators of their own trauma. Rarely does the literature explore the intersectional impacts of racism and sexism on the mental health of adolescent African American girls. What is given even less attention are the Black maternal practices (BMP) that seek to mitigate those negative societal factors. This chapter contributes empirical data that privileges the applied experiential knowledge of African American mothers and their approach to intersectional identity development. Heideggerian phenomenological study used an intersectional (Crenshaw, 1989) and Black feminist (Collins, 2000) lens to center on the narratives of ten African American mothers of adolescent daughters. Findings reveal three central themes in the BMP of intersectional identity development of African American daughters that contribute to the mental health of African American adolescent girls. Those themes are a) the development of positive race-esteem and self-esteem, b) developing positive racialized images of beauty, c) nurturing their daughter's unique self. The chapter closes with adolescent mental health implications for social work policy, practice, and research. The central aim of this chapter is to contribute to the promotion of the psychological well-being of African American adolescent girls.

Black maternal practice

This chapter takes the position that the intersectional identity and lived experiences of African American mothers inform their maternal thinking (Ruddick, 1989) in ways that inform their maternal practice. The day-to-day physical work associated with child rearing, referred to as reproductive labor by Collins (2000), called care-work by Ganz (2014), and mother-work by Toni Morrison (O'Reilly, 2004) is expanded in this study and referred to as Black maternal practice. BMP has two primary domains: a) intersectional child socialization and b) intersectional child

DOI: 10.4324/9780429276613-13

identity development. This chapter focuses exclusively on intersectional identity development. Motherhood holds within it concepts of communal survival, power, and identity (Collins, 2000). In particular, Toni Morrison defines it as "a political enterprise that assumes as its central aim the empowerment of children" (O'Reilly, 2004, p. 1).

Intersectional identity development

In Black maternal identity development, mothers undertake the multilayered task of constructing their children's individual and collective race–gender identity. African American mothers have the added task of cultivating a strong sense of racial pride in resistance to popularized images in the media that make certain aspects of their culture hyper visual while completely misrecognizing other aspects. Black mothers balance supporting the exploration of who their child is as a unique person while also socializing them within the context of how society will view and interpret their race–gender identity. The literature (Bailey-Fakhoury, 2014; Chaney & Brown, 2015; Fouquier, 2009; Lewis & Swift, 2014; McLanahan, 1988; Rastogi & Wampler, 1999) suggests that the experiences of motherhood are impacted not only by the intersectional identity of the mother but may also by the race and gender identity of the child she mothers. The race–gender, mother–child dyad plays a role in the lived experiences and meanings that Black women apply to motherhood.

Mothering daughters

The literature reveals that Black mothers have a significant influence on their daughter's development (Bailey-Fakhoury, 2014; Collins, 1987; Everett, Marks, & Clarke-Mitchell, 2016; Turnage, 2004; Hinton-Johnson, 2004; O'Sullivan, Meyer-Bahlburg, & Watkins, 2001; Ridolfo, Chepp, & Milkie, 2013). For instance, in a study designed to examine maternal parenting behaviors and child coping in African American families among a sample of 83 mother–child dyads, findings revealed that child gender moderated the association between maternal parenting behavior and child coping. Specifically, maternal parenting behaviors were more important for girls' coping strategies than for boys' coping strategies. Furthermore, Collins writes, "Black women's efforts to provide a physical and psychic base for their children can affect mothering styles and the emotional intensity of Black mother-daughter relationships" (Collins, 2000, p. 187). A review of the literature on Black mother–daughter relationships demonstrates two distinct areas where Black mothers have a significant influence on the identity development of their daughters. Those two areas are their daughter's race-esteem and self-esteem.

Self-esteem. In a qualitative study of 17 Black adult daughters, the participants reported receiving positive messages from their mother and grandmother about their self-worth and value (Everett et al., 2016). In a like manner, using survey data collected in 1994 from a nationally representative sample of US Black (N=1,330) and White (N=3,797) girls and their mothers, Ridolfo et al. (2013) found that Black adolescent girls have a higher self-esteem than White adolescent girls. Their study also found the quality of mother–daughter relationship to be a significant contributor to the rates of higher self-esteem. In addition, the study also reported that those daughters' perceptions of their "mothers' encouragement of their independence was significantly associated with self-esteem" (p. 504). Similarly, Turnage's (2004) study of 105 African American urban senior girls revealed a positive direct relationship between the daughters' Global Self-Esteem scores and their 'Trust of Mother' score. The identity development that mothers provide is not completely separate from developing an understanding of racialized gender identity. Likewise, mothers tend to cultivate their child's gender identity in affiliation with a particular culture.

Race-esteem. Because young Black girls are regularly exposed to images that do not affirm their race–gender identity, particularly their hair and varied skin complexions (Jones & Shorter-Gooden, 2003; Lewis & Swift, 2014), the work of developing high race-esteem is one of particular importance. The rejection that a Black girl might feel from the world and possibly internalize can be countered through the identity development of Black children, making the development of race-esteem in young Black girls a mother's counteraction based on societal views. Turnage's (2004) study of 105 African American daughters revealed that participants who scored high on self-esteem assessment also scored high on ethnic identity achievement. In addition, Everett et al. (2016)'s results suggest that, "Black mothers exercise agency when they raise their daughters to think positively about themselves, to value their self-worth, and to be proud of their race." Lewis and Swift (2014) also found that intergenerational transmissions of behavior and values might be enacted while young Black girls are getting their hair combed. The practice of hair combing and what is said about the girl's natural state of hair may reinforce or empower against the negative concepts seen in the media about their natural attributes. Similarly, in Bailey-Fakhoury's (2014) study of Black mothers with daughters in predominantly White schools, she found that mothers engage in strategies that reflect dimensions of maternal practices – presence, imaging, and code switching. Mothers found these strategies helpful in influencing the development of positive race–gender identity in their daughters. Collins (1987) suggests that White perspectives on motherhood not only put Black women in a no-win situation but also, when internalized, leads to lower self-esteem that mothers could then pass on to their daughters and provides a powerful mechanism for controlling Black communities.

Culturally relevant lens

The lens used to guide this study is intersectionality (Crenshaw, 1989) and Black feminist thought (BFT) (Collins, 2000). Intersectionality emphasizes the importance of reviewing overlapping systems of oppressions and their proximity to power and privilege. "Ongoing tensions characterize efforts to mold the institution of Black motherhood to benefit intersecting oppressions of race, gender, class, sexuality, and nation and efforts by African-American women to define and value our own experiences with motherhood" (Collins, 2000, p. 176). The point of overlap highlights their distinctiveness as a group. More importantly, shared experiences, history, and level of access to opportunity, privilege, and disadvantage provide the group with a collective and unique standpoint. Consistent with the primary tenants of BFT, this research studied key social–cultural elements that contributed to the unique standpoint of Black women; implicit in BFT's application is the utilization of qualitative, narrative research approach with an emphasis on empowerment, thus allowing the individuals to participate in their own self-evaluation and actualization. In practice, BFT replaces the artifices of Black womanhood with images of self-valuation. BFT is used as a lens and not a theory because the concepts out of which the theory is constructed are derived from data collected during the research process and not chosen prior to beginning the research (Corbin & Strauss, 2015, p. 6).

Methodology

The essence of maternal decisions is in part based in emotion and beliefs that generate thought and lead to action, "The world that mothers and children see and name separately and together is constructed by feeling" (Ruddick, 1989, p. 69). These feelings are based in personal perspectives that are best captured through qualitative means. While quantitative means are suitable for tracking the trend of actions, phenomenology is a more appropriate tool for uncovering the phenomenon of Black motherhood through personal perspectives and lived experiences.

Research questions

This chapter addresses two research questions; first, what is the essence of the Black maternal practices of African American mothers of daughters between the ages of 10 and 18 years old? second, what can we learn from African American mothers about intersectional identity development that could lead to the improved mental health of African American cis-gendered girls? In response to the research questions you'll also find how both the mother's intersectional identity and the intersectional identity of her child(ren) impacted what and how motherhood is enacted.

Sampling

All the participants self-identified as African American mothers of adolescent daughters between the ages of 10 and 18 who live in the Northeast Region of the United States. The 11 states that make up the U.S. Northeast Region are Connecticut, Delaware, Maine, Massachusetts, Maryland, New Hampshire, New Jersey, New York, Pennsylvania, Rhode Island, and Vermont. Neither random nor representative samplings were used in this study, as the goal in qualitative research is not to generalize.

Inclusion criteria

The primary criteria for inclusion in this study were women who self-identify as Black mothers of adolescent daughters. Other inclusion criteria required that the African American mothers lived in the Northeast Region of the United States and have no sons.

Designing the tool

Upon approval of the Institutional Review Board, three Black mothers were recruited to participate in a semi-structured interview on Black motherhood as a pilot to help shape the interview guide. In accordance with a phenomenological approach, the questions were broadly stated in unstructured recorded interviews (Kleiman, 2004) without specific reference to the existing literature (Creswell, 2009). After reading through the transcriptions of the pilot interviews, an evaluation of the data was conducted to discern whether or not the research questions were effective in soliciting data that was rich and relevant to the study. The pilot participants provided insight into what questions should be included in the interview guide and how it should be worded.

Data collection

Establishing a nonhierarchical relationship between the interviewer and the interviewee is important in feminist research (Fouquier, 2009). Therefore, after each participant via online form gave consent, recorded interviews were conducted via phone in a nonhierarchical conversational style that encouraged open dialogue and lasted approximately an hour. Recorded interviews were transcribed to allow for the researcher to focus on the conversation, take notes or memos (Creswell, 2009), and capture any additional insights (Padgett, 2008). A recording number and pseudonyms were given to each participant at the completion of each interview.

Data analysis

Concept clarification is an ongoing process in qualitative research (Rubin & Babbie, 2007), and the phenomenological process is one of intentionality, reduction, description, and search for essence (Giorgi, 1997; Laverty, 2003) as was reflected in the data analysis. The focus of this hermeneutic phenomenological study was to uncover and interpret the Black maternal practice of intersectional identity development among Black mothers of daughters (Moustakas, 1994; Patton, 1990; 2002).

Trustworthiness

The three main threats to trustworthiness are researcher bias, reactivity, and response bias (Padgett, 2008). Member checking was used to determine the accuracy of the qualitative findings through taking the final emergent themes back to some of the African American mothers and allowing them to determine whether their responses were captured accurately.

Limitations and delimitations of the study

Hermeneutic studies are harder to pin down and are subject to more debate due to their highly interpretive nature (Rubin & Babbie, 2007). Also, some may consider the participants an indirect source of information capable of filtering. Filtering can lead to response bias and thereby limit the study. Another concern in qualitative study is often reactive effects, wherein respondents are responding to the interviewer and/or shaping their responses to tell the researcher what they want to hear. To guard against the reactivity that can occur with researcher's presence on participant's responses (Padgett, 2008) participants were given the option of completing a telephone interview or in-person interview.

Researcher bias and other considerations

In keeping with Collins's (1986) concept of the "outsider within," it deserves note that the researcher fits all of the demographics of the population in which she is researching. "Many Black intellectuals, especially those in touch with their marginality in academic settings, tap this standpoint in producing distinctive analyses of race, class, and gender" (p. S15). The researcher's identity and proximity to the population being evaluated serves as a strength in a study of this nature. Padgett (2008) further notes that while sharing similar demographics does not guarantee rapport, she cautions that researcher–participant disparities deserve attention in the design of qualitative research. Collins (2000) urges social scientists to interrogate their own individual consciousness. In keeping with the framework and approach I maintained a research journal.

Findings

Description of the sample

The ten mothers who participated in this study were all African American mothers of adolescent cis-gendered daughters. While participants did have some aspects of shared identity around race, gender, and mothering daughters, they varied in marital status and income. The mothers were between the ages of 30 and 43 and resided in the Northeast Region of the United States. Exactly half of the participants were divorced. Other marital statuses included three mothers who reported being single and never married, one married, and one mother in a domestic partnership. Most (eight) of the mothers in this study had only one daughter, while two of the mothers reported having two or more daughters. The aforementioned demographics

TABLE 10.1 Demographics

Pseudonyms	Mom's Age	City/State	Marital Status	Daughter's Age
Silhouette	30–34	Baltimore, MD	Divorced	12
Monica	35–39	Baltimore, MD	Single (never married)	14
Riri	40–43	Baltimore, MD	Divorced	13 & 18
Jill	35–39	Haymarket, VA	Single (never married)	10
Spectrum	40–43	Baltimore, MD	Divorced	15
Roberta	35–39	Waterbury, CT	Single (never married)	10
Guinan	30–34	Baltimore, MD	Divorced	8,10, & 14
Amazonia		Baltimore, MD	Divorced	13
Quanisha	35–39	Philadelphia, PA	Married	14
Quinn	30–34	Brooklyn, NY	Domestic partnership (unmarried spousal relationship	15

are displayed in Table 10.1. To protect the individual identity of each participant, pseudonyms are given in the first column of the table.

Summary themes and sub-themes

The following section will provide an overview of themes as they relate to the research questions and conceptual framework. Themes that emerged in the intersectional identity development of African American adolescent daughters were a) developing positive race-esteem and gender-esteem; b) developing positive racialized images of beauty; c) honoring their daughter's unique self (see Figure 10.1).

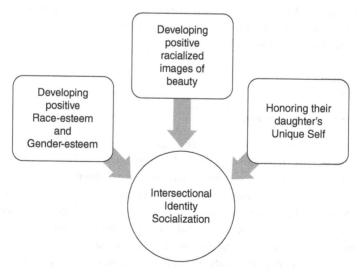

FIGURE 10.1 Overview of themes

Intersectional identity development in African American daughters

The Black mothers in this study developed their daughter's identity in two main aspects. They developed their daughter's group identity as well as their individual identity. "Black mothers socialize their daughter's to be independent, strong and self-confident" (Prof. Gloria Wade-Gales as cited in Collins (1987, p. 55). The group identity development is both racialized and gendered. Mothers also report that at times expectations placed on their daughters by their associated group identity conflicted with their unique self-identity. In those cases, mothers tended to prioritize their daughters' unique self-identity over their group identity. Group identity and individual identity are both intersectional.

Theme 1: developing positive race-esteem and gender-esteem to counter misrecognition

This research found that a key aspect in developing the identity of Black daughters is mitigating the negative impacts of racism, sexism, and classism that come with mis-recognition by cultivating a positive race-esteem and gender-esteem. Their strong sense of both self-esteem and race-esteem is itself an act of resistance to an outside world that they perceive not to value or affirm them. This research addresses the question put forth by Arendell (2000) where she asks, "How do women actively resist the dominant ideologies of mothering and family?" (p. 1202). RiRi, whom I had the pleasure of interviewing in person at an art exhibit in Baltimore, cried on several occasions recalling the joys and fears of being a mother. She also discussed the inseparable nature of being both Black and being a woman. She explained:

> So, my kids are older and I kind of want to start over, kind of want to take a stand back and teach them the responsibilities of not only being a woman but being a black woman and teach them how to have some ownership of that and how to show others and how important it is to be proud and to be black because I think surviving so much, I kind of forgot that part of myself.

Monica is originally from Columbus Oh, and currently lives in Baltimore, MD with her mother and 14-year-old daughter. She became a mother when she was 25 years old and feels it is particularly important to instill confidence and self-worth in her daughter specifically as it relates to race. When asked what the question "What does Black motherhood mean to you," she shared:

> I think it means that I feel more responsible to instill that confidence. I feel . . . again I keep using that word "responsible" but really for making sure that she knows who she is; that she understands her value; that she understands her worth and so it's more about trying to, to dispel these myths that you know white is better and smarter and prettier and that is incredibly challenging given that I went through it as a child myself

so I can relate . . . you know add the word black to me it's our personal responsibility of making sure that this person knows well quickly and their worth and we've got to put in extra effort especially as an African American to make sure that they understand that they are every bit as good as another person on the planet.

Theme 2: developing positive racialized images of beauty

Collins (1987) states, "Black girls learn by identifying with their mothers" (p. 53). How mothers self-define informs how they in turn develop the identity of and socialize their daughters. Key to the development of intersectional identity development is the development of a strong sense of self-esteem, race-esteem, and gender-esteem in the face of images that do not affirm their own natural beauty. In fact, over half of the mothers in the study shared that they refrain from the use of texture altering chemicals in their natural hair as a way of modeling self-love and embracing African American womanist beauty. "Young Black girls are consistently exposed to images that are not affirming of their own natural attributes especially related to their hair length and texture" (Lewis & Swift, 2014, p. 58). Hair and skin were major aspects of how beauty was performed. Much of the focus on developing positive racialized images of beauty was related to skin color and hair texture.

Roberta lives in Waterbury, Connecticut with her ten-year-old. Her daughter has felt unattractive not only because of her dark skin but also because she has eczema. She shared:

> *I have a daughter so there were issues with trying to make sure she knows she's beautiful. And it's not just something outside its inside, cause she's also darker skinned and she has eczema. So there are issues now that she's getting over older with. People are questioning what's wrong with her skin and some days she feels ugly.*

Quinn found that after her daughter compared her hair and appearance to others it made her feel "unpretty." She shared some strategies to encourage positive self-concepts.

> *After learning one of my daughters felt unpretty based on images she has seen (long hair specifically), I've had power sessions where I have them talk about all their greatness and attach it to a sentence, "I am _____," to remind them looks aren't everything but it is what we say, do, and how we make others feel that really matters.*

Monica, who self-identifies as biracial stresses the importance of her daughter being proud of her African American heritage:

> *I explain to her that you know she's beautiful even though that she comes from you know race from both sides. I'm biracial. She likes to consider herself biracial as well so we talk about that as well and the fact that she's not half white since she more gravitate to that side as white and why's really assessing her a lot about things; things her hair.*

Guinan shares a strategy she used to affirm her daughter's natural beauty and self-esteem:

> *Since my oldest daughter was about five she has noticed the difference and complaining a lot about her hair and skin. To the point where she said she hated herself. And then for that year I took her to Disney world because she wanted to be like a princess there and she didn't believe that she was. So I made it a point to take her to Disney world to show her that she was definitely not the . . . 07:59 and sit in line and all of the princesses called her princess. And then a year after that princess . . . 08:10 came out and she was I guess it confirmed what I said. But they always struggle with their hair and not knowing what to do with it themselves, not being able to just lookin the mirror and do it without some sort of chemical or blow-dryer or something like that. It's a little depleting to their self-esteem.*

Theme 3: honoring their daughter's unique self

Mothers in this study demonstrated a strong awareness of the ways in which dominant culture concepts are problematic for their own daughter's self-expression. They also expressed a desire to not be complicit in limiting their daughter's unique self. The misrecognition that Black mothers experience makes them particularly sensitive to the ways in which others impose limiting expectations and definitions. Motherhood for the mothers in this study was just as much about learning as it was about teaching. Many of the mothers articulated that they did not merely teach their daughters about the outside world and what their racialized identity means in that world, but that they also paid attention to and cultivated who their daughters expressed themselves to be. They also shared having challenges around allowing for some freedom of expression yet coming to the conclusion to honor their daughter's unique self. Mothers are balancing socializing their daughters for survival all the while working to not diminish their daughter's authentic self.

Jill teaches her daughter to self-define beyond racialized gender roles.

> *We've had conversations about things, I guess people are going to put on you like ideals they have about girls in a way that . . . you know when someone says, girls don't do that, girls aren't supposed to play with . . . So we've had those conversations when she was little about hey, you know, you can do what you want to do and let people know you can do what you want to do. So you don't have to fit into anyone's mold.*

Amazonia is l earning ways to allow her daughter's uniqueness to shine.

> *It's like trying to allow her personality and her finding her way, and allowing her uniqueness to shine without me stifling it with what my beliefs should be. I believe you she in bed by ten, though she has proven that this is her personality and this works for her and nothing is lacking. So I do not worry about it but I do constantly try to juggle*

when to step in and navigate things differently and when to allow her to just be free to figure out and find her way.

Mis-recognition is largely about visibility. It is just as much about not being visible as it is about hyper visibility that leads to inaccurate assessments (Harris-Perry, 2011). Silhouette is aware of how the appearance of her daughter might make her hyper visible. The following comments on the style choice of her 13-year-old daughter:

> *[T]here is some stuff that she wear and in my head I'm like what the hell but that how she feels comfortable, that is what she is comfortable with I don't want to kill that it look absolutely ridiculous but of course will say so but for the most part I kind a let her allow her to develop her own sense style, her own sense of person and you know it do make you happy it make you comfortable?*

Roberta, a single mother who recently received her masters' degree, talked about the balancing act of nurturing her daughter's inner voice in a way that will serve her as an adult and balancing that with the idea that she might be discriminated against or targeted for speaking up for herself. She shared:

> *She's very outspoken. So you get into that angry black girl or black women being loud or bossy or obnoxious. And I always say that her attitude will serve her well in the world. So I try not to – it's a fine line of disciplining her to not kill that spirit and her still keeping that kind of her voice. Keep her voice . . .*

One thing that is evident is that the role of African American mothers in the development of their daughters is crucial to self-concept and healthy identity development. The development of self-esteem in Black girls is not altogether mutually exclusive from the development of race–gender esteem. In fact, studies show a strong connection between a strong sense of race pride and self-concept in young Black girls (Prof. Gloria Wade-Gales as cited in Collins, 1987, p55). I posit that to be able to develop a strong sense of self-confidence in an African American daughter in opposition to the regular bombardment of media images that do not affirm her as a little black girl is a successful act of resistance (Lewis & Swift, 2014).

Policy. I believe this study demonstrates the need for an intersectional approach to healthy identity development in African American adolescent girls. Having found much correlation in the literature about the merits of positive racialized gender identity development and Black maternal practices, I'd like to open the discussion up by examining the relative merit of intersectional programming for African American girls.

Practice

The findings in this study can provide great insight into how to support the psycho-social development of African American adolescent girls. It can also provide social work practitioners with more insight into how to support mothers and families of color. These findings also suggest that developing programs to support families and serve adolescent girls requires particular intent around nurturing their intersectional identity. The intended readership for this article is not exclusive to African American mothers and social workers; it can also prove useful to others in the 'helping professions' (i.e. K-12 teachers and nonprofit organizations) who are interested in exploring methods in youth development and promoting youth well-being.

Research

Researching the lived experiences of Black women as valid sources of knowledge. When information is produced about or in reference to a group without their input, it puts the experiences of the group being examined in the margins and centralizes the standpoint of the researcher. The researcher decides what is relevant, significant, and worthy of public attention. Similarly, the researcher's peers who review then disseminate/publish the information to make the same decisions. Each process is a filtering process. "The voices of Black women have historically been silenced in social science research" (Bailey-Fakhoury, 2014, p. 61); thus, leaving them out of the power of knowledge production. The more that Black women are considered to be a valid source of knowledge production, the more insight researchers will be able to gain about lived experiences at the intersections and how those experiences inform meaning making and behavior.

Women of African descent in America and in other countries have traditionally used cocoa butter for the protection, prevention, and healing of their skin from the damage caused by the external environment. Similarly, African American mothers use Black maternal practices to mitigate the effects of racialized gender trauma.

References

Arendell, T. (2000). Conceiving and investigating motherhood: Decade's of scholarship. *Journal of Marriage and Family, 62*(4), 1192–1207.

Bailey-Fakhoury, C. (2014). Navigating, negotiating, and advocating: Black mothers, their youth daughters, and White schools. *Michigan Family Review, 18*(1), 57–59.

Chaney, C., & Brown, A. (2015). Is Black motherhood a marker of oppression or empowerment? Hip-Hop and R&B lessons about "mama". *Journal of Hip Hop Studies, 2*(1), 8–39.

Collins, P. H. (1986). Learning from the outsider within: The sociological significance of Black feminist thought. *Social Problems, 33*(6), S14–S32.

Collins, P. H. (1987). The meaning of motherhood in Black culture and Black mother/daughter relationships. *SAGE, 4*(2), 42–60.

Collins, P. H. (2000). *Black feminist thought: Knowledge consciousness, and the politics of empowerment* (2nd ed.). New York: Routledge.

Corbin, J. M., & Strauss, A. (2015). *Basics of qualitative research.* Los Angeles: Sage Publications.

Crenshaw, K. (1989). Demarginalizing the intersection of race and sex: A Black feminist theory and antiracist politics. *The University of Chicago Legal Forum,* 1241–1299.

Creswell, J. W. (2009). *Research design: Qualitative, quantitative, and mixed methods approaches.* Thousand Oaks, CA: Sage Publications.

Davin, A. (1978). Imperialism and motherhood. *History Workshop*, (5), 9–65.

Everett, J. E., Marks, L. D., & Clarke-Mitchell, J. F. (2016). A qualitative study of the Black mother-daughter relationship: Lessons learned about self-esteem, coping and resilience. *Journal of Black Studies*, 1–17.

Fouquier, K. F. (2009, October 5). *Invisible motherhood: A Heideggerian hermeneutical analysis of motherhood among three generations of African American women* (Dissertation). Georgia State University, Georgis.

Ganz, J. (2014). Mammies, maids & mothers: Representations of African-American and Latina women's reproductive labor in weeds. In D. Davis-Maye, A. D. Yarber, & T. E. Perry (Eds.), *What the village gave me: Conceptualizations of womanhood* (pp. 20–35). Lanham, MD: University Press of America.

Giorgi, A. (1997). The theory, practice, and evaluation of the phenomenological method as a qualitative research procedure. *Journal of Phenomenological Psychology, 28*(2), 235–251.

Harris-Perry, M. V. (2011). *Sister citizen: Shame, stereotypes, and Black women in America*. New Haven: Yale University Press.

Hinton-Johnson. (2004). African American mothers & daughters: Socialization, distance, & conflict (W. Glenn, R. Ginsberg, & D. King, Eds.). *The Alan Review, 31*(3).

Hymowitz, K. (2005, Summer). The Black family: 40 years of lies. *City Journal, 15*(3).

Jones, C., & Shorter-Gooden, K. (2003). *Shifting: The double lives of Black women in America*. New York: HarperCollins Publishers Inc.

Kleiman, S. (2004). Phenomenology: To wonder and search for meanings. *Researcher, 11*(4), 7–19.

Laverty, S. M. (2003). Hermeneutic phenomenology and phenomenology: A comparison of historical and methodological considerations. *International Journal of Qualitative Methods*, 21–35.

Lewis, M. L., & Swift, A. L. (2014). Combing my kinks: A culturally informed program to strengthen mother-daughter relationships. In D. Davis-Maye, A. D. Yarber, & E. T. Perry (Eds.), *What the village gave me: Conceptualizations of womanhood* (pp. 55–69). New York: University Press of America.

McLanahan, S. S. (1988). Family structure and dependency: Early transitions to female household headship. *Population Association of America, 25*(1).

Moustakas, C. E. (1994). *Phenomenological research methods*. Thousand Oak, CA: Sage Publications.

O'Reilly, A. (2004). *Toni Morrison and motherhood: Politics of the heart*. New York: State University of New York Press.

Ortiz, M. R. (2009). Hermeneutics and nursing research: History, process, and exemplar. *Southern Online Journal of Nursing Research, 9*(1).

O'Sullivan, L. F., Meyer-Bahlburg, H. F., & Watkins, B. X. (2001). Mother-daughter communication about sex among urban African American and Latino families. *Journal of Adolescent Research, 16*(3), 269–292.

Padgett, D. K. (2008). *Qualitative methods in social work research* (2nd ed.). Thousand Oaks, CA: Sage Publications.

Patton, M. (1990). *Qualitative evaluation methods* (2nd ed.). Thousand Oaks, CA: Sage Publications.

Patton, M. (2002). *Qualitative research & evaluation methods* (3rd ed.). Thousand Oaks, CA: Sage Publications.

Rastogi, M., & Wampler, K. S. (1999). Adult daughters' perceptions of mother-daughter relationships: A cross-cultural comparison. *Family Relations, 48*(3), 327–336.

Ridolfo, H., Chepp, V., & Milkie, M. A. (2013). Race and girls' self-evaluation: How mothering matters. *Sex Roles, 68*, 496–509.

Rubin, A., & Babbie, E. R. (2007). *Research methods for social work*. Belmont, CA: Thomson Higher Education.

Ruddick, S. (1989). *Maternal thinking: Toward a politics of peace*. Boston, MA: Beacon Press Books.

Turnage, B. F. (2004). African American mother-daughter relationships mediating daughter's self-esteem. *Child and Adolescent Social Work Journal, 21*(2), 155–173.

PART 4

In the trenches

Community advocacy

11

BEING AN INFORMAL CAREGIVER

A multigenerational issue across the life span

Tina Jordan

This chapter is designed to expand knowledge and understanding of caregiving, while discussing major trends, issues, and concerns regarding caregiving for the aging population. Intergenerational dynamics of caregiving for the aging as well as common interventions/practice models currently used to address caregiving for the aging population and ideas and insight for social workers, policy makers, sociology and psychology majors, nurse practitioners, health care professionals, and caregivers across the nation will be discussed.

According to the National Alliance for Caregiving (2020) before 1977, caregivers were an unseen, unheard, and unrecognized title. Now, over 53 million Americans, 21.3% of the adult population, serve as informal caregivers (2020). A caregiver is defined as a person (paid or unpaid) who provides care for a dependent adult, child, or family member with an illness or disability. This individual assists the care receiver (usually at home) with daily living activities and offers support as it relates to the specific health issue of the client, patient, or family member. Some of the responsibilities of a caregiver include assisting with basic personal care, food preparation, managing finances, housekeeping, and organizing health care appointments. This list is not conclusive or restricted because each care receiver has specific needs which a caregiver must provide (2020).

Caregiving is broken down into four general categories: informal, professional, private, and independent. Informal caregivers provide in-home care to their family members or friends (usually without pay) (Pickard, Inoue, Chadiha, & Johnson, 2011). Professional caregivers are licensed medical professionals employed to assist care receivers, usually in an in-home-based capacity (often referred to as home health care professionals, such as physical therapists or nurses). Private caregivers (often referred to as private-duty companions, in-home caregivers, live-in caregivers, or private-duty caregivers) are paid to provide care in the home and can provide medical care if trained to do so (Pickard et al., 2011). Private caregivers

DOI: 10.4324/9780429276613-15

usually provide non-medical support. Lastly, independent caregivers are those hired directly by the family to provide in-home care. Independent caregivers are also able to provide medical care if trained to do so.

Current state of caregiving

Caregiving often begins before conception, continuing in the womb when a child is being nurtured until birth (Goodman & Silverstein, 2002). This care is given throughout all developmental stages and ends after death. Caregiving responsibilities for family members who have major health or mental health issues have received a substantial amount of attention over the last 30 years. Despite the many services available to the aging population, many impaired aging adults rely solely on informal caregiving (from family and friends). Additionally, often no training has been provided to these individuals nor are they compensated for their services. Many family members are placed into the act of caregiving because a loved one, parent, child, or close friend has become unable, in many ways, to take proper care of themselves.

Elder care was once a family matter and those without family relied heavily on the people in their extended family and their communities. As "baby boomers" reach the pivotal age of 65 and life expectancies are increasing, changes in elder care and resources continue to expand (Goodman & Silverstein, 2002). While many seniors are aging rapidly and unable to perform daily activities on their own, there are equally as many seniors who are healthy, active, and able to complete daily activities. Many elderly people choose to continue to live at home as they age and do for themselves.

According to Schulz, Beach, Czaja, Martire, and Monin (2020), people in need of assistance can have a variety of needs such as assistance with medications, assistance with daily living skills, assistance with getting to appointments, and more. Figure 11.1 illustrates a prototypical longitudinal trajectory for older adult caregiving. The caregiver may be a family member or a friend or a medical professional. For the person needing assistance it is important to develop a strong support system and thoroughly assess the needs to find a caregiver most suitable.

Knowledge and skill

Initially, the care for a family member or a loved one required no skill set or knowledge base on how to provide care. Conversely, the knowledge and skill set were usually determined by the care-receivers' need. Additionally, the caregiver adjusted their lives and schedules to meet the needs of the care-receiver.

There are a host of free online informal caregiving training courses. These courses have been designed to assist the informal caregiver in general areas of caring for themselves and caring for the care receiver (Kelly, 2019). The courses include interactive questions and answers sessions, "how to" sessions, self-care, daily care, and planning for care videos. The courses are free of charge and include vignettes,

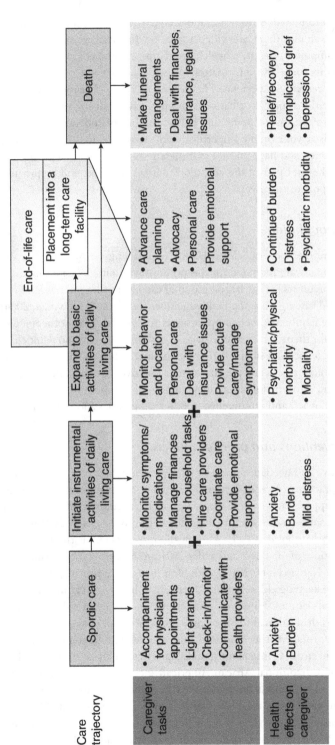

Chronic disease care trajectory: caregiver tasks and health effects. Note that caregiver tasks are additive over time from the early to the late stages of a caregiving career. Figure adapted with permission from Schulz & Tompkins (2010).

FIGURE 11.1   Chronic disease care trajectory

Source: Figure adapted with permission from Schulz & Tompkins (2010).

trainings, presentations, video tutorials, and webinars regarding topics related to caregiving. For example, there are video topics on financial assistance, how to locate medical equipment, that is, wheelchairs, ramps, canes, beds, and more.

In addition to resource and information videos, there are videos of caregivers who share their caregiving experiences. Moreover, there are chat rooms in which you could ask questions such as, what is the proper way to lift my mom from the chair to the bed?, or what is the best brand of bladder control undergarments?. The information that is at your online fingertips is priceless, but often new caregivers are very overwhelmed and have no idea that these resources and services are available to them. In the later part of the chapter, resources and links will be provided that will offer support to caregivers.

Problem and population

New caregivers are often overwhelmed by the responsibility of becoming a caregiver. However, many are recruited for this position without adequate support or training. Family caregivers are the largest group of caregivers who offer a significant amount of love and care for an aging family member (Feinberg & Newman, 2004). This title offers the family member an opportunity to "give back" to someone who has provided care for them at least at one stage of development (e.g., an adult child-caring for a parent or an adult sibling caring for an older sibling or family member). While this position offers joys and pleasures to the caregiver, consequently, caregiving can also result in a host of limitations including social seclusion, financial anxiety, emotional anguish, grief, and interference in other family roles and responsibilities.

Common interventions and practice models

To provide effective and needed support to family caregivers, it is crucial to utilize evidence-based practices (African-centered practices), interventions, and practice models used to support caregivers. Caregiving practices amongst African American communities can be traced back to ancient African societies (Wells-Wilbon & Simpson, 2009; Pickard et al., 2011). One of the most notable is the lower rates of institutionalization of disabled and elder African Americans (Seeman, Merkin, Crimmins, & Karlamangla, 2010). Although many government policies have altered the practice keeping elder African Americans at home with family members over the last several decades. However, such changes are more prevalent in urban and suburban areas than in small town or rural areas (Seeman, et al., 2010).

In small town or rural African American communities, families remain far closer knit that in urban areas. Consequently, social practices such as caregiving have retained many more traditional African American social behaviors than in urban or suburban areas. Throughout the nation in which there are African Americans in small town and rural areas, there are often far more advanced aged elders who are not institutionalized than what is more common in urban or suburban areas (Seeman et al., 2010). However, the availability of Medicare and Medicaid has altered that pattern somewhat. Moreover, there has been an emerging movement to facilitate the maintenance of elderly African Americans in their own homes or with family members rather than institutionalization (2010).

In the case of disabled African Americans of all age groups, keeping them at home with family members remains the caregiving option of choice particularly in small town and rural areas (Pickard et al., 2011; Seeman et al., 2010). Actually, there are similar patterns of the caregiving practice among African Americans who reside in urban and suburban areas. However, it must be noted that some important factors that appear to influence the degree to which African Americans have a greater tendency to keep their stabled family members at home are family size, composition, and economic status (2010). According to the Caregiving in the U.S. 2020 report, African American caregivers tend to be younger, are often unmarried, have poorer health, and frequently have to balance caregiving with full-time jobs. This results in African Americans having more burdensome caregiving situations than their non-Hispanic, white, or Asian caregiver counterparts. However, research conducted by Liu et al. (2020) indicated an increased sense of well-being among African American caregivers when compared to their white counterparts. This has been attributed to the value of "community" and the expectation that African American caregivers will have more support from family and the larger community. Despite the resilience demonstrated by African American caregivers, it is imperative that we explore interventions for addressing issues of stress, anxiety, and depression that often occur with caregiving responsibilities (Brewster et al., 2020).

Cognitive behavioral intervention

Cognitive behavioral intervention (CBI) is a practice used by many caregivers that allows caregivers to manage their own behaviors, thoughts, and emotions during the caregiving process (Rothbaum, Meadows, Resick, & Foy, 2000). This intervention is extremely helpful to the caregivers because as anxiety, grief, and negative thoughts of the caregiving process begin to escalate, using this intervention model will often de-escalate many of the negative thoughts and emotions that caregivers experience (Schulz et al., 2020) thus positioning the caregiver to change his/her way of thinking and behaviors. Research has also found that CBIs improved overall symptoms of depression anxiety, stress, and dysfunctional thoughts while also improving factors such as life satisfaction, behavioral activation, self-efficacy, and appraisal of problem behaviors (Schulz et al., 2020). Some of the practices frequently used with CBI include:

- *Journaling and thought recording:* allows caregivers to recognize and change useful and negative thoughts and behaviors. The purpose of journaling and thought recording is to allow the caregiver to view their thoughts and to make efforts to do what is necessary to change negative thoughts and negative thought patterns into positive ones. These thoughts are written and are easy to change (Rothbaum et al., 2000).

- *Relaxing and stress reduction techniques:* provide caregivers with ways of releasing stress. While this sounds extremely easy to most of the population, caregivers are not afforded this opportunity because their stress is usually associated with the responsibility of being a caregiver. However, crafting, reading, listening to music, taking long walks or long drives, calling a friend, taking an extended bath are all examples of stress releasing activities. In the same way, getting a full body, facial, or hand message, reading or writing are all excellent ways to minimize stress.
- *Cognitive restructuring or reframing:* is especially important to caregivers because it allows the caregivers to identify issues or concerns regarding caregiving, challenge those thoughts or views that are not positive, and then change them (Kelly, 2019). It is a particularly useful technique that allows caregivers to understand their unhappy or unpleasant feelings by taking control of their thoughts and changing the unpleasant thoughts to pleasant ones. This process will allow the caregiver to minimize stress and unhealthy thoughts during the caregiving process. An example of some cognitive restructuring techniques are as follows.

    - Relax – the caregiver should take their mind to a peaceful and positive place while thinking of positive people, places, or things (Kelly, 2019).
    - The caregiver should immediately identify the issue that has caused the disruption of their peace (2019).
    - The caregiver should then analyze how the disruption has made them feel – being extremely specific in their descriptions of their emotions/mood because then they will be able to easily change them once they have been identified (2019).
    - The caregiver must examine their thoughts of the issue(s) and then be able to identify why those issues or thoughts have disrupted their peace (2019).
    - The caregiver must find objective supporting evidence by objectively looking at what happened, writing down how it made them feel, discussing what led to their negative thoughts, and then find positive ways to change their thoughts to positive ones (2019).

Behavioral experiments

Behavioral experiments are techniques used to gather information regarding specific beliefs of a person. It is a planned experiment to test the accuracy of a belief that a person has, usually resulting in a less than 100% accuracy of the belief. Using this technique to gather information and evidence can minimize beliefs and assumptions that caregivers have regarding their care receiver or another family member while caregiving (Mental Health America, 2010).

- *Role playing*

    Role playing is a frequently used intervention where specific skills are practiced by acting out an issue or problem to see evidence-based practice to determine the best outcome or treatment (Rothbaum et al., 2000). In the role of a caregiver, this technique is especially important because it offers the caregiver an opportunity to receive training as it relates to caregiving, use real-life experiences and issues that arise during the caregiving process, and problem solve. Among other especially important aspects, caregivers also role play to learn how to effectively communicate their needs, dislikes, wants, and feelings. This technique allows for the caregiver to determine areas that may need improvement or to learn different ways to be productive, access resources, set goals, and to improve their overall well-being (Rothbaum et al., 2000).

Supportive interventions

While many caregivers have different ethnic, religious, and cultural backgrounds, supportive interventions are one of the most important practice models used by a family caregiver (Pickard et al., 2011; Rothbaum et al., 2000). Support groups bring people together who are or have experienced similar experiences. The group offers the caregiver an opportunity to share his or her thoughts, coping strategies, resources, other supports, dos and "don'ts." This group of individuals provides firsthand knowledge of the subject area and can offer examples and best practices. Support groups for family caregivers confirm that the caregiver is not alone and has a resource that can be used to confide in others. There are many support groups for caregivers. Additionally, group therapy is a particularly important practice model. Group therapy is a form of psychotherapy in which groups of people with similar issues or concerns meet to discuss those issues while being supervised by a therapist (Mental Health America, 2010). Both groups offer emotional support while discussing sensitive topics that may be difficult to discuss or share with family members. Please note that there are many different types of caregiver support groups. When trying to decide on the best support group, you may want to carefully review the following:

1) Does the group discussions, goals, and activities meet your needs?
2) Is the group led by a professional or a person with professional credentials?
3) What time and how frequent are the sessions?
4) How long has the group been established?
5) Is the group facilitator culturally competent?
6) Are fees associated with attendance?
7) Is the group session offered virtually for those who may not be able to physically visit a location?

Family support

Family support is a very crucial component for caregivers. Family members are often the persons assigned to assist a family member in a crisis – leading to caregiving. The selection of this person often encompasses several variables. These variables include strengths that aid in the selection process of the caregiver (Mental Health America, 2010). Family support may include respite (or another family member stepping in while the caregiver takes a break or a vacation). Respite care is critical for the caregiver. It allows the caregiver time to be alone/enjoy themselves/ or to simply catch up on personal goals.

Caregiving across the life span

In the African American community, grandparents have been accustomed to the formal role of caregiving of grandchildren for centuries. This inherited duty of African American grandparents can be dated back to the time of slavery. Goodman and Silverstein (2002) contend that, "African-American grandparents have historically served as kin keepers and have often raised their grandchildren as a result of African tradition, family survival during slavery, and the parents' search for economic opportunities in the North" (p. 676). Situations such as these caused many African American grandparents to be strongly involved in their grandchildren's life during that time period. It was seen as a form of a mechanism for retaining the family together as they endured hardship.

As time evolved and history has changed itself, adult children are now providing care for their parents and children simultaneously. The Life Course Perspective discusses how a person grows and ultimately changes over time (Mental Health America, 2010). This theoretical framework is used often in therapy and is extremely helpful when explaining the stages of development and how many people were reared (values and morals) to care for their aging family members.

Women and men as caregivers

Historically, there has been a gender divide as it relates to gender roles for nurturers and caregivers. Those roles generally fell on the shoulders of women. This section will discuss the similarities and differences between women and men in the role of a caregiver. According to the Family Care Giver Alliance (2020), over 68% (the majority) of caregivers in the United States are women. Historically, women have been seen as caregivers and nurturers. Many women have been socialized to care for individuals (physically and emotionally), while men have generally been socialized to provide care and to protect the individuals in their family. While both genders have had the responsibilities and titles of a caregiver, there are significant differences between the levels of stress, guilt, care provided, patience, and emotional, financial and physical support offered by both (2020).

Women caregivers

The social roles for women have changed over the past three decades. Progressively, women are working out of the home, and many are business owners, entrepreneurs, presidents, vice presidents, and CEOs (National Alliance for Caregiving, 2020). The aforementioned roles, coupled with parenting, often conflict with the role of being a caregiver, specifically if the care receiver lives in the home with the caregiver. The stress level of women caregivers is statically high due to the physical and emotional strain of providing care for the care-receiver, children, herself, and others, simultaneously.

Men caregivers

Most men are able and willing to provide care for their family members in a time of need but are often overlooked due to the social perception and stereotypical ideals of caregiving. Men have often been discredited as being caretakers and providers. However, over the past three decades, men have also found themselves in the unanticipated role as a caregiver. The stress level for men is high due to the physical and emotional strain of being a caregiver. Additionally, men are also subjected to financial strain, while caring for others in the family as well as small children.

According to Feinberg and Newman (2004) and The Center for Disease Control (2020), agreeably men and women caregivers are similar in that both have reported that they:

- Provide care for a parent or in law
- Provide daily living activities for the care receiver (e.g., managing medications, grocery shopping, maintaining the personal hygiene of the care receiver, as well as transportation for the care receiver) and provide financial support
- Adjusted their personal and work schedules to provide care for the care receiver
- Women are more involved in the personal care of the care receiver such as hygiene and dressing, while men are more involved with the financial aspect of caring for the care receiver

On the other hand, significant differences between the two genders have also been noted in that:

- Most men provide long distance care for the care receiver (CDC, 2020);
- Men are less likely to discuss guilt, emotional fatigue, stress, and issues regarding the role of a caregiver with others (CDC, 2020);
- Men are less likely to use resources and funding from local, state, or government funding to assist with the care of the care receiver;
- Men are less likely to seek counseling as a caregiver (p.1).

Issues of racism and poverty

African Americans have reported being ignored in medical settings, in addition to having resources and support withheld or selectively disbursed (Pickard et al., 2011). Many have reported that the request for assistance has gone unheard (from their municipality, local or state government). Many have reported being unable to access resources that are available due to their geographical location and having transportation issues. That prevented them from accessing resources.

Many African Americans receive support from their families and friends. This is not because this is what they choose to do, it is because unfortunately there are systems in place that prompt individual, institutional, and interpersonal racism. Health care systems prompt individual, institutional, and interpersonal racism. For example, individual racism in the health care system is shown when personal biases are shared regarding a group of people (National Alliance for Caregiving, 2009). Often, assumptions are made regarding a person's ability to perform a task for their loved ones, understand treatment options and or regimens, or to comply with treatment modalities. In the same way, institutional racism in the health care system refers to unfair qualities and discriminatory practices as it relates to access to goods, services, and opportunities, which creates health disparities (Goodman & Silverstein, 2002).

Lastly, interpersonal racism in the health care system refers to biases that happen when people discuss their private racial beliefs that usually affect their public interactions. Moreover, many have reported having service delivery that have been sub-par, at best. While this issue can be discussed under many headings, the fact remains that there are groups of people who feel that they are not receiving the same level of support, knowledge, and resources as a caregiver because of their race. Statistically, African Americans caregivers are younger than their counterparts. This information is relevant to understand and hopefully eradicate the issue of racism as it is related to caregiving (FCA, 2020).

Poverty

According to The National Family Caregiver Association (2020), women who are informal caregivers are 2.5 times more likely than non-caregivers to live in poverty. Numerous articles

have been written to discuss whether or not caregiving increases poverty. Unfortunately, the hard truth is that it does. According to the National Alliance for Caregiving (2020), women who are caregivers are 2.5 times more likely than non-caregivers to live in poverty and five times more likely to receive Supplemental Security Income (SSI). Caregivers are also living below the poverty line because many have had to use direct out-of-pocket expenses to provide care for their family member(s). Tapping into pensions and reallocating funds to provide care for their care receiver has been another variable that has increased the poverty rate of caregivers (2020).

Out-of-pocket prescriptions costs, food, supplies, materials, personal hygienic items, special care products (e.g., wheelchairs, walkers, ramps,) and other essential items that care-receivers need, often place caregivers at a financial disadvantage. Thus, the importance of access to resources to ensure that caregivers are not voluntarily placing themselves in the category of poverty because they are being excluded or ignored and exhausting their life savings in order to care for a family member is paramount (Pickard et al., 2011). Conversely, the interventions discussed earlier in the chapter (cognitive behavioral intervention, group therapy, family support intervention, and role play, etc.) will be compared to the seven principles of *Ma'at* (an African-centered approach). It is especially important to honor traditions and religion in the African American community.

After defining each principle, the corresponding intervention/technique will be listed (in parenthesis for comparison) keeping in mind that the concepts in parentheses have been mentioned earlier in the chapter under the definition of intervention and models used to assist the caregivers. By definition, an African-centered approach is simply affirming and integrating common cultural experiences, values, morals, and interpretations. For many African American caregivers, caregiving responsibilities include many individuals in the family outside of those immediate members. It is important to discuss the African-centered approach for the future of African American caregivers in order to include a cultural intervention that will assist in the aid of not only the caregiver but also the care receiver (Wells-Wilbon & Simpson, 2009).

African-centered principles of *Ma'at*

Truth

Truth in this approach is defined as the ability to understand the difference between what is real and what is not (Karenga, 2006). This principle is interpreted as all living creatures are sacred and all human beings deserve respect and honor. This principle can be used to assist the caregiver in determining their boundaries and abilities as it relates to being a primary informal caregiver. Often, caregivers are burdened and burnt out due to their unwillingness to determine what is true and what is untrue as it relates to caregiving and the burden that this role has on a person. Additionally, this principle can be used to challenge negative thoughts and to turn those thoughts to positive ones using this principle (cognitive reframing).

Justice

This principle discusses the equal rights for all persons (Karenga, 2006). That each person has the right to equal treatment and to have their basic needs met (food, shelter, water, safety, medical care, equal opportunities, equal health care, and access to health care and resources) (2006). More frequently than not, African American caregivers experience racism that prohibits them from receiving the same opportunities for access to resources, financial assistance, and care as their counterparts. Using this principle will assist in identifying areas that are obvious as a breach in justice to eradicate, or at best minimize, racism for caregivers (behavioral experiments).

Harmony

This principle expresses the need for animals, planets, etc. to move together in ways to align with authenticity (Karenga, 2006). It is paramount that each element of Mother Nature is authentic, and synergy has occurred when each entity is true to itself and its purpose. Caregivers must operate using this principle to ensure that they maintain their mental and physical health. Often, caregivers become burnt out or exhausted because they do not utilize this principle as often as they should. Being true to oneself, knowing their limitations, asking for and seeking help, caucusing family members to assist when personal time is needed or required is important (Kelly, 2019) (group therapy, role play, supportive intervention).

Balance

This principle is a state in which inside and outside environments are all aligned with Mother Nature. A point where opposites meet, and new possibilities come into being (Karenga, 2006). Caregivers are aligned with the responsibilities of caregiving as well as providing care for their care receiver. Caregivers are exposed to new people, treatment options, medications, and medical routines. It is the caregiver's responsibility to ensure that they act in the best interest of the care receiver at all times. Additionally, the caregiver must take care of themselves in order to provide care for others (Kelly, 2019) (group therapy, cognitive behavior intervention, family intervention, supportive intervention).

Order

Order is the way in which goals or items are aligned that are organized to produce various results (Karenga, 2006). Preparing for the care of a care receiver is critical. Using this principle to ensure that the caregiver has his/her ideals, lifestyle, and values in order will make way for a smoother transition into caregiving (Wells-Wilbon & Simpson, 2009). While many receive this title untimely, many aspects of caregiving can be established to maintain some level of order to the process and to the caregiver (supportive interventions, family therapy, group therapy).

Reciprocity

This principle discusses the concept that there is a cause and effect and that what goes up must come down and to remember to treat others as you would like to be treated (Karenga, 2006). This concept is important as it relates to caregiving and the fact that most caregivers are adult children of the care receiver. Remembering when the care receiver actually provided care for the caregiver is the driving force for many caregivers. While there is always a level of guilt in care caregiver (Mom sacrificed so much for me and yet I have to compartmentalize her care because

I am working – I have to work to provide the best care for her) is real (group therapy, role play, journaling, and thought recording).

Righteousness

Righteousness is defined as doing what one knows is right (Karenga, 2006). This principle is very important to caregivers. Knowing that you have someone's life in the palm of your hands and making a conscious decision to do no harm to them is vital. This concept also refers to the caregiver not imposing harm to themselves and reaching out for assistance when things get rough. It is important to schedule an appointment to speak with someone about the fears associated with being a caregiver, the dos and don'ts of caregiving, not being afraid to embrace your religious beliefs as it relates to caring for one other, receiving your values, beliefs, and intergenerational tutelage that may affect the decisions that you make as a caregiver (Kelly, 2019) (group therapy, role play, journaling, supportive intervention, family therapy, behavioral experiments, and cognitive reframing). In the same way, Wells-Wilbon and Simpson (2009), contend that one must go back and begin to trace the beginning of family patterns that originated in Western Africa in order to understand the reasoning behind the nurturing of a family member and the guilt that one experiences when they are not able to assist a family member in need. The seven principles of *Ma'at* could and should be used to assist African American informal caregivers as they travel the road of caregiving.

Resources

* Caregiving 101: On Being a Caregiver – Family Caregiver Alliance
* Support Groups for Caregivers and Older Adults at Iona
* The costs of becoming a primary caregiver | Fidelity
* Managing health care and its costs | Understanding caregiving | Fidelity
* Resources and Support for Family Caregivers – NFCR
* Stress Meter www.providence.org/for-employees/covid-19-resources

References

Brewster, G. S., Epps, F., Dye, C. E., Hepburn, K., Higgins, M. K., & Parker, M. L. (2020). The effect of the "Great Village" on psychological outcomes, burden, and mastery in African American caregivers of persons living with dementia. *Journal of Applied Gerontology*, *39*(10), 1059–1068.

Family Caregiver Alliance/ National Alliance for Caregiving. (2020). Retrieved February 13, 2021, from www.caregiver.org.

Feinberg, L. F., & Newman, S. L. (2004). A study of 10 states since passage of the National Family Caregiver Support Program: Policies, perceptions, and program development. *The Gerontologist*, *44*(6), 760–769.

Goodman, C., & Silverstein, M. (2002). Grandmothers raising grandchildren: Family structures and well- being in culturally diverse families. *The Gerontologist*, *42*(5), 676–689.

Karenga, M. (2006). Maat, the moral ideal in ancient Egypt: A study in classical African ethics. *British Journal for the History of Philosophy, 21*(3), 421–442. ISBN(s): 0415947537 9780415947534 04156. . .

Kelly, S. (2019). Cognitive behavior therapy with African Americans. In G. Y. Iwamasa & P. A. Hays (Eds.), *Culturally responsive cognitive behavior therapy: Practice and supervision* (pp. 105–128). American Psychological Association. https://doi.org/10.1037/0000119-005

Liu, C., Badana, A. N., Burgdorf, J., Fabius, C. D., Roth, D. L., & Haley, W. E. (2021). Systematic review and meta-analysis of racial and ethnic differences in dementia caregivers' well-being. *The Gerontologist, 61*(5), e228–e243.

Mental Health America. (2010). Retrieved December 20, 2020, from https://mhanational.org/caregiving-AfricanAmerican-communities

National Alliance for Caregiving. (2009). Retrieved January 12, 2021, from www.caregiving.org/

Pickard, J. G., Inoue, M., Chadiha, L. A., & Johnson, S. (2011). The relationship of social support to African American caregivers' help-seeking for emotional problems. *The Social Service Review, 85*(2), 246–265. https://doi.org/10.1086/660068

Rothbaum, B. O., Meadows, E. A., Resick, P., & Foy, D. W. (2000). *Cognitive-Behavioral Therapy*. In E. B. Foa, T. M. Keane, & M. J. Friedman (Eds.), Effective treatments for PTSD: Practice guidelines from the International Society for Traumatic Stress Studies (pp. 320–325). The Guilford Press.

Schulz, R., Beach, S. R., Czaja, S. J., Martire, L. M., & Monin, J. K. (2020). Family caregiving for older adults. *Annual Review of Psychology, 71*, 635–659.

Seeman, T. E., Merkin, S. S., Crimmins, E. M., & Karlamangla, A. S. (2010). Disability trends among older Americans: National Health and Nutrition Examination surveys, 1988–1994 and 1999–2004. *American Journal of Public Health, 100*(1), 100–107.

The Center for Disease Control. (2020). *Productive aging and work*. Retrieved November 8, 2020, from www.cdc.gov/niosh/topics/productiveaging/default.html.

The National Alliance for Caregiving & AARP. (2020). *Caregiving in the U.S. 2020*. Retrieved November 14, 2020, from www.aarp.org/content/dam/aarp/ppi/2020/05/full-report-caregiving-in-the-united-states.doi.10.26419-2Fppi.00103.001.pdf

Wells-Wilbon, R., & Simpson, G. M. (2009). Transitioning the caregiving role for the next generation: An African-centered womanist perspective. *Black Women, Gender & Families, 3*(2), 87–105.

12

TRAUMA AND EDUCATION AMONG YOUNG BLACK MALES

Exploring African-centered rites of passage programming as a protective factor

David Miller, Deidre McDaniel

According to the United States Census Bureau (2019) 35.5% of all Black families live in poverty, compared to 21.5% of Whites. Further, Black youth also tend to be raised in single-parent households and grow up in unsafe neighborhoods more than their White counterparts (Bowen & Bowen, 1999; Garbarino, Dubrow, Kostelny, & Pardo, 1992). This data is alarming and provides a bleak forecast for Black male youth growing up in communities often forgotten by mainstream society. Furthermore, Black male youth are also disproportionately overrepresented in underfunded schools, which are predominantly located in communities of color (Noguera, 2014; Vaughans, 2021). At every level of society, Black male youth face landmines beginning as early as grade school. Numerous scholars contend that there is a direct correlation between Black male students' academic challenges in schools and the negative perception teachers have adopted about Black male students (Ladson-Billings, 2011; Carey, 2019). These negative perceptions lead to higher rates of school suspensions, disparities in high school completion, and underrepresentation in rigorous or gifted and talented courses for Black male students (Wald & Losen, 2003; Rowley et al., 2014). Further, Black males are more susceptible to being misdiagnosed with learning disabilities or behavior issues which fast-tracks them for special education services in schools (Skiba et al., 2015). Nationwide, over 20,000 Black male students are inappropriately classified as mentally retarded. For Black male students, special education courses are viewed in many schools as a "life sentence."

Young Black males also face societal challenges such as racial profiling in schools, navigating encounters with the police, and community violence (Bronson & Carson, 2019; Garland, 2001; Zeng, 2019; Noguera, 2003). For Black male youth, the ongoing pressures and exposure to police and community violence create trauma from living in dangerous environments. The deaths of Ahmaud Arbury, Rayshard Brooks, George Floyd, and Andrew Brown are consistent examples of

DOI: 10.4324/9780429276613-16

the challenges Black males face within larger society related to encounters with police. Growing up Black and male in the United States forces youth to have a healthy suspicion of the "cops and the robbers." Furthermore, recent studies suggest that adolescents who live in low-resourced neighborhoods feel like they have limited options for responding to stressful and anxiety-provoking situations because of limited or ineffective coping skills (Robinson, Droege, Case, & Jason, 2015). In this chapter, African-centered Rites of Passage (ROP) programming is discussed as a much-needed protective factor in the lives of Black male youth. African-centered ROP programming builds on the work of Frantz Fanon, Carter G. Woodson, Marcus Garvey, Elijah Muhammad, Malcolm X, Maulana Karenga, and a host of other Black freedom fighters and activists which focused on "psychological liberation" (Baldwin, 1989; Fanon, 1965; Myers & Speight, 2010). Lloyd and Williams (2017) point out that African-centered interventions provide essential skills development in life management, self-esteem, and promote anti-substance use behavior. As the educational system can be a traumatic environment for Black male youth, African-centered ROP programming facilitates psychological health and well-being by providing an alternative youth development intervention that promotes racial identity while strengthening healthy social and cognitive functioning that helps young Black males cope with many traumatic experiences from childhood to adulthood (Hill, 1992; Warfield-Coppock & Harvey, 1989; Kelsey, 1991; Gilbert et al., 2009; Delaney, 1995).

Brief history

The South Carolina Negro Act of 1740 was the first law of record that legally prohibited the education of enslaved Africans (Rasmussen, 2010). This crucial piece of legislation set a precedent in cementing the subordination of enslaved Africans and African Americans via educational suppression. At that time, Black literacy was feared as a threat to the legitimacy and continuation of the system of slavery and continued with the institution of Jim Crow laws and segregated school systems. As such, education and literacy within the Black community have served as a form of resistance and liberation from oppression. However, much of the research on education among young Black males has focused on recidivism, academic challenges in school, youth violence, and the school-to-prison pipeline (Ferguson, 2001; Losen & Martinez, 2013; Ladson-Billing, 2006, 2011). Some might wonder why academia would focus so much research on pathologies and deficits versus examining the strengths and resiliency of young Black males. Within this deficits-based framework, Bryan (2017) points out that the school-to-prison pipeline begins early in the lives of young Black males. The school playground-to-prison pipeline (SPTPP) explains a phenomenon that occurs in the lives of Black boys who attend racially diverse schools (Bryan, 2017). The "school to prison pipeline (SPP) nomenclature was popularized in the 1980s to describe zero-tolerance policies that implement harsh penalties in schools for students of color" (Morris, 2012; Wade & Ortiz, 2016). Moreover, young Black males are characterized as at-risk, endangered, incorrigible, beyond love, and damaged beyond repair (Brown, 2016; Polite & Davis, 1999). Further narratives describe young Black males as violent, uneducated, disinterested in school, hopeless, and destined for failure (Bonilla-Silva, 2006; Hopkins, 1997; Knaus, 2007). In general, young Black males are bombarded with negative messages that marginalize Black life (Hazell & Clarke, 2008). These messages have shaped public perceptions of young Black males and contribute to racial profiling in schools.

Racial profiling in schools

Nationally, Black students comprise 15% of the U.S. school population; however, 35% of all suspended students are Black (U.S. Department of Justice & U.S. Department of Education, 2018). Furthermore, 50% of Black students who are suspended were involved in school-related arrests or referred to law enforcement (U.S. Department of Justice & U.S. Department of Education, 2018). Increases in school suspensions and expulsions and the overrepresentation of Black students in special education indicate that school systems have become tough waters to navigate for Black students and a difficult place to be affirmed and recognized (Webster & Knaus, 2021). The failures of school districts to address educational outcomes among Black male students are well documented. The literature demonstrates that disproportionate numbers of Black male children suspended from schools for minor disruptions and misbehavior are racially motivated (Skiba, et al., 2002). Conversely, many of the same minor offenses would not warrant a suspension among White students like talking in class to peers, not having proper school supplies, tardiness, and truancy (Fitzgerald, 2015; Morrison & D'Incau, 1997).

Gilliam (2005) coined the term "pushed out" to describe the national trends related to Black male students' suspensions in preschool. According to the U.S. Department of Education (2016), racial disparities in suspensions from prekindergarten classrooms represent alarming trends among Black children. Meek and Gilliam (2016) assert that racial profiling among children starts as young as infancy and toddlerhood. These findings indicate that Black children are at the highest risk of being expelled from early care and education programs. According to the Office for Civil Rights (2016), Black boys represent 19% of preschool enrollment; however, they represent approximately 45% of the preschool population that receives one or more out-of-school suspensions. Black male students navigating the school climate and coping with the realities of being viewed "as a problem" is a constant reality. The overrepresentation of Black male suspension to White students is glaring. Black male students are suspended three times more often than their White peers (Skiba et al., 2002). Furthermore, the targeting of Black male students is reinforced by data suggesting that many school staff and administrators view students as potential criminals versus students (Hirschfield, 2008). To this end, young Black males navigating school culture have created a "perfect storm" for inherent teacher bias, low expectations, and insufficient resources to support their healthy social and academic development. Black male students are forced to attend schools with more armed school police and metal detectors than school counselors thereby normalizing police interference in their everyday lives (Price, 2009).

Navigating encounters with the police

Whether it's navigating draconian disciplinary policies in schools or getting home safely from walking to the store, young Black males are constantly under surveillance. Scholars contend that racial discrimination remains a significant obstacle for Black youth and that they experience racial incidents at a greater frequency than their White counterparts (Coker et al., 2009; Fisher et al., 2000; Greene et al., 2006). In a study conducted by Seaton et al. (2011), 97% of Black youth reported experiencing regular discriminatory treatment within a two-week time period. Subsequently, scholars suggest that racial animus may lead to social and psychological challenges, such as anxiety and depression, lower levels of general well-being, poor academic performance, and community disengagement (Sellers et al., 2006; (Seaton et al., 2011; Neblett et al., 2006; Bulhan, 1985). Moreover, for Black parents raising a male child, conversations about navigating encounters with police or "The Talk," are crucial and potentially lifesaving as police are three times more likely to kill Black males than White males. As police shootings have become the leading cause of death for Black men, fear and mistrust among Black parents about police and the judicial system are at an all-time high (Buehler, 2017; Edwards et al., 2019). These traumatic encounters within school systems and communities in general bear witness to the need for interventions that center liberating Black youth from oppressive systems.

An African-centered intervention: ROP programs

Due to the challenges faced by Black students, it is imperative to create and cultivate an environment for culturally specific pedagogy in schools and community-based institutions that give rise to Afrocentric models and ideals. African-centered ROP programs date back to the early 1960s in the United States, in the form of afterschool programs, charter schools, independent schools, and homeschooling collectives (Gilbert, Harvey, & Belgrave, 2009; Whaley & McQueen, 2019). Maulana Karenga, the founder of *Kwanza* and the *Nguzo Saba*, is also credited with implementing one of the earliest ROP models in Watts, California (Hill, 1987). Simba Wachanga was also known as United Simba (U.S. organization), which means young lions in Kiswahili (Hill, 1987). For many scholars, Afrocentric youth development and educational interventions are viewed as realistic alternatives instilling racial pride, building on strengths, focusing on a greater sense of community, and the vital role of culture in the lives of Black youth (Durden, 2007; Lomotey, 1992; Madhubuti, 1994; Murrell, 1999). African-centered ROP programs seek to develop and strengthen racial literacy among Black male youth through culturally specific interventions. The term "racial literacy" was postulated by legal theorist Lani Guinier to describe the detrimental effects of institutional racism and stereotyping (Sealey-Ruiz & Greene, 2015; Guinier, 2004).

The terms Afrocentric, African-centered, and African are used interchangeably in the literature to describe a framework that adopts African-centered approaches into interventions (Lateef, Amoako, Nartey, Tan, & Joe, 2021). ROP programs are used to describe the developmental transitions from childhood to adulthood (Lateef, 2021; Gavazzi, Alford, & McKenry, 1996). ROP programs emerged as interventions to address the declining significance of Black families and insulate Black youth from crime, drug abuse, community violence, and incarceration (Harvey & Hill, 2004). More specially, African-centered youth development and ROP programs expose Black youth to rituals and values that address racism/White supremacy and elevate racial pride (Gilbert et al., 2009; Grills et al., 2016). Typically, an African-centered ROP program focuses on three core areas of socialization that were damaged during enslavement and continued racialized oppression: 1) sense of history; 2) sense of community; and 3) sense of Supreme Being (Hill, 1992). Throughout the African-centered ROP process, members are referred to as initiates to symbolize the new journey they will embark upon. For example, facilitating African-centered ROP programs with young Black males would heavily focus on deconstructing popular myths and stereotypes associated with manhood and masculinity (Goggins, 2012). Additionally, content and rituals would be offered to young Black males such as (Hill, 1992; Goggins, 2012):

- Honoring the ancestors (pouring libations)
- Understanding the role of elder (permission from the elders)
- Redefining manhood from an African-centered lens
- African/African American history and culture
- Study skills
- Understanding racism/White supremacy
- Discovering and practicing family rituals and traditions
- Visiting significant African American historical sites
- Economic development (money, banking, and finances/entrepreneurship)
- Male and female relationships (roles and responsibilities of husbandry)
- Cooking
- Fishing/hunting
- Farming/gardening
- Geography
- Basic self-defense
- African language (call and response in Kiswahili)

African-centered ROP programs provide young Black males a framework for understanding the "Maafa" and the period of enslavement. The *Maafa* is a Kiswahili term that describes a "disaster, terrible occurrence or great tragedy referring to the Transatlantic Slave Trade or Middle Passage" (Ani, 1994). Thus, an African-centered ROP program seeks to disrupt systemic racism, White supremacy, bigotry, and discrimination through an intentional process that provides young Black males a healthier knowledge of self and contextualizes African and African American history and healthy coping skills to manage oppression (Chapman-Hilliard & Adams-Bass, 2016). Perkins (2005) builds on the notion that supporting young Black males requires intentional efforts to address the racial trauma Black people have faced in the United States. Perkins (2005) believes that the *Maafa* and the socialization of Western values and rituals have contaminated Black youth. Thus, a "new harvest" is needed that reflects Afrocentric values and norms necessary to transition Black youth from healthy childhood to healthy adulthood in the midst of racism and oppression (Perkins, 2005).

The *Nguzo Saba*, also known as the seven principles, developed by Maulana Karenga (1988), has become an essential framework for understanding, teaching, and cultivating an African-centered way of life for Black youth. The *Nguzo Saba* is a core set of values centered around mutual aid, community, economic development, and family. These values become the essential building blocks for helping Black youth cope with growing up in a toxic society and provide a "moral compass" to view the larger community. Hill (1992) believes that the *Nguzo Saba* is a vital value system for Black people in America to reclaim their history, humanity, and daily lives. These beliefs are consistent with African-centered scholars and practitioners who posit that as Black people, we are solely responsible for developing community solutions and processes to address healthy community development and combating racism/White supremacy (Asante, 2003; Karenga, 1988; Schiele, 1997).

Empirical research on African-centered interventions

While research gaps exist featuring empirical studies documenting Afrocentric interventions, several scholars highlight the effectiveness of these models in shaping identity development and positive psychosocial development among Black youth (Whaley & McQueen, 2019; Jones & Neblett, 2016; Belgrave & Brevard, 2015). Lateef (2021) purports that American culture has failed to empower Black youth; thus, African-centered programs are needed to build self-confidence and utilize African American history and culture to instill racial pride. Asante and Mazama (2010) assert that addressing identity among Black students and focusing content on the culture and history of Black people through educational interventions affirm their heritage and can provide a rich foundation for learning. Other researchers make a compelling argument supporting the significance of racial and cultural programming using Afrocentric educational interventions in addressing the achievement gap between White and Black students (Bowman, et al., 2018; Miller-Cotto & Byrnes, 2016; Santos & Collins, 2015; Shockley, 2011; Hill, 2020). Since most Black students in the United States are educated by Eurocentric values and curricula in schools which negatively impact racial identity, self-esteem, and self-efficacy, African-centered curriculum would serve as a useful tool in countering these negative effects (Lateef et al., 2021; Byrd & Chavous, 2011).

Conclusion

Antiquated educational theories and Eurocentric curriculums seek to undermine the social and cognitive development of young Black males. This chapter underscores the hardships that young Black males encounter within the education system and the need for African-centered programs that foster racial identify, self-esteem, liberation, and self-efficacy. The positioning of young Black males at the lower rungs of society normalizes their underachievement and perpetuates racist systems (Jenkins, 2006). A deeper analysis of educational and quality-of-life data suggests that most of the current interventions fail to address the unique needs of young Black males' lives adequately. Therefore, more empirical research supporting African-centered frameworks as a tool for addressing the causal impact of racism and oppression is required to advance educational aspirations of young Black males. In the wake of social and racial unrest in the United States, it is an opportune moment for educators to rethink current teaching methodologies and modalities for educating Black males within the context of racist and oppressive systems.

References

Ani, M. (1994). *Yurugu: An African-Centered critique of European cultural thought and behavior.* Trenton, NJ: Africa World Press.

Asante, M. K. (2003). *Afrocentricity: The theory of social change.* Chicago, IL: African American Images.

Asante, M. K., & Mazama, A. (2010). *Afrocentric infusion for urban schools: Fundamental knowledge for teachers.* Philadelphia, PA: Ankh Scientific Institute.

Baldwin, J. A. (1989). The role of Black psychologists in Black liberation. *Journal of Black Psychology, 16,* 67–76. https://doi.org/10.1177/009579848901600106

Belgrave, F. Z., & Brevard, J. (2015). *African American boys: Identity, culture, and development.* New York, NY: Springer.

Bonilla-Silva, E. (2006). *Racism without racists: Color-blind racism and the persistence of racial inequality in the United States* (2nd ed.). Washington, DC: Rowman & Littlefield.

Bowen, N. K., & Bowen, G. L. (1999). Effects of crime and violence in neighborhoods and schools on the school behavior and performance of adolescents. *Journal of Adolescent Research, 14,* 319–342.

Bowman, B., Comer, J., & Johns, D. (2018). Addressing the African American achievement gap: Three leading educators issue a call to action. *Young Children, 73*(2).

Bronson, J., & Carson, E. A. (2019). *Prisoners in 2017 (NCJ252156).* Retrieved from www.bjs.gov/content/pub/pdf/p17.pdf

Brown, K. D. (2016). *After the "at-risk" label: Reorienting educational policy and practice.* New York, NY: Teachers College Press.

Bryan, N. (2017). White teachers' role in sustaining the school-to-prison pipeline: Recommendations for teacher education. *The Urban Review, 49*(2), 326–345.

Buehler, J. W. (2017). Racial/ethnic disparities in the use of lethal force by U.S. police, 2010 – 2014. *American Journal of Public Health, 107*(2), 295–297. https://doi.org/10.2105/ajph.2016.303575

Bulhan, H. A. (1985). Black Americans and psychopathology: An overview of research and theory. *Psychotherapy: Theory, Research, Practice, Training, 22*(2 Suppl.), 370–378. https://doi.org/10.1037/h0085517

Byrd, C. M., & Chavous, T. (2011). Racial identity, school racial climate, and school intrinsic motivation among African American youth: The importance of person-context congruence. *Journal of Research on Adolescence, 21*(4), 849–860. https://doi.org/10.1111/j.1532-7795.2011.00743.x

Carey, R. (2019). Imagining the comprehensive mattering of black boys and young men in society and schools: Toward a new approach. *Harvard Educational Review, 89,* 370–396. https://doi.org/10.17763/1943-5045-89.3.370

Chapman-Hilliard, C., & Adams-Bass, V. (2016). A conceptual framework for utilizing black history knowledge as a path to psychological liberation for black youth. *Journal of Black Psychology, 42*(6), 479–507. https://doi.org/10.1177/0095798415597840

Coker, T. R., Elliott, M. N., Kanouse, D. E., Grunbaum, J. A., Schwebel, D. C., Gilliland, M. J., & Schuster, M. A. (2009). Perceived racial/ethnic discrimination among fifth-grade students and its association with mental health. *American Journal of Public Health, 99,* 878–884.

Delaney, C. H. (1995). Rites of passage in adolescence. *Adolescence, 30,* 891–898.

Durden, T. R. (2007). African-centered schooling: Facilitating holistic excellence for Black children. *The Negro Educational Review, 58*(1/2), 23–34.

Edwards, F., Lee, H., & Esposito, M. H. (2019). Risk of being killed by police use of force in the United States by age, race – ethnicity, and sex. *Proceedings of the National Academy of Sciences, 116*(34), 16793–16798.

Fanon, F. (1965). *The wretched of the earth.* New York, NY: Grove Press.

Ferguson, R. F. (2001). Analysis of Black-White GPA disparities in Shaker Heights, Ohio. *Brookings Institute Papers on Educational Policy, 4,* 347–414.

Fisher, C. B., Wallace, S. A., & Fenton, R. E. (2000). Discrimination distress during adolescence. *Journal of Youth and Adolescence, 29,* 679–695. https://doi.org/10.1023/a:1026455906512

Fitzgerald, T. (2015). *Black Males and racism: Improving the schooling and life chances of African Americans.* New York, NY: Paradigm.

Garbarino, J., Dubrow, N., Kostelny, K., & Pardo, C. (1992). *Children in danger: Coping with the consequences of community violence.* Hoboken, NJ: Jossey-Bass/Wiley.

Garland, D. 2001. *Mass imprisonment: Social causes and consequences.* London: Sage Publications.

Gavazzi, S. M., Alford, K. A., & McKenry, P. C. (1996). Culturally specific programs for foster care youth: The sample case of an African American rites of passage program. *Family Relations, 45*(2), 166. https://doi.org/10.2307/585287

Gilbert, D. J., Harvey, A. R., & Belgrave, F. Z. (2009). Advancing the Africentric paradigm shift discourse: Building toward evidence-based Afrocentric interventions in social practice with African Americans. *Social Work, 54*(3), 243–252. https://doi.org/10.1093/sw/54.3.243

Gilliam, W. S. (2005). *Pre-kindergarteners left behind: Expulsion rates in state prekindergarten systems.* Yale University Child Study Center. Retrieved from www.ziglercenter.yale.edu/publications/National%20Prek%20Study_expulsion_tc m350-34774_tcm350-284-32.pdf.

Goggins, L. (2012). *Brining the light into a new day: African-Centered rites of passage.* Akron, OH: Saint Rest Publications.

Greene, M. L., Way, N., & Pahl, K. (2006). Trajectories of perceived adult and peer discrimination among Black, Latino, and Asian American adolescents: Patterns and psychological correlates. *Developmental Psychology, 42,* 218–236. https://doi.org/10.1037/0012-1649.42.2.218.

Grills, C., Cooke, D., Douglas, J., Subica, A., Villanueva, S., & Hudson, B. (2016). Culture, racial socialization, and positive African American youth development. *Journal of Black Psychology, 42*(4), 343–373. https://doi.org/10.1177/0095798415578004.

Guinier, L. 2004. From racial liberalism to racial literacy: Brown v. board of education and the interest-divergence dilemma. *The Journal of American History, 91*(1), 92–118.

Harvey, A. R., & Hill, R. (2004). Africentric youth and family rites of passage program: Promoting resilience among at-risk African American youths. *Social Work, 49*(1), 65–74.

Hazell, V., & Clarke, J. (2008). Race and gender in the media: A content analysis of advertisements in two mainstream black magazines. *Journal of Black Studies, 39*(1), 5–21. https://doi.org/10.1177/0021934706291402.

Hill, P. (1987, October 13). *Passage to Manhood: Rearing the Male African-American Child.* [Paper Presentation]. The National Black Child Development Institute17th Annual Conference, Detroit, MI, United States.

Hill, P. (1992). *Coming of Age: African American male rites-of-passage.* Cleveland, OH: East End Neighborhood House.

Hill, H. (2020). *Culturally responsive teaching is promising; But there's a pressing need for more research.* Education Week. Retrieved from www.edweek.org/ew/articles/2020/03/09/culturally-responsive-teachingis-promising-but-theres.html.

Hirschfield, P. J. (2008). Preparing for prison?: The criminalization of school discipline in the USA. *Theoretical Criminology, 12*(1), 79–101. https://doi.org/10.1177/1362480607085795

Hopkins, R. (1997). *Educating Black males: Critical lessons in schooling, community, and power.* New York, NY: State University of New York.

Jenkins, T. (2006). Mr. Nigger: The challenges of educating Black males within American society. *Journal of Black Studies, 37*(1), 127–155.

Jones, S. C., & Neblett, E. W. (2016). Racial-ethnic protective factors and mechanisms in psychosocial prevention and intervention programs for Black youth. *Clinical Child and Family Psychology Review, 19*, 134–161.

Karenga, M. (1988). *The African American holiday of Kwanzaa: A celebration of family, community & culture.* Los Angeles, CA: University of Sankore Press.

Kelsey, M. (1991). *Rites of passage: Road to adulthood.* Columbus, OH: Africentric Personal Development Shop.

Knaus, C. (2007). Still segregated. Still unequal: Analyzing the impact of no child left behind on African American students. In S. J. Jones (Ed.), *The state of Black America 2007* (pp. 1–11). Harlem, NY: National Urban League.

Ladson-Billings, G. (2006). From achievement gap to education debt: Understanding achievement in U.S. schools. *Educational Researcher, 35*(7), 3–12. https://doi.org/10.310 2/0013189X035007003.

Ladson-Billings, G. (2011). Boyz to men: Teaching to restore Black boys' childhood. *Race, Ethnicity, and Education, 14*(1), 7–15.

Lateef, H. (2021). What is African-centered youth development? A content analysis of Bantu perspectives. *Journal of Ethnic & Cultural Diversity in Social Work,* 1–11. https://doi.org/10.1080/15313204.2020.1870600

Lateef, H., Amoako, E. O., Nartey, P., Tan, J., & Joe, S. (2021). Black youth and African-Centered interventions: A systematic review. *Research on Social Work Practice.* https://doi.org/10.1177/10497315211003322

Lloyd, A. B., & Williams, B. V. (2017). The potential for youth programs to promote African American youth's development of ethnic and racial identity. *Child Development Perspectives, 11*(1), 29–38. https://doi.org/10.1111/cdep.12204

Lomotey, K. (1992). Independent Black institutions: African-Centered education models. *The Journal of Negro Education, 61*(4), 455–462.

Losen, D. J., & Martinez, T. E. (2013). *Out of school & off track: The overuse of suspensions in American middle and high schools.* Los Angeles, CA: The Center for Civil Rights Remedies.

Madhubuti, S. (1994). African centered pedagogy. In H. Madhubuti & S. Madhubuti (Eds.), *African-centered education: Its value, importance, and necessity in the development of Black children* (pp. 13–27). Chicago, IL: Third World Press.

Meek, S. E., & Gilliam, W. S. (2016). Expulsion and suspension in early education as matters of social justice and Health Equity. *NAM Perspectives, 6*(10).

Miller-Cotto, D., & Byrnes, J. (2016). Ethnic/racial identity and academic achievement: A meta- analytic review. *Developmental Review, 1,* 51–70. https://doi.org/10.1016/j.dr.2016.06.003

Morris, M. W. (2012). *Race, gender, and the school to prison pipeline: Expanding our discussion to include Black girls.* The African American Online Policy Forum. Retrieved from www.otlcampaign.org/sites/default/files/resources/Morris-Race-Genderand-the-School-to-Prison-Pipeline.pdfwww.otlcampaign.org/sites/default/files/resources/Morris-Race-Gender-and-the-School-to-Prison-Pipeline.pdf

Morrison, G., & D' Incau, B. (1997). The web of Zero-Tolerance: Characteristics of students who are recommended for expulsion from school. *Education & Treatment of Children, 20*(3), 316–335.

Murrell, P. C. (1999). Chartering the village: The making of an African-centered charter school. *Urban Education, 33*(5), 565–583.

Myers, L. J., & Speight, S. L. (2010). Reframing mental health and psychological well-being among persons of African descent: Africana/Black psychology meeting the challenges of fractured social and cultural realities. *Journal of Pan African Studies, 3*(8), 66–82.

Neblett, E. W., Jr., Philip, C. L., Cogburn, C. D., & Sellers, R. M. (2006). African American adolescents' discrimination experiences and academic achievement: Racial socialization as a cultural compensatory and protective factor. *Journal of Black Psychology, 32,* 199–218. https://doi.org/10.1177/0095798406287072.

Noguera, P. A. (2003). The trouble with Black boys: The role and influence of environmental and cultural factors on the academic performance of African-American males. *Urban Education, 38,* 431–459. https://doi.org/10.1177/0042085903038004005

Noguera, P. A. (2014). Confronting the urban in urban school reform. *Urban Review, 28*(1), 1–19. Retrieved from www.doi.org/10.1007/BF02354375.

Perkins, U. E. (2005). *Harvesting new generations: The positive development of Black youth.* Chicago, IL: Third World Press.

Polite, V. C., & Davis, J. E. (Eds.). (1999). *African American males in school and society: Practices and policies for effective education.* New York, NY: Teachers College Press.

Price, P. (2009). When is a police officer an officer of the law? The status of police officers in schools. *Journal of Law and Criminology, 99*(2), 541–570.

Rasmussen, B. (2010). Attended with great inconveniences: Slave literacy and the 1740 South Carolina negro act. *Publications: Modern Language Association, 125*(1), 201–203.

Robinson, W. L., Droege, J. R., Case, M. H., & Jason, L. A. (2015). Reducing stress and preventing anxiety in African American adolescents: A culturally-grounded approach. *Global Journal of Community Psychology Practice, 6*(2).

Rowley, S. J., Ross, L., Lozada, F. T., Williams, A., Gale, A., & Kurtz Costes, B. (2014). Framing Black boys: Parent, teacher, and student narratives of the academic lives of black boys. In L. S. Liben & R. S. Bigler (Eds.), *Advances in child development and behavior* (Vol. 47, pp. 301–332). http://dx.doi.org/10.1016/bs.acdb.2014.05.003

Santos, C., & Collins, M. (2015). Ethnic identity, school connectedness, and achievement in standardized tests among Mexican-origin youth. *Cultural Diversity & Ethnic Minority Psychology, 22.* https://doi.org/10.1037/cdp0000065

Schiele, J. H. (1997). The contour and meaning of Afrocentric social work. *Journal of Black Studies, 27*(6), 800–819. https://doi.org/10.1177/002193479702700605

Sealey-Ruiz, Y., & Greene, P. (2015). Popular visual images and the (mis) reading of Black male youth: A case for racial literacy in urban preservice teacher education. *Teaching Education, 26*(1), 1–22.

Seaton, E. K., Neblett, E. W., Upton, R. D., Hammond, W. P., & Sellers, R. M. (2011). The moderating capacity of racial identity between perceived discrimination and psychological well-being over time among African American youth. *Child Development, 82,* 1850–1867. https://doi.org/10.1111/j.1467-8624.2011.01651.x

Sellers, R. M., Copeland-Linder, N., Martin, P. P., & Lewis, R. L. H. (2006). Racial identity matters: The relationship between racial discrimination and psychological functioning in African American adolescents. *Journal of Research on Adolescence, 16,* 187–216. https://doi.org/10.1111/j.1532-7795.2006.00128.x

Shockley, K. (2011). Reaching African American students: Profile of an Afrocentric teacher. *Journal of Black Studies, 42*(7), 1027–1046. https://doi.org/10.1177/0021934711403739

Skiba, R. J., Chung, C. G., Trachok, M., Baker, T., Sheya, A., & Hughes, R. (2015). Where should we intervene? Contributions of behavior, student, and school characteristics to out-of-school suspension. In D. J. Losen (Ed.), *Closing the school discipline gap: Equitable remedies for excessive exclusion* (pp. 132–146). New York, NY: Teachers College Press.

Skiba, R. J., Michael, R. S., Nardo, A. C., & Peterson, R. L. (2002). The color of discipline: Sources of racial and gender disproportionality in school punishment. *Urban Review, 34*(4), 317–342.

United States Census Bureau. (2019). *U.S. census bureau releases 2014–2018 ACS 5-year estimates.* Retrieved from www.census.gov/programs-surveys/acs/news/updates/2019.html.

U. S. Department of Education Office for Civil Rights. (2016). *2013–2014 civil rights data collection: A first look.* Retrieved from www2.ed.gov/about/offices/list/ocr/docs2013–2014-first-look.pdf

U.S. Department of Justice & U.S. Department of Education. (2018). *Joint – dear colleague letter.* Retrieved from https://www2.ed.gov/about/offices/list/ocr/letters/colleague-201401-title-vi.html

Vaughans, K. C. (2021). Black boys in the eye of the storm. *The Psychoanalytic Study of the Child, 74*(1), 47–58. https://doi.org/10.1080/00797308.2020.1859300.

Wade, D. T., & Ortiz, K. S. (2016). Punishing trauma: How schools contribute to the carceral continuum through its response to traumatic experiences. In K. J. Fasching-Varner, L. L. Martin, R. W. Mitchell, K. P. Bennett-Haron, & A. Daneshzadeh (Eds.), *Understanding, dismantling, and disrupting the prison-to-school pipeline* (pp. 183–194). Washington, DC: Lexington Books.

Wald, J., & D. J. Losen. (2003). Defining and redefining the school-to-prison pipeline. *New Directions for Youth Development, 99,* 9–15. https://doi.org/10.1002/yd.51.

Warfield-Coppock, N., & Harvey, A. (1989). *Teenage pregnancy prevention: A rites of passage resource manual.* New York, NY: New York Commission for Racial Justice

Webster, C., & Knaus, C. B. (2021). I don't think they like us: School suspensions as anti-Black male practice. *Journal of African American Males in Education, 12*(1), 66–88.

Whaley, A. L., & McQueen, J. P. (2004). An Afrocentric program as primary prevention for African American youth: Qualitative and quantitative exploratory data. *The Journal of Primary Prevention, 24*(2), 253–269. https://doi.org/10.1023/B:JOPP.0000042389.22212.3a

Zeng, Z. (2019). *Jail inmates in 2017.* U.S. Department of Justice, Office of Justice Programs, Bureau of Justice Statistics. (NCJ 251774). Retrieved from www.bjs.gov/content/pub/pdf/ji17.pdf

13

UPONYAJI

Restoring the spirits of foster care and adopted children who have experienced loss

Tiffany Y. Lane, Jazlyn A. Bain, Stephanie Oyler

The 1995 film, *Losing Isaiah* directed by Stephen Gyllenhaal, depicts an African American boy, Isaiah, a newborn addicted to drugs abandoned in an alleyway by his biological mother. Due to Isaiah's birth parents' absence, he was placed in foster care and later adopted by a White upper-middle-class family. The remainder of the movie is centered on the contentious court case between two mothers who want legal custody.

Losing Isaiah was controversial for many reasons. It depicted a stereotypical African American woman addicted to drugs and could not care for her son. It highlighted the cultural and racial differences between Isaiah and his adoptive family and its impact on his identity. Some maintain that the film reinforces the idea of colorblindness and the White savior narrative, which depicts a White person "going the extra mile to help people of color who cannot or will not help themselves" (Hughey, 2012, p. 761). Isaiah understandably grieves the loss from his adopted family. After reunification, it was hard for Isaiah to resume attachment with his birth mother.

As portrayed in the movie, many African American foster and adopted children experience losses that can significantly impact their social, psychological, and emotional health. However, the movie did not show his ongoing use of mental health services after his traumatic grief and loss. Sadly, Isaiah's story resembles many African American children in the child welfare system.

Social workers are charged to support those in need, particularly vulnerable groups such as African American children in foster care and children preparing for adoption. At times, these children's and youth's emotional needs are secondary to ensuring their safety and permanency; however, experiencing loss and trauma that children endure is vital to their long-term well-being. The National Association of Black Social Workers (2020) reminds us that "ensuring that the needs of children who experience or who are at risk for maltreatment are addressed is critical

DOI: 10.4324/9780429276613-17

as the impact of adverse childhood experiences cascades throughout the lifetime" (para. 2). From a mental health perspective, mainstream therapeutic models such as trauma-informed cognitive behavioral therapy, play therapy, and therapeutic foster care are used to address loss and trauma issues for foster children regardless of their racial and ethnic backgrounds.

Section 1.05 of the Social Work Code of Ethics (National Association of Social Workers, 2017) outlines the commitment to cultural awareness and diversity. It highlights that social workers' "role to understand their clients' cultures and be able to demonstrate competence in the provision of services that are sensitive to clients' cultures and to differences among people and cultural groups," as such cultural-based models should be at the forefront of therapeutic interventions. The National Association of Black Social Work (NABSW) demands cultural-sensitive practices in child welfare services and kinship care to preserve families (Association of Black Social Workers, 2003). NABSW charges Black social workers to intentionally use their knowledge and skills to improve people of African ancestry's quality of life through human service delivery in fields such as child welfare (National Association of Black Social Workers, n.d.). NABSW's vision adopts an African-centered lens informed by the *Nguzo Saba* – the seven principles of *Kwanza*: unity, self-determination, collective work and responsibility, cooperative economics, purpose, creativity, and faith (Official Kwanzaa, n.d.). In the essence of *Kwanza*'s principles, this chapter will provide an overview of the African American children in the child welfare system and common interventions utilized to address trauma and loss issues and offer critiques of those models/interventions through an African-centered lens.

Foster care and adoption

Public child welfare services are a range of services that states offer to ensure children's and youth's safety. The services also support family systems to make sure they have the resources to care for their children. The public child welfare agencies partner with private, public, and community-based organizations to ensure that the appropriate services are rendered to children and their families. Services include but are not limited to childcare, parenting classes, and mental health services.

According to the Child Welfare Information Gateway (2018), child welfare agencies usually:

- Support or coordinate services to prevent child abuse and neglect
- Provide services to families that need help protecting and caring for their children
- Receive and investigate reports of possible child abuse and neglect; assess child and family needs, strengths, and resources
- Arrange for children to live with kin (i.e., relatives) or with foster families when safety cannot be ensured at home

- Support the well-being of children living with relatives or foster families, including ensuring that their educational needs are addressed
- Work with the children, youth, and families to achieve family reunification, adoption, or other permanent family connections for children and youth leaving foster care

The sectors of the child welfare system that this chapter focuses on are foster care and foster care adoption. *Foster care* is an interim living arrangement facilitated by a child welfare agency for children and youth whose parents cannot care for them and need support. Children and youth in foster care could be placed with foster families, kinsfolk, emergency shelters, independent living facilities, and group homes (The Annie Casey Foundation, 2020; Child Welfare Gateway Information Center, 2020). *Foster care adoption* is when a child in foster care will not be reunified with their biological parents because the court terminated their rights. Foster parents or an adoptive family could adopt the children (Considering Adoption, n.d.).

Common practices

General interventions vary for foster care children and are based on the presenting concerns and related issues per case. Children and youth in foster care utilize mental health and behavioral health care services more often than other children who have Medicaid insurance. They are more likely to be diagnosed with mental health disorders, which perhaps is related to their losses, experiences leading to placement in care, trauma, and significant transitions (Rosenbach, Lewis, & Quinn, 2000). If traumatic events are not treated and tackled, the outcomes are gloomy and could put children and youth at further risk (Johnson & Chipungu, 2016). Mental health interventions tend to focus on their behaviors and possible trauma issues due to maltreatment. Some common interventions used to support children and youth in care are behavioral health services such as therapeutic foster care, trauma-focused cognitive behavioral therapy, and play therapy.

Therapeutic foster care

Therapeutic foster care, also known as treatment foster care, is specialized care provided by foster parents to support an eclectic range of children and youth, typically those with considerable emotional, behavioral, or social concerns and or take medications (Child Welfare Gateway, n.d.). Children and youth in these settings have been identified as needing a higher level of care. Therapeutic foster care parents are trained on an ongoing basis and receive more supports and services. The trainings prepare foster parents to address complex situations related to the children's past trauma or abusive circumstances. Some children and youth in traditional and therapeutic foster placement may be referred to community-based agencies for therapy.

Trauma-focused cognitive behavioral therapy

Trauma-Focused Cognitive Behavior Therapy (TF-CBT) is an evidence-based cognitive-behavioral therapy that focuses on the emotional and mental health needs of children, youth, adults, and families by addressing the harmful effects of trauma (Murray, Cohen, & Mannarino, 2013; Psychology Today, 2020). It has been used to support children and youth who experienced sexual abuse and any form of severe trauma. Depending on the child's needs and their caregiver, TF-CBT is intended to occur for 12–16 sessions. Some techniques include psychoeducation, exploring loss and grief, relaxation techniques, cognitive coping, and trauma narrative and processing (Murray et al., 2013). TF-CBT can involve non-offending caregivers who have a healthy relationship with the child or youth, such as a parent, foster parent, or any adult who provides parental support in the child's everyday life during the child's therapeutic and healing process (Ramirez et al., 2014).

Play therapy

Play therapy is an intervention used to address mental health and behavioral concerns with children aged 4–12. Play therapy is an approach that expands on children's communication and learning process, and it is utilized when children are unable to articulate, explore, and process their feelings (Drisko, Perri, Kelly, & Nielson, 2020). The play and activity serve as a way for children to convey their needs, wants, and fears. Some modalities of play therapy are child-centered play therapy and cognitive-behavioral play therapy.

African Americans in child welfare

Historically, African American children were nearly excluded from openly segregated child welfare services (Roberts, n.d.). African American communities formed kinship networks (including fictive kin) to care for children in need (Everett, Chipungu, & Leashore, 2004; Hill, 2006; Roberts, 2002). Churches provided aid for children and their families by supporting orphanages and community outreach programs (Brice, 2017). African American children's existence in the child welfare system increased by the 1960s (Hill, 2006). The child welfare system operated from a Eurocentric framework and perspective that did not acknowledge African American traditions, customs, and cultures. The system's practices and expectations on how families should rear their children placed African Americans at risk of discrimination and involvement in the child welfare system. The incline of African American families involved in the child welfare systems is predictable, considering the conflicting views of mainstream ideas of family structure and practices. Despite efforts in the social work profession and related fields to promote cultural competence, humility, and sensitivity, African Americans have been disproportionately represented in the child welfare system.

The Adoption and Foster Care Analysis & Reporting System (2020) reveals that from 2010 to 2019, Black children have made up at least 20% or more of the foster care and adoption system. African American children are two times more likely to enter foster care than White children. The Child Welfare Information Gateway report (2016) summarizes potential justifications for the disparity, including higher poverty rates and caseworkers' racial and cultural biases. Race and culture also influence child welfare decision-making through entrenched stereotypical ideas about Black family "dysfunction," mainly related to parenting styles and family composition (Roberts, 2002).

Implicit biases and cultural misunderstandings among child welfare workers may affect decisions regarding African Americans' involvement in the child welfare system (Child Welfare Gateway, 2016). Biases can also impact the type of interventions used to help children and families in need. Historically, mental health and other services for African American children in foster care have been ineffective due to the lack of training and education of cultural understanding, disempowering engagement during the referral process, and family and community involvement. The general interventions lack consideration of cultural, explicit needs and historical contexts (Manning, Cornelius, & Okundaye, 2004). Despite the information known about African American children in care, there are minimal culturally based interventions considered to address issues associated with maltreatment.

Critique

Although the social work profession suggests cultural-based intervention models, there are limited child welfare agencies that use frameworks centered on racial and ethnic identities. Social workers and agencies have expressed an awareness of discrimination and racism that African Americans and other marginalized groups have endured while utilizing universal models; however, that is not culturally focused practice. It's been suggested that these methods do not "seek to support, nurture, and understand the emotional, spiritual, and developmental needs of Black families to advance the collective interests of African people" (Graham, 1999, p. 105–106). The mainstream frameworks adopted by agencies and social workers to support foster care youth are rooted in a Eurocentric moral theory and policy perspective. Graham (1999) suggests that

> [T]he existing tools for social work practice are grounded within ethnocentric epistemologies and, as the foundation for social work theory and practice, are ill-equipped for the task of nurturing and developing African families and their children, psychologically, socially, or spiritually.
>
> *(p. 119)*

Social work lacks the exploration of all philosophical concepts that are relevant to the African diaspora, which would encourage insight about themselves and their emotional responses to overcome circumstances, assess cultural misorientation, engage and build systems, create opportunities, and implement policies to advance family and the community (Fairfax, 2017). Simply infusing African-centered concepts into mainstream interventions to address matters associated with loss and trauma of foster and adopted African American children is insufficient.

The social work profession's mission is "to enhance human well-being and help meet the basic human needs of all people, with particular attention to the needs and empowerment of people who are vulnerable, oppressed, and living in poverty" (NABSW, 2020). Dr Molefi Kete Asante (2009) suggests that Afrocentric practitioners operate upon the understanding of what is in the "best interest of black people, that is, black people as a historically oppressed population" (para. 6). African-centered frameworks and practices in social work must center African ideals, philosophies, and values in its most organic state. As such, it is imperative to analyze behaviors and interventions for its Afrocentric origin.

African-centered approach

"Afrocentric social work can be defined as a method of social work practice based on traditional African philosophical assumptions that are used to explain and to solve human and societal problems" (Schiele, 1997). The framework centralizes the interest of African people. Functioning through an African-centered paradigm calls for awareness to center the "African," precisely Black thought, patterns, ideologies, and values, as demonstrated in the upmost forms of African principles (Asante, 2009). Traditional social work professionals maintain professional boundaries with less intimacy and connection to the client. African-centered or Afrocentric practitioner approach to working with clients adopts a different approach to the help or "healing" process. Rowe and Woodson (2018) advise that healing can be done

> through helping us [African Americans] take back our individual and collective identities and stories, especially those that replicate and reflect our true and righteous African heritage. The goals also allow us to restore our spirits, sense of self, sense of wonderment, and potential.
>
> *(para, 23)*

The healing process is an organic process for emotional health (Phillips, 1990).

An African-centered practitioner must first personify the African ideologies and values, as demonstrated in the upmost forms of African principles. Asante (2003) offers breakthrough strategies toward collective consciousness that African-centered practitioners should exemplify in their work with children and youth dealing with trauma and loss: "victorious thought, love of own culture first, positive race behaviors, reflect own motifs in dress [African material], personal spiritual growth, respect for people, historical continuity, and relate all to Africa" (p. 130). In an African-centered practitioner's mind, the question is, "What is the best interest of the African and the African community [client systems]?". Afrocentric practitioners seek to analyze, reconstruct, and develop images and behaviors in the best interest of African people.

Collective work and responsibility are the essences of the interaction and healing of the client system. Integrating communalism and spirituality into the helping process is a protective factor that can decrease risk (Chipungu et al., 2000).

Spirituality is central to efficiently working with the client system (Bent-Goodley, 2005). Spirituality is an unseen facet that links all human beings to each other and a creator (Schiele, 1994) – healing spaces require a level of calmness and relaxation for both the practitioner and the client systems. Many children in care have a history of chaotic environments, so serenity in the helping process is crucial. Afrocentric practitioners should be mentally prepared to work with client systems to ensure harmony and balance in the helping relationship. The therapist (practitioner) can engage in centering or relaxation exercises to tap into their spiritual forces (Phillips, 1990). The person-to-person alignment is principal to the African values and essential to address issues centered on trauma and loss – in a one-on-one session and a group setting.

The methods used by child welfare agencies, who have adopted the African-centered approach to work with African American families, focus on therapeutic and communal strategies to support children and their families. For example, a foster care agency used some techniques from NTU psychotherapy. NTU psychotherapy "is based on core principles of Ancient African and Afrocentric world view, nurtured through African-American culture and augmented by concepts and techniques in Western psychology." NTU is a Central African idea derived from the Bantu people. It is described as the essence of life, in that it connects the universe (Phillips, 1990, p. 55–56). NTU applies the African principles of *harmony, interconnectedness, cultural awareness, and genuineness*. It recognizes that therapy is a healing process, and the goal is to help client systems restore natural order and alignment. Harmony is the idea that people are mentally healthy and aligned with life's forces (Phillips, 1990); connecting with the spiritual forces is essential (Bent-Goodley, 2005). Interconnectedness suggests a mutual alliance among people, and they are one (Graham, 1999). Cultural awareness is the ability to maintain balance and authentic consciousness of cultural self. Genuineness is the idea of being authentic and displaying "realness" and is the basis for valuable relationships (Phillips, 1990). The NTU psychotherapy model provides concepts and tasks to address loss and healing issues among children and youth in foster care. It empowers client systems to adopt *Kwanza*'s seven principles, which are considered the proper and practical guidelines for healthy living for Africans. Although there are limited African-centered models that directly address loss that foster care children endured, the following sections will apply African-centered values, concepts, and traditions to offer healing methods for foster care children.

Model rites of passage

Rites of passage experiences in African culture are customary and serve as an opportunity to adopt African cultural norms and concepts that can be ultimately actualized. Rites of passages support the ideals of awareness of their situation, and it provides a safe space to connect socially and spiritually perhaps and begin the healing process. It supports the *Kwanza* ideals of unity, collective responsibility, and self-determination. Foster care agencies have adopted four-week transition rites of passage programs to help children transition into foster care homes. The program lasts for four weeks, and during that time, they engage in cultural rituals and ceremonial activities that introduce *Kwanza*'s principles. Programs have incorporated a welcoming ceremony and a crossover ceremony for a child to signify completion and new beginnings into the agency's rites of passage program (Gregory & Phillips, 1997).

Ideally, in rites of passage experiences, the entire "community" should be involved, especially for ceremonies. The family system includes the foster parents and agency workers and therapists. It is essential to cultivate a space of relaxation and calmness. The ceremonial and ritual activities should be well thought out and incorporate traditional African concepts and traditions. The words should empower the clients and foster care parents to adopt an African-centered viewpoint on the value of communalism and fundamental goodness. Creating a programmatic creed that embodies African concepts may provide a base for ceremonies. *Marking* is the necessary component of the rites of passage program. Marking is when a "person delineates a cultural boundary around a particular cultural space in human time" (Asante, 2009). Marking can be incorporated by proclaiming African American heroes in history, using symbols, and displaying African fabric. Techniques in the rites of passage program could include libation to empower and center the children and youth and engage foster parents and agency workers in the ceremony. "Libation is conducted through the pouring of liquid unto the earth for circular connectedness and is accompanied by the calling forth of the names of ancestors" (Gregory & Phillips, 1997). Incorporating group reflections in the program provides a space for children and youth to express their feelings related to loss and transitions support interconnectedness. Their reflections can be shared at the crossing over ceremony to acknowledge self-awareness in the context of their circumstances.

Cultural awareness exercises

Imagine being taken from your home and family. Regardless of the circumstances leading to the removal, it can be a traumatic incident. It can be a time for African American children and youth in care where they feel alone and trying to figure out where they belong. It is vital to help them discover who they are to build on their strengths and address areas they can work on in the healing process in a healing space. Self-awareness is an essential component of the therapeutic process. Cultural awareness is being aligned with the needs, importance, and affirmative development of the African community. A healthy cultural awareness requires that a person is authentic and in agreement with self. Helping children and youth in care understand who they are and their culture can support their self-esteem during times of confusion, loss, and transitions.

Cultural projects and activities promote a positive sense of self (Chipungu et al., 2000). Cultural awareness exercises can be implemented in a one-on-one session or group setting. However, a group setting cultivates a sense of unity, community, and extends interconnectedness. For older foster care youth who may never be reunified with their families and possibly age out of care, the group setting may benefit their transition to self-sufficiency. Self and cultural awareness models used with similar populations (youth) introduced the seven principles of *Kwanza* to help members "understand themselves, others, and the world in which they live" (Harvey & Coleman, 1997. p 203). To extend this group exemplar, the group therapist could introduce African Americans and Africans who have made contributions to the African community; this can be implemented by showing imagery through pictures, videos, books, and visits to museums and landmarks in the communities. For example, a practitioner facilitating a group session centered on loss and resilience might decide to create a museum in the meeting space and post pictures of African and African American pioneers and ancestors on the meeting space walls. The facilitator could discuss the pioneers or have the group members go around the room and read pioneers' and ancestors' brief biography posted near their picture. This empowerment activity introduces them to their heritage and connections to their ancestors and emphasizes cultural awareness.

An African-centered framework calls for practitioners to restore African people to their traditional greatness (Official Kwanza, n.d.). Concepts of resilience and perseverance should be integrated into the group discussions, particularly for those in foster care who may be dealing with feelings of hopelessness. It has been suggested that exposure to African ancestry and *Kwanza* principles has increased the youth's consciousness of unity, self, and purpose (Harvey & Coleman, 1997). Encouraging client systems to connect with their ancestors' journeys is an empowering tool, as it gives them a sense of connection and purpose. It centers the children and youth who experience loss and transitions and positions them to relate with their ancestors' calamities and victories. Empowering clients to express resilient, powerful stories can help them address trauma (Rowe & Woodson, 2018).

Self-awareness exercises are a self-discovery tool that is meaningful and reinforces self-determination. These exercises should be progressive and organic and allow time and space to process with facilitators/practitioners. The activities can be interactive in a group or one-on-one settings with a practitioner. Some topics to discuss are family history, what it means to be "real," identifying personal characteristics, behaviors, values, feelings related to placement in care, coping strategies, describing things they enjoy, and their personal and community goals. Connecting the *Kwanza* principles and other African values to the clients' responses and experiences are crucial, and it is suggested that the facilitator/practitioner guide the process.

Affirmations that encourage positive regard for self and the African community can be part of the healing process. In the spirit of self-determination, creativity, and purpose, clients can form affirmations that incorporate their strengths and community strengths. Affirmations is a spiritual act and typically stated verbally to exude confidence and power. Ideally, the practitioner should provide examples of affirmations and demonstrate how to speak them into existence boldly. Declaring affirmations can be an activity during therapeutic sessions (one-on-one and group) and perhaps signify the beginning or end of a session.

Conclusion

African-centered approaches to address loss among children involved in the child welfare system deviate from mainstream interventions and can be considered "controversial" in social work practice, mainly due to the absence of the Eurocentric view. However, African Americans' concerns and outcomes in the child welfare system call for cultural intervention. The African-centered perspective does not adopt the idea that the African American family is the issue. Asante (2003) contests that the system dictates what occurs with an individual. If possible and healthy for the child in care, the practitioner should include the biological and foster family systems, including elders, in the healing process. Collective work and responsibility and unity are critical to the progression. Family (natural, foster, or adoptive) involvement can encourage healthy communication and address the family unit's roles and responsibilities. Creating a healthy environment for the child to thrive and deal with loss and trauma requires family members to understand the importance of self and others. Connecting client systems with cultural-based services are essential. Asante (2003) asserts that being Black does not mean one is Afrocentric and subscribe to the *Kwanza* principles. With that in mind, African-centered practitioners in diverse capacities must refer to agencies that uphold the African-centered values and practices. Building networks are essential to African-centered practice. Cultural-based services include but are not limited to mental health services, community centers (with a range of programs), afterschool programs, and spiritual-based agencies.

Suggested websites and readings

Adoptee LIT: https://adopteelit.com/
Afrocentricity: www.asante.net/articles/1/afrocentricity/
African Centered Education: https://senecavillagemontessori.com/resources/
Asante, M. (2003). *Afrocentricity: The theory of social change* (4th ed.). African American Images.
Asante, M. (2002). *100 greatest African Americans*. Amherst: Prometheus Books.
Official Kwanza Site: www.officialkwanzaawebsite.org/

References

Adoption and Foster Care Analysis & Reporting System. (2020). *Adoption & foster care statistics*. Retrieved from www.acf.hhs.gov/cb/research-data-technology/statistics-research
Asante, K. M. (2003). *Afrocentricity: The theory of social change* (4th ed.). Chicago, IL: African American Images.

Asante, K. M. (2009, April 13). *Afrocentricity*. Retrieved from www.asante.net/articles/1/afrocentricity/

Association of Black Social Workers. (2003, January 10). *Preserving families*. Retrieved from https://cdn.ymaws.com/www.nabsw.org/resource/collection/0D2D2404-77EB-49B5-962E-7E6FADBF3D0D/Preserving_Families_of_African_Ancestry.pdf

Bent-Goodley, T. B. (2005). An African-centered approach to domestic violence. *Families in Society, 86*(2), 197–206. https://doi.org/10.1606/1044-3894.2455

Brice, T. (2017). Child welfare practice: An African-centered approach. *Journal of Human Behavior in the Social Environment, 27*(1/2), 81–91. https://doi.org/10.1080/10911359.2016.1263092

Child Welfare Gateway. (2016, November). *Racial disproportionality and disparity in child welfare*. Retrieved from www.childwelfare.gov/pubpdfs/racial_disproportionality.pdf

Child Welfare Gateway. (2020). *Treatment foster care*. Retrieved from www.childwelfare.gov/topics/outofhome/foster-care/treat-foster/#:~:text=Treatment%20foster%20care%20is%20designed,receive%20additional%20supports%20and%20services.

Child Welfare Information Gateway. (2018, June). *What is child welfare? A guide for educators*. Retrieved from www.childwelfare.gov/pubPDFs/cw_educators.pdf

Chipungu, S. S., Hermann, J., Sambrano, S., Nistler, M., Sale, E., & Springer, J. F. (2000). Prevention programming for African American youth: A review of strategies in CSAP's national cross-site evaluation of high-risk youth programs. *Journal of Black Psychology, 26*(4), 360–385. https://doi.org/10.1177/0095798400026004002

Considering Adoption (n.d.). *Adoption process*. Retrieved October 27, 2020, from https://consideringadoption.com

Drisko, J., Perri, C., Kelly, L., & Nielson, J. (2020). Is individual child play therapy effective? *Research on Social Work Practice, 30*(7), 715–723. http://doi.org/10.1177/1049731519854157

Everett, J. E., Chipungu, S. P., & Leashore, B. R. (2004). *Child welfare revisited: An Africentric perspective*. New Brunswick, NJ: Rutgers University.

Fairfax, C. N. (2017). African philosophy: The center of African-centered social work. *Journal of Human Behavior in the Social Environment, 27*(1/2), 7–14. https://doi.org/10.1080/10911359.2016.1252599

Graham, M. J. (1999). The African-centered worldview. *Journal of Black Studies, 30*(1), 103. https://doi.org/10.1177/002193479903000106

Gregory, S. D. P., & Phillips, F. B. (1997). "Of mind, body, and spirit": Therapeutic foster care – An innovative approach to healing from an NTU perspective. *Child Welfare, 76*(1), 127–142.

Gyllenhaal, S. (Director). (1995). *Losing Isaiah* [Motion picture].

Harvey, A. R., & Coleman, A. A. (1997). An Afrocentric program for African American males in the juvenile justice system. *Child Welfare, 76*(1), 197–211.

Hill, R. B. (2006, October 1). *Synthesis of research on disproportionality in child welfare: An update*. The Annie E. Casey Foundation. Retrieved from www.aecf.org/resources/synthesis-of-research-on-disproportionality-in-child-welfare-an-update/

Hughey, M. W. (2012). Racializing redemption, reproducing racism: The odyssey of magical negroes and white saviors. *Sociology Compass, 6*(9), 751–767. https://doi.org/10.1111/j.1751-9020.2012.00486.x

Johnson, K. Y., & Chipungu, S. S. (2016). Child welfare in urban environments. In R. Wells-Wilbon, A. R. McPhatter, & H. F. O. Vakalahi (Eds.), *Social work practice with African Americans in urban environments*. (pp. 37–54). New York, NY: Springer Publishing Company.

Manning, M. C., Cornelius, L. J., & Okundaye, J. N. (2004). Empowering African Americans Through Social Work Practice: Integrating an Afrocentric Perspective, Ego Psychology and Spirituality. *Families in Society*, *85*(2), 229–235. https://doi.org/10.1606/1044-3894.325

Murray, L. K., Cohen, J. A., & Mannarino, A. P. (2013). Trauma-focused cognitive behavioral therapy for youth who experience continuous traumatic exposure. *Peace and conflict: Journal of peace psychology: The journal of the Division of Peace Psychology of the American Psychological Association*, *19*(2), 180–195. https://doi.org/10.1037/a0032533.

National Association of Black Social Workers. (2020). *Mission statement*. Retrieved from www.nabsw.org/page/MissionStatement

National Association of Social Workers. (2017). *Code of ethics*. Retrieved from https://www.socialworkers.org/About/Ethics/Code-of-Ethics/Code-of-Ethics-English

Official Kwanzaa Website. (n.d.). *Kwanza*. Retrieved from www.officialkwanzaawebsite.org/

Phillips, F. (1990). NTU Psychotherapy: An Afrocentric approach. *Journal of Black Studies*, *17*(1), 55–74. https://doi.org/10.1177/00957984900171005

Psychology Today. (2020). *Trauma-focused cognitive behavior therapy*. Retrieved from www.psychologytoday.com/us/therapy-types/trauma-focused-cognitive-behavior-therapy

Ramirez de Arellano, M. A., Lyman, D. R., Jobe-Shields, L., George, P., Dougherty, R. H., Daniels, A. S., . . . Delphin-Rittmon, M. E. (2014). Trauma-focused cognitive-behavioral therapy for children and adolescents: Assessing the evidence. *Psychiatric Services*, *65*(5), 591–602. https://doi.org/10.1176/appi.ps.201300255

Roberts, D. (2002). *Shattered bonds: The color of child welfare*. New York: Basic Books.

Roberts, D. (n.d.). *Race and class in the child welfare system*. PBS. Retrieved from www.pbs.org/wgbh/pages/frontline/shows/fostercare/caseworker/roberts.html

Rosenbach, M., Lewis, K., & Quinn, B. (2000). *Health conditions, utilization, and expenditures of children in foster care: Final report*. Office of the Assistant Secretary for Planning and Evaluation. Retrieved from https://aspe.hhs.gov/report/health-conditions-utilization-and-expenditures-children-foster-care

Rowe, T., & Woodson, K. (2018, June 19). How to heal African-Americans' traumatic history. *The Conversation*. Retrieved from https://theconversation.com/how-to-heal-african-americans-traumatic-history-98298

Schiele, J. H. (1994). Afrocentricity implications for higher education. *Journal of Black Studies*, *25*(2), 150–169. https://doi.org/10.1177/002193479402500202

Schiele, J. H. (1997). The contour and meaning of Afrocentric social work. *Journal of Black Studies*, *27*(6), 800–819. https://doi.org/10.1177/002193479702700605

The Annie E. Casey Foundation. (2020, February 5). *What is foster care?* Retrieved from www.aecf.org/blog/what-is-foster-care

The Office of Children Advocates. (2016). *Don't call me resilient: What loss & grief look like for children and youth*. Retrieved from https://cyc-net.org/pdf/Loss-and-Grief-FINAL-web.pdf

14

ADDRESSING SUBSTANCE USE THROUGH AFRICAN-CENTERED PRACTICE APPROACHES

*Anthony Estreet, Paul Archibald,
Len Price, Korey Johnson*

African Americans have historically experienced negative consequences as a result of substance use. These negative consequences have primarily been the results of the adverse health outcomes as well as disproportioned policies which criminalized this substance use. As a result of the so called War on Drugs, many minority communities, specifically African Americans, faced unequal outcomes such as higher arrest and incarceration rates (Alexander, 2010; Lusane & Desmond, 1991). Despite levels of substance use among the African American community remaining lower than their non-Hispanic white counterparts, these racial disparities were experienced in terms of arrests and incarcerations for drug use, possession, and low-level sales (Alexander, 2010). African Americans continue to face barriers to treatment and recovery from substance use as a result of issues such as racism, discrimination, poverty, treatment access, and stigma (Verissimo & Grella, 2017). Research also shows that the prevalence of help-seeking behaviors is lower among African Americans. This chapter explores the issues of substance use among African Americans and describes the incorporation of African-centered practice approaches for consideration to address current substance use rates. This chapter will highlight existing barriers to treatment and propose alternative approaches to increase help-seeking and overall engagement.

African Americans and substance use

There is a complex history between African Americans and substance use. Despite African Americans representing approximately 13% of the U.S. population, rates of substance use among African American continue to demonstrate that more work is needed in this area. According to the National Survey on Drug Use and Health (NSDUH) (U.S. Department of Health and Human Services, Substance Abuse and Mental Health Services Administration, Center for Behavioral Health Statistics and

DOI: 10.4324/9780429276613-18

Quality, 2020), among people aged 12 or older in the United States, past year marijuana use in African Americans (19.3%) was higher than the national average (17.5) and the highest among ethnically diverse groups. This represents an almost 7% increase in marijuana use from 2002. Similarly, rates of past year opioid use, specifically heroin use (.28) among people aged 12 or older was higher than the national average (.27%) among African Americans. Conversely, this represented a decrease in heroin use of approximately .05% when compared to previous data from 2002. In reviewing additional opioid use among African Americans, the NSDUH report shows that prescription pain reliever use among African Americans (3.2%) was lower than the national average (3.5%). Similar to the decreases noted with heroin use, prescription opioids use among African Americans also significantly decreased from 4.4% in 2015 to 3.2% in 2019.

As we examine current trends in substance use among African Americans it is imperative to note that according to Schiele (1996), the African-centered paradigm of human service does not view the use of drugs as inherently disruptive to human and societal relationships. Within many traditional African societies, the use of mood-altering substances was permitted as long as it did not compromise the individual's ability to function and contribute to the collective survival of the community (Christmon, 1995; Lusane, 1991). In fact, within its holistic viewpoint, the paradigm recognizes the importance of African-centered rituals, ceremonies, and other important social events that would include the use of mood-altering substances (Schiele, 1996). However, the paradigm does acknowledge that excessive use of substances is a problematic and destructive force for the individual, family, community, and wider social environment. It is when the use becomes problematic and uncontrollable that it begins to reach the threshold of becoming a substance use disorder.

According to the Substance Abuse and Mental Health Services Administration (SAMHSA), substance use disorders occur when the recurrent use of alcohol and/or drugs causes clinically significant impairment, including health problems, disability, and failure to meet major responsibilities at work, school, or home (2020). According to data from the NSDUH, rates of illicit substance use disorder among African Americans aged 12 or older in the United States were higher than the national average (3.3% and 3.0% respectively). Moreover, African Americans represented higher rates of marijuana use disorder (2.3%) compared to the national average (1.8%). Comparatively, rates of marijuana use disorders among African Americans are down from 2.6% in 2002. Similarly, the rate of opioid use disorders (OUDs) among African Americans was lower (.5%) than the national average (.6%). This represents a decline from previously recorded data from 2015 which reported rates of OUDs at .8%. These decreases in SUDs are consistent even when looking at legalized substances such as alcohol. According to the data, the rate of African Americans having an alcohol use disorder (AUD) (4.6%) in the past year was significantly lower than the national average (5.3). This represents a significant decrease from 2002, when the rate of AUD among African Americans was 7.1%. In general, African Americans had lower rates of substance use disorders (7.2%) than the national average (7.4). Consequently, this did not represent a change from the previous rate in 2015. While substance use among African Americans continues to be a complex issue, research has shown that African Americans are seeking and accessing treatment at far greater rates that the national average. The rate of treatment access for African Americans was 5.6% which was higher than the national average of 4.7%. Substance use disorder treatment data show that African Americans experiencing AUD increased in the number of people receiving treatment from 2015 when compared to 2019 (5.4% & 5.6% respectively). Consequently, the rate of treatment for illicit substance use was 5.6% which was significantly lower than the national average of 9.9% and even less than their non-Hispanic white counterparts (12.3%). Moreover, African Americans experience a decline in the number of people receiving treatment (5.6%) when compared to African Americans receiving treatment in 2015 (10.5%).

African Americans impacted by substance use also experience a myriad of challenges such as racism and discrimination, trauma, homelessness, unemployment, and financial instability. These additional challenges can lead to co-occurring behavioral health challenges such as mental health symptoms including thoughts of suicide. According to the 2019 NSDUH report, in 2019, 6.5 million African Americans had a mental illness and/or substance use disorder which is an increase of more than 10% from the previous year. Within this group, approximately 65% of young adults (18–25) with severe mental illness did not receive any treatment. Similarly, approximately 42% of African American adults aged 26–49 with severe mental illness received no treatment. These staggering numbers are alarming considering that within these same groups, approximately 456,000 young adults had serious thoughts of suicide while another 549,000 adults had similar thoughts. These numbers represent significant increases over ten years from 2009. These statistics are concerning and represent the complexity of behavioral health challenges among substance use in African Americans (Verissimo & Grella, 2017).

African-centered approaches for substance use: a life course perspective

Substance use within the African American community impacts not only the individuals but also their family, community, and the environments in which they operate. As such, it is imperative that we explore African-centered practice approaches with a lens that takes into account the complexities of these issues. One such lens that provides these opportunities for exploration is the Social-Ecological Model (Barati et al., 2021). This model accounts for influences as various levels to include the individual, interpersonal, community, and societal levels. Moreover, this model allows for adaptations of both the African-centered paradigm and the life course perspective as the issues of substance use among African Americans intersect with gender, age, education, etc. Figure 14.1 conceptualizes the adaptation of the model with the incorporation of the life course perspective. The inclusion of the life course perspective to understanding substance use and the health disparities

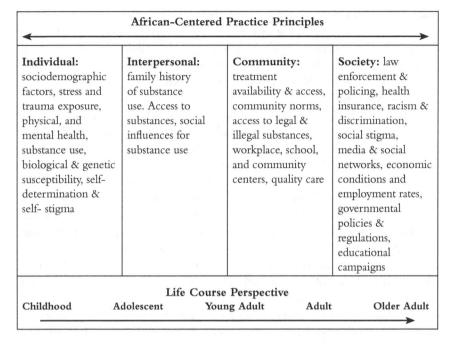

FIGURE 14.1 African-centered ecological life course perspective

within the African American community allows for a greater understanding of how socially patterned physical, environmental, and socioeconomic exposures at different stages of human development shape health within and across generations.

> Life course approaches are informed by developmental and structural per-spectives. Developmental perspectives emphasize how socially patterned exposures to risk factors during sensitive life stages shift health trajectories, whereas structural perspectives emphasize how social identity and position within socially patterned environments disproportionately allocate risk fac-tors and resources, resulting in altered health trajectories.
>
> *(Jones et al., 2019)*

Integrating African-centered practice with the transtheoretical model – stages of change

One approach to addressing substance use in general that can easily be adapted within an African-centered practice approach is the Transtheoretical Model of Change (TTM). This behavioral change approach, which was originally developed to address smoking cessation, has more widely been applied within the existing substance use treatment approaches (Krebs, Norcross, Nicholson, & Prochaska, 2018). The TTM approach is an integrated approach which allows individuals to assess and establish their level of commitment to the change process or current stage of change. This self-evaluation process is consistent with the principle of *Kujich-agulia* (self-determination), which encourages people to define, name, create, and speak for themselves. Instead of the treatment professional pushing a prescribed agenda, individuals are able to engage in a process where they can define and establish their own goals.

Central to the TTM approach is the process by which individuals modify a problem behavior (i.e. substance use disorder) or acquire a positive behavior (abstinence or reduction in use). The TTM asserts that individuals progress intentionally through a change cycle based on informed decision-making and can enter or exit the change process at various points within the stages of change (Krebs et al., 2018). In an African-centered practice approach, the principles of *Umoja*, *Ujima*, *Nia*, *Kuumba*, and *Imani* could be applied to this process. As people progress through the change cycle, they would consult with and use the support of their family and community. In general, the overarching principles within this adaptation are *Imani* or faith in the ability to overcome their substance use; and *Nia* the belief that through this process of substance use reduction we are working to improve and restore the larger community. Moreover, drawing on the collective work, individuals could benefit from greater creativity around behavioral change actions and supports. Overall, by engaging in this change process and reducing their substance use, individuals would be in a better position to engage in cooperative *economics* or *Ujamaa* by returning to work or supporting businesses in their community instead of spending on substance use.

The process of behavioral change is facilitated through ongoing cognitive and behavioral processes that an individual is guided through during their treatment episode. These ten processes are often associated with the model as follows: (1) consciousness raising, (2) dramatic relief, (3) self-reevaluation (4) environmental reevaluation, (5) social liberation, (6) self-liberation, (7) helping relationships, (8) counter-conditioning, (9) reinforcement management, and (10) stimulus control. As part of an African-centered practice approach, we propose the inclusion of the seven healing center commitments: relationships, culture, agency, aspirations, restorations of identity, assets, and meaning which would provide for more culturally relevant and trauma-responsive treatment approaches (Ginwright, 2018). Central to the TTM is the assumption that individuals who enter into the behavioral change event typically move through various stages of change (Krebs et al., 2018). In this approach, individuals progress through the following six stages (Table 14.1): pre-contemplation, contemplation, preparation, action, maintenance, and termination. In substance use disorder treatment, the stage of termination is not often used given the fact that treatment and recovery from addiction is an ongoing and continuous process which should consistently be worked on. With this in mind, maintenance is usually the final stage that is discussed within this model for substance use disorders. The inclusion of African rites of passages as individuals achieve their goals along the stage of change would serve as a culturally responsive motivator and encourage continued connection with the treatment and recovery process.

TABLE 14.1 Stages of Change

Stage of Change	Definition	Treatment Goal
Pre-contemplation	Not yet considering change or is unwilling or unable to change	Raising awareness
Contemplation	Sees the possibility of change but is ambivalent and uncertain	Resolving ambivalence and encouragement to choose change
Determination	Committed to changing. Still considering what to do	Help identify appropriate change strategies
Action	Taking steps toward change but has not stabilized in the process	Help implement change strategies and learn to eliminate potential recurrence of use
Maintenance	Has achieved goals and is working to maintain change	Develop new skills for maintaining recovery
Recurrence	Experienced a recurrence of the symptoms	Cope with the consequences and determine what to do next

Promising African-centered practice approaches

Culturally relevant and trauma responsive prevention and treatment options for addressing substance use among African Americans are an important area for expansion in both program development and research. While quite a few programs have been developed using African-centered principles, many have not been adopted into the mainstream public health arena. As a result, there continues to be a gap in access to culturally responsive treatment for African Americans. This section reviews some promising African-centered practice approaches that could easily be adapted and implemented for large-scale public use. As part of furthering the discussion regarding these approaches, we will also review the importance of continued research and evaluation which contributes to these approaches becoming evidenced-based practices.

Substance use prevention

In a review of African-centered drug preventions and interventions, Chipungu et al., (2000), suggest the following three major components from the African-centered framework:

1) The utilization of culturally responsive projects and activities which highlight accurate and relevant historical concepts that promotes a positive sense of self.
2) The incorporation of components that increase a positive sense of self and community while also reducing societal pressures and negative stereotypes. The incorporation of values, specifically communalism and spirituality, increases protective factors and resiliency while decreasing risk factors.

3) The incorporation of African-centered values such as spirituality, collective community well-being, self-determination, and creativity while also working to increase protective factors and resiliency while decreasing risk-factors and barriers.

An example of an African-centered prevention approach for substance use among youth is that of the MAAT Afrocentric Adolescent and Family Rites of Passage Program. As described by Harvey and Hill (2004), this program was developed with the specific goals to "reduce the incidence and prevalence of substance abuse and antisocial attitudes and behaviors" (p. 65). This prevention approach provides and accounts for the life course perspective. While this prevention program was developed for African American youth aged 11–15, there is also a strong family component which supports the idea of collective work and responsibility. Youth in the prevention program are able to engage with their family who can also share their experiences with substance use and provide family history which could be beneficial. As a strength-based, family centered afterschool program, youth engaged in rites of passage program that focused on the principle of *Ma'at* (truth, balance, order, harmony, righteousness, morality, and justice) and engaged in family empowerment and enhancement activities, as well as individual and family counseling. According to a multi-year study of this prevention program, youth demonstrated significant increases in knowledge about substance use, self-esteem, racial identity, cultural awareness, and community involvement. Family members who participated in the student program also demonstrated significant increases in parenting skills.

As we work to create more culturally relevant and trauma-responsive prevention programs for youth, it is imperative that we continue to develop and adapt programs that incorporate in utilizing these critical components of the African-centered practice approach. Research has demonstrated that a one-size-fits-all prevention approach does not take into account the unique experiences that African Americans experience as it relates to substance use. Moreover, many of the prevention approaches do not account for the larger societal issues as depicted in the African-centered ecological life course perspective. Another barrier to the implementation of African-centered prevention approaches is that they fail to meet the threshold of becoming an "evidence based practice" (EBP). As such, many treatment programs won't adopt and implement approaches they are not able to get reimbursed for by insurances. It is imperative that African-centered practice approach continue to be developed and engage in consistent evaluative and replicable approaches. It is through this process that African-centered prevention programs can begin moving closer to meeting the criteria for EBPs (Schiele, 2000).

Moving toward EBPs

As previously mentioned, for these African-centered practice approaches to have greater recognition and uptake by health care providers, we have to start moving them toward becoming evidence based. The idea of EBP is not a new one and is a result of a shift in the mid-1990s following public criticism of ineffective prevention programming (Shelton, Cooper, & Stirman, 2018). Following this shift, the substance use field became more unified in utilizing programs that were theoretically and empirically sound which resulted in greater implementation and transferability across the substance use care continuum. In addition, the overall field of substance use prevention became a more unified theoretically based discipline (Shelton et al., 2018). As such, in 2003, the National Institute of Drug Abuse (NIDA) provided guidance and structure for youth prevention programs that should be taken into consideration when discussing, planning, and implementing community-based substance use prevention programs (Table 14.2).

TABLE 14.2 National Institute of Drug Abuse: Preventing Drug Use Among Children and Adolescents

Principle 1 – Prevention programs should enhance protective factors and reverse or reduce risk factors.

Principle 2 – Prevention programs should address all forms of drug abuse, alone or in combination, including the underage use of legal drugs (e.g., tobacco or alcohol); the use of illegal drugs (e.g., marijuana or heroin); and the inappropriate use of legally obtained substances (e.g., inhalants), prescription medications, or over-the-counter drugs.

Principle 3 – Prevention programs should address the type of drug abuse problem in the local community, target modifiable risk factors, and strengthen identified protective factors.

Principle 4 – Prevention programs should be tailored to address risks specific to population or audience characteristics, such as age, gender, and ethnicity, to improve program effectiveness.

Principle 5 – Family based prevention programs should enhance family bonding and relationships and include parenting skills; practice in developing, discussing, and enforcing family policies on substance abuse; and training in drug education and information. Family bonding is the bedrock of the relationship between parents and children. Bonding can be strengthened through skills training on parent supportiveness of children, parent–child communication, and parental involvement.

Principle 9 – Prevention programs aimed at general populations at key transition points, such as the transition to middle school, can produce beneficial effects even among high-risk families and children. Such interventions do not single out risk populations and, therefore, reduce labeling and promote bonding to school and community.

Principle 10 – Community prevention programs that combine two or more effective programs, such as family based and school-based programs, can be more effective than a single program alone.

Principle 11 – Community prevention programs reaching populations in multiple settings – for example schools, clubs, faith-based organizations, and the media – are most effective when they present consistent, community-wide messages in each setting.

Principle 12 – When communities adapt programs to match their needs, community norms, or differing cultural requirements, they should retain core elements of the original research-based intervention which include: structure (how the program is organized and constructed); content (the information, skills, and strategies of the program); and delivery (how the program is adapted, implemented, and evaluated).

(Continued)

TABLE 14.2 (Continued)

Principle 6 – Prevention programs can be designed to intervene as early as preschool to address risk factors for drug abuse, such as aggressive behavior, poor social skills, and academic difficulties.

Principle 7 – Prevention programs for elementary school children should target improving academic and social–emotional learning to address risk factors for drug abuse, such as early aggression, academic failure, and school dropout. Education should focus on the following skills: self-control; emotional awareness; communication; social problem-solving; and academic support (especially in reading).

Principle 8 – Prevention programs for middle or junior high and high school students should increase academic and social competence with the following skills: study habits and academic support; communication; peer relationships; self-efficacy and assertiveness; drug resistance skills; reinforcement of anti-drug attitudes; and strengthening of personal commitments against drug abuse.

Principle 13 – Prevention programs should be long term with repeated interventions (i.e., booster programs) to reinforce the original prevention goals. Research shows that the benefits from middle school prevention programs diminish without follow-up programs in high school.

Principle 14 – Prevention programs should include teacher training on good classroom management practices, such as rewarding appropriate student behavior. Such techniques help to foster students' positive behavior, achievement, academic motivation, and school bonding.

Principle 15 – Prevention programs are most effective when they employ interactive techniques, such as peer discussion groups and parent role-playing, that allow for active involvement in learning about drug abuse and reinforcing skills.

Principle 16 – Research-based prevention programs can be cost-effective. Similar to earlier research, recent research shows that for each dollar invested in prevention, a savings of up to $10 in treatment for alcohol or other substance abuse can be seen.

Substance use treatment

In addition to increasing African-centered prevention approaches, we have to also consider the importance of treatment approaches. Research has indicated that African Americans have experienced the greatest consequences from engaging in illicit substance use when compared to their white counterparts (Alexander, 2010). As previously demonstrated, African Americans impacted by illicit substance use disorder engage in treatment at rates lower that the national average and their non-Hispanic white counterparts. As such it is imperative to gain a better understanding of the treatment needs related to African American substance users. One such explanation is around treatment access. African Americans have far greater barriers to accessing treatment such as transportation, child care, insurance, racism, provider discrimination and stigma, as well as the criminal justice system. Research has indicated that African Americans believe that that they are less likely to benefit from a formalized treatment approach when compared to their white counter-parts (Jackson, Stephens, & Smith, 1997). One of the consistently stated barriers to initiation and engagement in substance use disorder treatment among African Americans is the lack of treatment which specifically addresses sociocultural factors that are often experienced by this diverse population (Longshore, Grills, Annon, & Grady, 1998). As such, research and practitioners alike have been advocating for the development of more culturally diverse and sensitive treatment approaches (Hodge, Jackson, & Vaughn, 2012). Utilizing an African-centered treatment approach to address substance use would meet this call to action. According to Jackson et al. (1997), some of the key elements that have been included in the development of African-centered practice approaches include: 1) strong emphasis of spirituality, 2) harmony with nature, 3) rites of passages, 4) interconnectedness with previous generations, 5) self-identity and dignity, and 6) the overall respect for traditions.

One aspect of treatment that has become a significant indicator of treatment-related outcomes is engagement. According to Lizardi and Stanley (2010), engage-ment is the process of being committed to the treatment process and being an active and present participant in a collaborative journey engaged in behavioral change and improve one's life. Given that much of the research asserts that African Americans are less likely to engage in and be retained in treatment, African-centered practice approaches should address this issue. One such approach that focuses on engage-ment in the general population is Screening, Brief Intervention, and Referral to Treatment (SBIRT). SBIRT is an approach to deliver early intervention and treat-ment to people with substance use disorders and those at risk of developing these disorders (Manuel et al., 2015). This approach has been used in several research studies within the African American community and has shown great success in being able to screen, identify, and engage African Americans into some form of substance use treatment (Green, 2018). Much of the appeal of the SBIRT model is that is a time-limited approach that can be applied in a variety of settings (Babor et al., 2007). The components of this approach are as follows:

- **Screening**: quickly assesses the severity of substance use and identifies the appropriate level of treatment.
- **Brief intervention**: focuses on increasing insight and awareness regarding substance use and motivation toward behavioral change.
- **Referral to treatment**: provides those identified as needing more extensive treatment with access to specialty care.

Today, SBIRT is the current trending screening and engagement approach within the substance use landscape. There was a previous approach similar to SBIRT devel-oped in 1998 that utilized African-centered principles to address substance use. The Engagement Project (EP) combined African-centered principles with a stage of change approach. Developed as a brief intervention for engagement, this intervention was developed, "to engage clients in a psychosocial process conducive to recovery from illicit drugs" (Longshore et al., 1998, p. 320). Similar to the SBIRT model, EP is a brief intervention that incorporates motivational interviewing skills and dyadic counseling. It specifically targets African American substance users with no prior treatment experience or those who were in the pre-contemplation or contemplation stage of change. As part of this approach, African-centered practice principles such as the *Nguzo Saba*, spiritualism, interdependence, transformative behaviors based on the principles of *Ma'at* and sociopolitical consciousness raising which reframed recovery as healing the larger community were incorporated into each aspect of the intervention (intake process, a meal, video, and 30-minute counseling session). The goal of this approach was the same as that of SBIRT – to make a successful referral for the individuals to receive additional services (Longshore et al., 1998).

Previous examples of African-centered practice approaches among African Americans have and continue to demonstrate high effectiveness as a means to address substance use. Even when we look at treatment approaches across the life course, African-centered practice approaches have been developed and shown significant outcomes with the targeted population. For example, the NTU project was developed to decrease risk factors and increase protective factors among African American girls (Cherry et al., 1998). Moreover, the JEMADARI program was developed for African American men in residential treatment with the goal of reducing drug- and sexual risk-related behaviors. Similar to many of the African-centered practice approaches, the JEMADARI program was developed using the *Nguzo Saba* (Gilbert, Harvey, & Belgrave, 2009). Additional support for the use of the Afrocentric approach with substance use disorders has demonstrated treatment approaches with both adolescent males (Kalonji, 2014; Liddle, Jackson-Gilfort, & Marvel, 2006) and women (Poitier, Niliwaambieni, & Rowe, 1997). Moreover, the African-centered practice approach for substance use disorders has been adapted to both inpatient residential and outpatient treatment (Jackson et al., 1997). Given the large number of African Americans who are impacted by substance use and the limited information currently available regarding African-centered prevention and treatment approaches for substance use, program development and implementation should be a primary goal to move these programs toward obtaining evidence-based status. This would be inclusive of rigorous research agenda which evaluates the overall effectiveness of these programs.

Conclusion

This chapter highlighted the benefits and utilization of African-centered practice approaches and the focus on the prevention and treatment of substance use across the life course. While there is a clear understanding of the complex issues associated with continued substance use, there are tools which could increase help-seeking and overall engagement. The utilization of these culturally relevant and trauma-responsive approaches are a great place to start as we focus on decreasing substance use among African Americans. As we close out this chapter, it is important to note that the proposed practice approaches do not address the full continuum of substance use treatment. One area that continues to be unaddressed within the

African-centered practice approach is that of substance use recovery. According to SAMHSA, recovery is "a process of change through which individuals improve their health and wellness, live self-directed lives, and strive to reach their full potential"(Lizardi & Stanley, 2010). Given that recovery is a significant milestone in the substance use treatment continuum, researchers and treatment providers should work to develop an African-centered practice approach that addresses the concept of recovery in substance use. One such approach that is utilized is the general recovery community recovery-oriented care. This approach utilizes four dimensions (promoting citizenship, organizational commitment, supporting personally defined goals, and strong working relationships) which could integrate well with an African-centered practice approach. Another aspect that should be explored as a recovery concept is the use of 12-step/self-help groups. Given the high degree of spirituality and community with this recovery framework, principles of the *Nguzo Saba* and *Ma'at* could be integrated to move this approach toward a more African-centered practice approach.

References

Alexander, M. (2010). The war on drugs and the New Jim Crow. *Race, Poverty & the Environment, 17*(1), 75–77.

Babor, T. F., McRee, B. G., Kassebaum, P. A., Grimaldi, P. L., Ahmed, K., & Bray, J. (2007). Screening, Brief Intervention, and Referral to Treatment (SBIRT) toward a public health approach to the management of substance abuse. *Substance Abuse, 28*(3), 7–30.

Barati, M., Bashirian, S., Mohammadi, Y., Moeini, B., Mousali, A., & Afshari, M. (2021). An ecological approach to exploring factors affecting substance use relapse: A systematic review. *Journal of Public Health*, 1–14.

Cherry, V. R., Belgrave, F. Z., Jones, W., Kennon, D. K., Gray, F. S., & Phillips, F. (1998). NTU: An Africentric approach to substance abuse prevention among African American youth. *Journal of Primary Prevention, 18*(3), 319–339.

Chipungu, S. S., Herman, J., Sambrano, S., Nistler, M., Sale, E., & Springer, J. F. (2000). Prevention programming for African American youth: A review of strategies in CSAP's national cross-site evaluation of high-risk youth programs. *Journal of Black Psychology, 26*, 360–385.

Christmon, K. (1995). Historical overview of alcohol in the African American community. *Journal of Black Studies, 25*(3), 318–330.

Gilbert, D. J., Harvey, A. R., & Belgrave, F. Z. (2009). Advancing the Africentric paradigm shift discourse: Building toward evidence-based Africentric interventions in social work practice with African Americans. *Social Work, 54*(3), 243–252.

Ginwright, S. (2018). The future of healing: Shifting from trauma informed care to healing centered engagement. *Occasional Paper, 25*.

Green, H. D. (2018). A community-based evaluation of screening, brief intervention, and referral to treatment (SBIRT) for the Black community. *Qualitative Health Research, 28*(3), 418–432.

Harvey, A. R., & Hill, R. B. (2004). Africentric youth and family rites of passage program: Promoting resilience among at-risk African American youths. *Social Work, 49*(1), 65–74.

Hodge, D. R., Jackson, K. F., & Vaughn, M. G. (2012). Culturally sensitive interventions and substance use: A meta-analytic review of outcomes among minority youths. *Social Work Research, 36*(1), 11–19.

Jackson, M. S., Stephens, R. C., & Smith, R. L. (1997). Afrocentric treatment in residential substance abuse care: The Iwo San. *Journal of Substance Abuse Treatment, 14*(1), 87–92.

Jones, N. L., Gilman, S. E., Cheng, T. L., Drury, S. S., Hill, C. V., & Geronimus, A. T. (2019). Life course approaches to the causes of health disparities. *American Journal of Public Health, 109*(S1), S48–S55.

Kalonji, T. (2014). The Nguzo Saba & Maat, a path for self-reconstruction and recoveredness: Exploring a Kawaida paradigm for healing addiction in the black community. *Journal of Pan African Studies, 7*(4).

Krebs, P., Norcross, J. C., Nicholson, J. M., & Prochaska, J. O. (2018). Stages of change and psychotherapy outcomes: A review and meta-analysis. *Journal of Clinical Psychology, 74*(11), 1964–1979.

Liddle, H. A., Jackson-Gilfort, A., & Marvel, F. A. (2006). An empirically supported and culturally specific engagement and intervention strategy for African American adolescent males. *American Journal of Orthopsychiatry, 76*(2), 215.

Lizardi, D., & Stanley, B. (2010). Treatment engagement: A neglected aspect in the psychiatric care of suicidal patients. *Psychiatric Services, 61*(12), 1183–1191.

Longshore, D., Grills, C., Annon, K., & Grady, R. (1998). Promoting recovery from drug abuse: An Africentric intervention. *Journal of Black Studies, 28*(3), 319–333.

Lusane, C., & Desmond, D. (1991). *Pipe dream blues: Racism and the war on drugs.* Cambridge, MA: South End Press.

Manuel, J. K., Satre, D. D., Tsoh, J., Moreno-John, G., Ramos, J. S., McCance-Katz, E. F., & Satterfield, J. M. (2015). Adapting screening, brief intervention and referral to treatment (SBIRT) for alcohol and drugs to culturally diverse clinical populations. *Journal of Addiction Medicine, 9*(5), 343.

National Institute on Drug Abuse. (2003). *Preventing drug abuse among children and adolescents: A research based guide for parents, educators, and community leaders.* Washington, DC: U.S. Department of Health and Human Services.

Poitier, V., Niliwaambieni, M., & Rowe, C. L. (1997). A rite of passage approach designed to preserve the families of substance-abusing African American women. *Child Welfare Perspectives: Serving African American children,* 169–191.

Schiele, J. H. (1996). Afrocentricity: An emerging paradigm in social work practice. *Social Work, 41*(3), 284–294.

Schiele, J. H. (2000). *Human services and the Afrocentric paradigm.* London: Psychology Press.

Shelton, R. C., Cooper, B. R., & Stirman, S. W. (2018). The sustainability of evidence-based interventions and practices in public health and health care. *Annual Review of Public Health, 39,* 55–76.

Substance Abuse and Mental Health Services Administration. (2020). Behavioral health barometer: United States, Volume 6: Indicators as measured through the 2019 National Survey on Drug Use and Health and the National Survey of Substance Abuse Treatment Services. HHS Publication No. PEP20-07-02-001. Rockville, MD: Substance Abuse and Mental Health Services Administration.

U.S. Department of Health and Human Services, Substance Abuse and Mental Health Services Administration, Center for Behavioral Health Statistics and Quality. (2020). *National Survey on Drug Use and Health 2016* (NSDUH-2016-DS0001). Retrieved from https://datafiles.samhsa.gov/

Verissimo, A. D. O., & Grella, C. E. (2017). Influence of gender and race/ethnicity on perceived barriers to help-seeking for alcohol or drug problems. *Journal of Substance Abuse Treatment, 75,* 54–61.

15

ADDRESSING HIV/AIDS IN THE BLACK COMMUNITY

Examining culturally responsive approaches

Jordan White, Anthony Estreet

HIV/AIDS has been a public health concern in the Black community for several decades dating back to the early 1980s, when Black people accounted for 12% of the U.S. population but accounted for more than a quarter of reported AIDS cases (Center for Disease Control, 2015; Crepaz, Dong, Wang, Hernandez, & Hall, 2018). It was not until 1998 that the Congressional Black Caucus (CBC) chaired by Congresswoman Maxine Waters (D-CA) declared the impact of HIV/AIDS in the Black community as a "a national crisis" (Arya, Behforouz, & Viswanath, 2009; Perry-Mitchell & Davis-Maye, 2017). As a result of ongoing advocacy, President Clinton launched the Minority HIV/AIDS initiative with substantial funding support and also declared HIV/AIDS to be a "severe and ongoing crisis" in the Black community (Arya et al., 2009).

At the time the "national crisis" was declared, the Center for Disease Control (CDC) reported that 162,193 Black Americans were living with HIV/AIDS in the United States while another 141,607 Black Americans had died from AIDS-related conditions. These numbers represented an overwhelming majority of Black women who made up an alarming 60% of HIV/AIDS cases among women (Perry-Mitchell & Davis-Maye, 2017). Almost 20 years later, and despite President Obama establishing the National HIV/AIDS strategy which provides increased federal support, these health disparities continue to persist. According to the CDC, Black Americans make up only 13% of the U.S. population, however, they account for nearly 42% (16,002) of all new HIV diagnoses in the United States and dependent areas. Furthermore, while women in general accounted for approximately 20% of new HIV cases in 2018, Black women accounted for 57% of those new diagnoses among women. Similarly, yet alarming statistics show that Black men who have sex with men (BMSM) are more affected by HIV than any other group in the United States and dependent areas. In 2018, BMSM accounted for 26% of the 37,968 new

DOI: 10.4324/9780429276613-19

HIV diagnoses and 37% of new diagnoses among all gay and bisexual men. These new diagnoses among BMSM primarily occurred between the ages of 13 and 34.

Consequently, these numbers look just as staggering in the mental health arena for Black Americans. According to the U.S. Department of Health and Human Services Office of Minority Health, suicide was the second leading cause of death for Black Americans aged 15–24 while the death rate from suicide for Black men was four times greater than that of Black women. Moreover, Black adults in the United States are more likely than white adults to report persistent symptoms of emotional distress, such as sadness, hopelessness, and feeling like everything is an effort. Black adults living below the poverty line are more than twice as likely to report serious psychological distress as those with more financial security. In 2018, 18.6% of white Americans received mental health services, compared to less than 9% of Black Americans. Similarly, more than 70% of white Americans received treatment after a major depressive episode compared to 61% of Black Americans. People living with HIV/AIDS (PLWHA) often have co-occurring behavioral health concerns such as mental health, trauma, substance abuse, or any combination of these factors in addition to additional health concerns. According to the National Institute of Mental Health (NIMH), having a diagnosis of HIV/AIDS and the associated stress of living with a serious illness can lead to a higher likelihood of developing a mood, anxiety, or cognitive disorder. These staggering statistics highlight the continuing issues regarding HIV/AIDS health disparities in the United States and the need for more culturally relevant and trauma-responsive interventions to address HIV/AIDS and the co-occurring conditions that occur within the Black community. This chapter will explore and discuss existing HIV/AIDS-related prevention and intervention strategies to utilize within the Black community. A special focus will be placed on those groups that are impacted most by HIV/AIDS which include BMSM and Black women. This chapter is meant to serve as a call to action and bring to light the importance of utilizing culturally responsive HIV-related interventions to address the staggering statistics related to HIV incidence and prevalence among Black Americans. Moreover, these identified approaches will incorporate the complex co-occurring issues such as mental health, substance use, poverty, racism, and discrimination, as well as stigma.

Advancing HIV/AIDS practice: an African-centered ecological systems approach

Complex issues such as the examination of health disparities related to HIV/AIDS in the Black community can benefit from a conceptual framework.

This framework helps to organize various factors and principles which can be applied to a model to create and communicate a better understanding of a concept. Within the area of African-centered practice with HIV/AIDS, this approach acknowledges the various levels of the systems perspective which include micro-, mezzo-, and macro-level factors and the overarching principles of African-centered practice. It acknowledges that interventions can occur at various levels and that

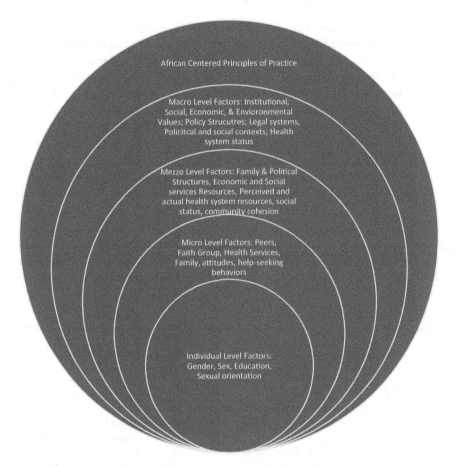

FIGURE 15.1   An African-centered ecological systems approach for understanding HIV/AIDS in Black Americans

barriers can also impact the implementation of these interventions at various levels. Within this approach, micro-level factors include gender, sex, education, sexual orientation, attitudes, help-seeking behaviors, etc. Mezzo-level factors include family and political structures, economic and social service resources, perceived and actual health system resources, social status and community cohesion, and perceptions of health systems. At the macro level, higher-level constructs such as institutional, social, economic, and environmental values, policy structures, and political and social contexts as well as health system status can impact interventions.

As we continue to address the issue of HIV/AIDS in the Black community, it is imperative to use a framework that is inclusive of all the levels and influences that can impact health outcomes and decision-making. An African-centered ecological systems approach takes many of these variables into account and also recognizes that these variables are often interconnected. Many of the health disparities that

Black Americans experience related to HIV/AIDS are typically a combination of many of these factors, such as poverty, racism, stigma, discrimination in health care system, medical mistrust, and access but also takes into consideration individual health decisions, perceptions of the health care system and risky behaviors (Bogart, Ransome, Allen, Higgins-Biddle, & Ojikutu, 2019). As we continue to develop, adapt, and implement HIV prevention and intervention measures, we must also ensure that these approaches are culturally responsive and inclusive of many of the principles and values that are found in the Black community. One such model (Table 15.1) that explores this approach is HIV/AIDS Risk Reduction among Heterosexually Active African American Men and Women (HIV-RAAP), a seven-session coeducational curriculum that incorporates cultural and gender sensitivity (Yancey et al., 2012). It is also important to note that many African-centered practice models have historically utilized trauma-informed care principles such as safety, trustworthiness and transparency, peer/mutual support, collaboration and mutuality, empowerment, voice, and choice, as well as cultural, historical, and gender issues. Many African-centered practice approaches understand the importance of

TABLE 15.1 An African-Centered Ecological Systems Approach for understanding HIV/AIDS in Black Americans

Sessions	Principle and Theory	Learning Objectives
1 Culture- and gender-related issues	• *Nguzo Saba*: *Kujichagulia* – self-determination • NTU • Theory of gender and power	★ List and understand the *Nguzo Saba* principles ★ Discuss cultural fit of African American men and women in their communities ★ Define gender roles as men and women ★ Identify personal values as African American men and women
2 HIV risk knowledge	• *Nguzo Saba*: *Nia* – purpose • NTU • Theory of gender and power	★ Define HIV and HIV-related concepts ★ Discuss the effect of HIV on participants' lives as African American men and women ★ Learn methods of self-protection from HIV/AIDS infection ★ Learn methods to assist partners in protecting themselves
3 Risk reductio behavior interventions	• *Nguzo Saba*: *Ujima* – collective work and responsibility • Theory of gender and power	★ Determine levels of personal risk for HIV and other STDs ★ Identify and discuss personal beliefs and attitudes about HIV ★ Identify ways to express views about positive sexual health practices

	Sessions	Principle and Theory	Learning Objectives
4	Condom barrier beliefs	• *Nguzo Saba: Kuumba* – creativity • Theory of gender and power	⋆ Discuss reasons why men and women choose to use or not use condoms ⋆ Identify relationship expectations of African American men and women ⋆ Identify ways to achieve sexual satisfaction using safer sex methods
5	Conversations with partners about condoms and AIDS concerns	• *Nguzo Saba: Imani* – faith • NTU • Theory of gender and power	⋆ Communicate and practice condom negotiation skills ⋆ Identify personal causes of unsafe sexual practices ⋆ Increase self-esteem in condom use communication
6	Safer sex peer norms	• *Nguzo Saba: Ujamaa* – cooperative economics • NTU • Theory of gender and power	⋆ Increase understanding of worldview on sex ⋆ Increase understanding of worldview on sex and the influence on personal sexual decisions ⋆ Increase awareness of African American men's and women's attitudes regarding sex
7	Celebration of unity and love	• Nguzo Saba: *Umoja* – unity • NTU	⋆ Identify methods to increase personal bond and support with partner ⋆ Identify problems, economic challenges, and social benefits that affect healthy lifestyles for African Americans ⋆ Identify methods to create a support network

addressing the historical traumas as well as the current complexities of many health and behavioral health issues.

HIV and BMSM

Reducing HIV infections among African Americans in the United States, and especially among BMSM, ranks among the nation's top public health priorities and is part of the national HIV/AIDS strategy (The White House Office of National AIDS Policy, 2010). According to research, Black men in the United States have the lowest life expectancy of all populations and have the highest rates of HIV mortality (Bond & Herman, 2016; Cunningham et al., 2017; Pathak, 2018). This is a long-standing inequity (Ransome, Kawachi, Braunstein, & Nash, 2016). In the fourth decade of the HIV epidemic, BMSM continue to be the population most affected by HIV/AIDS in the United States. HIV provides an important lens for understanding the health of BMSM as it is a health context often studied among sexual minority populations (Matthews et al., 2016; Maulsby et al., 2013; Oldenburg, Perez-Brumer, Reisner, & Mimiaga, 2015). BMSM are less than 1% of the U.S. population, but accounted for 26.1% of all HIV diagnoses and 59.9% of diagnoses among Blacks/African Americans in 2015 (Control & Prevention, 2015). The HIV care continuum is a model that outlines the steps or stages of HIV medical care from diagnosis to the goal of viral suppression (Skarbinski et al., 2015). It also shows the proportion of individuals living with HIV who are engaged in care at each stage. Compared to white MSM living with HIV, Black MSM are half as likely as to be retained in care. At every step of the HIV care continuum there are disparities in care between Black and white MSM.

BMSM face a one-in-two lifetime risk of HIV, and engagements in HIV prevention and care are often poor among BMSM (Hess, Hu, Lansky, Mermin, & Hall, 2017; Hoots, Finlayson, Wejnert, Paz-Bailey, & Group, 2017). Sustained viral suppression is critical for addressing HIV disparities (Hess et al., 2018). However, BMSM populations in particular are less likely to have sustained viral suppression compared to Latino MSM or White MSM (Crepaz et al., 2018). While 75% of BMSM have been diagnosed with HIV, only 16% are estimated to be virally suppressed compared to 34% of white MSM (Rosenberg, Millett, Sullivan, Del Rio, & Curran, 2014). Linkage and retention to HIV care require that patients navigate a series of complicated processes. Barriers for successful linkage to care exist at multiple levels (e.g. individual, interpersonal, community, and policy levels) (Herce, Chi, Liao, & Hoffmann, 2019; White, Yang, Tobin, Beyrer, & Latkin, 2020). BMSM will likely face challenges to linkage or retention in HIV care at some point in their lives (Levy et al., 2014; Singh, Mitsch, & Wu, 2017). Evidence suggests that improving HIV care outcomes is urgently needed for BMSM, but strategies are needed to address individual, psychosocial, and structural challenges or adversity hindering these outcomes.

Barriers to HIV/AIDS prevention and care contributing to the high rates of HIV infection among BMSM include sexually transmitted infections (STIs), unknown HIV serostatus (HIV testing), and adherence to antiretroviral therapy. Having an STI can significantly increase the chance of getting or transmitting HIV and HIV-positive individuals have higher risk for comorbidities and disease-related events than HIV-negative individuals (Alonso et al., 2019). These documented gaps inform health inequity among BMSM. Experiences of stigma, discrimination, marginalization, and negative cultural perceptions of homosexuality are documented factors that elevate BMSM's vulnerability to HIV infection. Previous studies have found that medical mistrust of the health care system, providers, public health officials, researchers, and/or the pharmaceutical industry is prevalent among BMSM (Cahill et al., 2017). Blacks and Hispanics on average have higher levels of distrust of physicians than do whites (Bogart et al., 2019; Kinlock et al., 2017). Distrust may lead to suboptimal HIV adherence.

Evidence-based African-centered HIV/AIDS practice models and prevention interventions among BMSM

Clearly, more attention needs to be focused on preventing HIV among BMSM given that BMSM continue to be disproportionately affected. An extensive body of literature grounded in fundamental cause theory suggests that programs should focus on "upstream" social and economic determinants as they relate to ethnic minority and LGBT health disparities for effective prevention and control of syndemic conditions (Bränström, Hatzenbuehler, Pachankis, & Link, 2016; Khan, Ilcisin, & Saxton, 2017). Multiple factors can co-occur and function synergistically to propagate HIV-related risk behaviors. To this end, social and behavioral interventions remain a critical component of HIV prevention efforts in the United States for BMSM (Maulsby et al., 2013). Common interventions and practice models used to address HIV among BMSM include HIV prevention health communication, peer support for HIV prevention, linkage to care and adherence. Many of the interventions and preventions activities are informed by BMSM and other community stakeholders (McCree et al., 2016). These factors have implications for how interventions and other activities for BMSM are targeted/tailored and delivered.

HIV interventions utilize a variety of channels and platforms to reach and disseminate information. Channels most often fall within the broader categories of interpersonal, community, mass media, and the internet (Noar, Palmgreen, Chabot, Dobransky, & Zimmerman, 2009). Interpersonal channels include individual or group educational and counseling sessions, workshops, small group discussions, and peer education. Community channels sometimes include an interpersonal component but often include outreach (conducted in person or by distributing print materials such as posters) in public venues, including gay pride events, bars, clubs, bathhouses, organizations, and testing centers. Mass media channels include newspapers, public service announcements (PSAs), and videos, among others. The internet provides for a number of web-based activities and tailored content. Using multiple channels may be helpful when trying to reach BMSM who do not identify as gay because they often do not frequent gay venues or seek out gay media or venues (McCree et al., 2016).

Programs also tap into existing community networks to increase credibility by disseminating prevention messages through respected community members. HIV prevention programs among BMSM have reported greater success when collaborating with respected community members and influential community organizations (Grieb, Donovan, White, Miller, & Dangerfield, 2020). Peers in the community or at organizations may assist or guide individuals through and around barriers in the complex cancer care system to help ensure timely diagnosis and treatment. BMSM peers can serve as examples or role models. In addition, they can support other BMSM in addressing challenges along the HIV care continuum and other environment/social determinant-related challenges. The following are examples of African-centered, evidence-based HIV prevention intervention specifically designed to address HIV/AIDS among BMSM:

1. *Many Men, Many Voices* (3MV) is a seven-session group-level intervention developed to prevent HIV and sexually transmitted diseases (STDs) among BMSM who may or may not identify themselves as gay. The intervention addresses factors that influence the behavior of BMSM: cultural, social, and religious norms; interactions between HIV and other STDs; sexual relationship dynamics; and the social influences that racism and homophobia have on HIV risk behaviors (Wilton et al., 2009). The goal of this intervention is to reduce unprotected insertive and receptive anal intercourse; reduced number of sex partners, increase consistent condom use, and increase testing for HIV and other STIs.

2. *D-UP: Defend Yourself!* is an efficacious community-level HIV prevention intervention for BMSM and addresses racism and homophobia and targeting the shifting of social and behavioral norms within the BMSM community. D-UP is a cultural adaptation of the *Popular Opinion Leader intervention* (POL) and is designed to change social norms and perceptions of BMSM regarding condom use. The intervention involves identifying well-liked "popular opinion leaders" or "POLs" in the BMSM community and training them on safer sex strategies. The intention of this intervention is that the POLs will use their innovation/social influence principles to diffuse their knowledge to others in one-on-one or small group conversations with peers (Jones et al., 2008). The goal of this intervention is to increase condom use with main and other sex partners among BMSM.

3. **Connect HIP** is an evidence-based intervention adapted for substance-using BMSM couples, originally developed for heterosexual couples *"Connect" (Wu et al., 2011)*. *Connect HIP* is a relationship-based intervention that teaches couples techniques and skills to enhance their quality of their relationship, communication, and shared commitment to safety and health. This intervention is based on the AIDS Risk Reduction Model which organizes behavior change into three phases – recognize risk, commitment to change, and act on strategies. It utilizes the ecological perspective which emphasizes the personal, relational, and societal influences on behavior. There is strong evidence from white male couples that HIV infection often occurs within primary relationships. MSM are more likely to engage in condom-less anal intercourse with primary partners than with outside partners (Frost, Stirratt, & Ouellette, 2008; Jin et al., 2009). Intervening with couples can offer advantages over individual interventions, including encouraging mutual responsibility and support for the partners to remain healthy using health promotion and risk reduction strategies. To date, there are few interventions designed to promote and motivate couples to engage in couples-care or couples-based prevention. Research in this area may reduce the burden and impact of HIV on BMSM couples. This research is vital for addressing health disparities among Black male populations in the United States.

BMSM continue to be at high risk for acquiring and transmitting HIV, yet very few interventions exist to address their unique prevention and intervention needs. Utilizing culturally responsive interventions that incorporate African-centered principles could be a way to engage, connect, and retain these men into the care continuum. Consequently, these interventions do not address the larger systematic challenges such as health care discrimination, stigma, and racism. However, these interventions could provide these men with the tools necessary to navigate and cope with the challenges associated with accessing care and prevention measures for HIV.

Evidence-based African-centered HIV/AIDS practice models and prevention interventions among Black women

As previously mentioned, Black women also continue to be disproportionately impacted by HIV. Research has shown that Black women account for approximately 60% of new HIV infections among US women, despite being less than 15% of the female population. In addition, the rates of sexually transmitted infections are highest among Black women and are consistently increasing. Similar to BMSM, Black women would benefit from culturally responsive prevention and treatment interventions that take into account the myriad of factors that contribute to poor health outcomes. According to research, Black women who have a history of criminal justice involvement are at significantly higher risk for acquiring an STI. Given these high rates of HIV incidence and prevalence among Black women, there needs to be more development, evaluation, and implementation of evidence-based culturally responsive prevention and treatment interventions to significantly reduce and potentially end HIV and the co-occurring conditions that often occur.

Drawing on the African-centered ecological systems approach, there are several approaches that have been developed to address and respond to HIV among Black women. Consistent with much of the previous African-centered practice work, many of these interventions were designed utilizing the seven principles of *Nguzo Saba* which are *Umoja* (Unity), *Kujichagulia* (Self-Determination), *Ujima* (collective work & responsibility), *Ujamma* (cooperative economics), *Nia* (purpose), *Kuumba* (creativity), and *Imani* (faith). Many of the *Nguzo Saba* principles are critical for the development of a culturally responsive intervention, which also allows for individuals to heal from systemic issues such as racism, discrimination, trauma, and stigma. The following are examples of culturally responsive approaches that incorporate African-centered and trauma-informed care principles.

1. *Healer Women Fighting Disease* **(HWFD)** is an African-centered, individual- and group-level intervention focused on HIV and substance use prevention with emphasis on self-love, wholeness, and cultural realignment. The target group is African American women between ages 13 and 55 who are

at risk of contracting and transmitting HIV through unsafe sexual activity and substance abuse. Utilizing the African-Centered Behavioral Change Model (ACBSCM) of *culturecology*, this intervention is based on the premise that behavior change must be grounded in an understanding of one's own culture which occurs through resocialization and culturalization. According to Nobles, Goddard, and Gilbert (2009), through the resocialization and culturalization process, prosocial and affirming conditions such as cultural pride and collectivity decrease the effects of the negative social conditions such as institutional racism, gender oppression, and economic inequities. The outcomes related to this intervention include increasing knowledge, attitudes, beliefs, and intentions related to HIV/AIDS and risky sexual behaviors, improved attitudes toward drug use, increased self-worth, decreased hopelessness, and depression.

2. *Sisters Informing Sisters about Topics on AIDS (SISTA) Project* is a small-group, gender-relevant, culturally sensitive group program for African American women designed to be implemented in a community setting. Based on social cognitive theory and the theory of gender and power, SISTA seeks to prevent HIV transmission by promoting consistent condom usage, increased sexual behavior self-control, increased sexual communication, and increased sexual assertiveness skills. Using a peer-led approach, peer health educators lead five two-hour sessions, focusing first on ethnic and gender pride, then moving on to provide knowledge about HIV/AIDS and skills training to promote sexual safety.

3. **Horizons** is a group-level, gender and culturally tailored evidence-based practice that is focused on addressing HIV/STI among Black American adolescent females seeking health services. The Horizons intervention is grounded in social cognitive theory and the theory of gender and power. It comprises two group sessions (4 hours each) and four phone calls (15 minutes each). The overall goal of the intervention is to reduce HIV and sexually transmitted infections, increase condom use, increase communication with male partners about safer sex choices, and increase male partners accessing STI services.

Many of the aforementioned evidence-based interventions for both BMSM and Black women are readily available for use and implementation. Consequently, many of these culturally responsive interventions are passed over for the larger scale "one size fits all" approach that is often taken by many large hospitals and treatment organizations. In order to make a significant impact addressing HIV/AIDS within the Black community, more specifically among BMSM and Black women who have a greater likelihood for becoming infected, we have to continue to replicate and adapt existing interventions as well as develop new ones. As social workers and health practitioners, it is imperative that we continue to contribute to the existing literature through the dissemination and application of these culturally responsive treatment interventions.

Moving forward with African-centered practice approaches to address HIV/AIDS among Black Americans

A part of the national policy to end the epidemic, social workers and health professionals have to consider the benefits of multidimensional approaches to address HIV/AIDS in the Black community. As described in the African-centered ecological systems approach, many of the challenges faced by Black Americans in addressing HIV/AIDS occur at varying levels from individuals all the way to macro-level issues such as institutional racism and policy. At the federal level, there needs to be a comprehensive shift in how we approach the HIV care continuums with regard to Black Americans. We need to reconsider messaging regarding pre-exposure prophylaxis (PrEP) and testing as well as prevention and interventions approaches. The use of approaches such as popular opinion leaders lends itself to the African-centered practice framework because it relies on the community to be a part of the solution to the issue of HIV/AIDS. Moreover, the POL approach can mitigate some of the barriers to testing and treatment such as medical mistrust, stigma, and institutional racism. Overall, this chapter highlighted the work that is being done in the HIV/AIDS arena to be more culturally responsive to the needs of the Black community. The African-centered evidence-based interventions highlighted in this chapter demonstrate a growing body of work that is being developed and disseminated to address a critical issue within the Black community. However, the continued overrepresentation of cases among Black Americans with regard to incidence and prevalence specifically among BMSM and Black women indicate much needs to improve with utilization of these interventions and addressing the complexities of HIV/AIDS within the Black community.

References

Alonso, A., Barnes, A. E., Guest, J. L., Shah, A., Shao, I. Y., & Marconi, V. (2019). HIV infection and incidence of cardiovascular diseases: An analysis of a large healthcare database. *Journal of the American Heart Association, 8*(14), e012241.

Arya, M., Behforouz, H. L., & Viswanath, K. (2009). African American women and HIV/AIDS: A national call for targeted health communication strategies to address a disparity. *The AIDS Reader, 19*(2), 79–C3.

Bogart, L. M., Ransome, Y., Allen, W., Higgins-Biddle, M., & Ojikutu, B. O. (2019). HIV-related medical mistrust, HIV testing, and HIV risk in the National Survey on HIV in the Black Community. *Behavioral Medicine, 45*(2), 134–142.

Bond, M. J., & Herman, A. A. (2016). Lagging life expectancy for Black men: A public health imperative. *American Public Health Association, 106,* 1167–1169. https://doi.org/10.2105/AJPH.2016.303251

Bränström, R., Hatzenbuehler, M. L., Pachankis, J. E., & Link, B. G. (2016). Sexual orientation disparities in preventable disease: A fundamental cause perspective. *American Journal of Public Health, 106*(6), 1109–1115.

Cahill, S., Taylor, S. W., Elsesser, S. A., Mena, L., Hickson, D., & Mayer, K. H. (2017). Stigma, medical mistrust, and perceived racism may affect PrEP awareness and uptake in black compared to white gay and bisexual men in Jackson, Mississippi and Boston, Massachusetts. *AIDS Care, 29*(11), 1351–1358.

Control, C. f. D., & Prevention. (2015). HIV surveillance report: Diagnoses of HIV infection in the United States and dependent areas, 2015. *Atlanta, GA, 500*, 25.

Crepaz, N., Dong, X., Wang, X., Hernandez, A. L., & Hall, H. I. (2018). Racial and ethnic disparities in sustained viral suppression and transmission risk potential among persons receiving HIV care – United States, 2014. *Morbidity and Mortality Weekly Report, 67*(4), 113.

Cunningham, T. J., Croft, J. B., Liu, Y., Lu, H., Eke, P. I., & Giles, W. H. (2017). Vital signs: Racial disparities in age-specific mortality among blacks or African Americans – United States, 1999–2015. *MMWR. Morbidity and mortality Weekly Report, 66*(17), 444.

Frost, D. M., Stirratt, M. J., & Ouellette, S. C. (2008). Understanding why gay men seek HIV-seroconcordant partners: Intimacy and risk reduction motivations. *Culture, Health & Sexuality, 10*(5), 513–527.

Grieb, S. M., Donovan, E., White, J. J., Miller, D., & Dangerfield, D. T. (2020). Increasing opportunities for spiritual and religious supports to improve HIV-related outcomes for Black sexual minority men. *Journal of Urban Health*, 1–11.

Herce, M. E., Chi, B. H., Liao, R. C., & Hoffmann, C. J. (2019). Re-thinking linkage to care in the era of universal test and treat: Insights from implementation and behavioral science for achieving the second 90. *AIDS and Behavior*, 1–9.

Hess, K. L., Hu, X., Lansky, A., Mermin, J., & Hall, H. I. (2017). Lifetime risk of a diagnosis of HIV infection in the United States. *Annals of Epidemiology, 27*(4), 238–243.

Hess, K., Johnson, A. S., Hu, X., Li, J., Wu, B., Yu, C., Zhu, H., . . . et al. (2016). Diagnoses of HIV infection in the United States and dependent areas, 2016. *HIV Surveillance Report, 2*(28), 1–125. Retrieved from http://www.cdc.gov/hiv/library/reports/hiv-surveillance.html

Hoots, B. E., Finlayson, T. J., Wejnert, C., Paz-Bailey, G., & Group, N. H. B. S. S. (2017). Updated data on linkage to human immunodeficiency virus care and antiretroviral treatment among men who have sex with men – 20 cities, United States. *The Journal of Infectious Diseases, 216*(7), 808–812.

Jin, F., Crawford, J., Prestage, G. P., Zablotska, I., Imrie, J., Kippax, S. C., . . . Grulich, A. E. (2009). Unprotected anal intercourse, risk reduction behaviours, and subsequent HIV infection in a cohort of homosexual men. *Aids, 23*(2), 243–252.

Jones, K. T., Gray, P., Whiteside, Y. O., Wang, T., Bost, D., Dunbar, E., . . . Johnson, W. D. (2008). Evaluation of an HIV prevention intervention adapted for Black men who have sex with men. *American Journal of Public Health, 98*(6), 1043–1050.

Khan, M., Ilcisin, M., & Saxton, K. (2017). Multifactorial discrimination as a fundamental cause of mental health inequities. *International Journal for Equity in Health, 16*(1), 43.

Kinlock, B. L., Parker, L. J., Bowie, J. V., Howard, D. L., LaVeist, T. A., & Thorpe Jr, R. J. (2017). *High levels of medical mistrust are associated with low quality of life among black and white men with prostate cancer*. Los Angeles, CA: Sage Publications.

Levy, M. E., Wilton, L., Phillips, G., Glick, S. N., Kuo, I., Brewer, R. A., . . . Magnus, M. (2014). Understanding structural barriers to accessing HIV testing and prevention services among black men who have sex with men (BMSM) in the United States. *AIDS and Behavior, 18*(5), 972–996.

Matthews, D. D., Herrick, A., Coulter, R. W., Friedman, M. R., Mills, T. C., Eaton, L. A., . . . Team, P. S. (2016). Running backwards: Consequences of current HIV incidence rates for the next generation of black MSM in the United States. *AIDS and Behavior, 20*(1), 7–16.

Maulsby, C., Millett, G., Lindsey, K., Kelley, R., Johnson, K., Montoya, D., & Holtgrave, D. (2013). A systematic review of HIV interventions for black men who have sex with men (MSM). *BMC Public Health, 13*(1), 625.

McCree, D. H., Beer, L., Prather, C., Gant, Z., Harris, N., Sutton, M., . . . Wortley, P. (2016). An Approach to Achieving the Health Equity Goals of the National HIV/AIDS Strategy for the United States Among Racial/Ethnic Minority Communities. *Public Health Reports, 131*(4), 526–530.

Noar, S. M., Palmgreen, P., Chabot, M., Dobransky, N., & Zimmerman, R. S. (2009). A 10-year systematic review of HIV/AIDS mass communication campaigns: Have we made progress? *Journal of Health Communication, 14*(1), 15–42.

Nobles, W. W., Goddard, L. L., & Gilbert, D. J. (2009). Culturecology, women, and African-centered HIV prevention. *Journal of Black Psychology, 35*(2), 228–246.

Oldenburg, C. E., Perez-Brumer, A. G., Reisner, S. L., & Mimiaga, M. J. (2015). Transactional sex and the HIV epidemic among men who have sex with men (MSM): Results from a systematic review and meta-analysis. *AIDS and Behavior, 19*(12), 2177–2183.

Pathak, E. B. (2018). Mortality among black men in the USA. *Journal of Racial and Ethnic Health Disparities, 5*(1), 50–61.

Perry-Mitchell, T., & Davis-Maye, D. (2017). Evidence-based African-centered HIV/AIDS prevention interventions: Best practices and opportunities. *Journal of Human Behavior in the Social Environment, 27*(1–2), 110–131.

Ransome, Y., Kawachi, I., Braunstein, S., & Nash, D. (2016). Structural inequalities drive late HIV diagnosis: The role of black racial concentration, income inequality, socioeconomic deprivation, and HIV testing. *Health & Place, 42*, 148–158.

Rosenberg, E. S., Millett, G. A., Sullivan, P. S., Del Rio, C., & Curran, J. W. (2014). Understanding the HIV disparities between black and white men who have sex with men in the USA using the HIV care continuum: A modelling study. *The Lancet HIV, 1*(3), e112–e118.

Singh, S., Mitsch, A., & Wu, B. (2017). HIV care outcomes among men who have sex with men with diagnosed HIV infection – United States, 2015. *MMWR. Morbidity and mortality weekly report, 66*(37), 969.

Skarbinski, J., Rosenberg, E., Paz-Bailey, G., Hall, H. I., Rose, C. E., Viall, A. H., . . . Mermin, J. H. (2015). Human immunodeficiency virus transmission at each step of the care continuum in the United States. *JAMA Internal Medicine, 175*(4), 588–596.

The White House Office of National AIDS Policy. (2010, July). *National HIV/AIDS strategy for the United States*. Retrieved March 9, 2021, from https://www.hiv.gov/federal-response/national-hiv-aids-strategy/overviewexternal icon

White, J. J., Yang, C., Tobin, K. E., Beyrer, C., & Latkin, C. A. (2020). Individual and social network factors associated with high self-efficacy of communicating about men's health issues with peers among black MSM in an urban setting. *Journal of Urban Health, 97*(5), 668–678.

Wilton, L., Herbst, J. H., Coury-Doniger, P., Painter, T. M., English, G., Alvarez, M. E., . . . Johnson, W. D. (2009). Efficacy of an HIV/STI prevention intervention for black men who have sex with men: Findings from the manymen, manyvoices (3MV) Project. *AIDS and Behavior, 13*(3), 532–544.

Wu, E., El-Bassel, N., McVinney, L. D., Hess, L., Remien, R. H., Charania, M., & Mansergh, G. (2011). Feasibility and promise of a couple-based HIV/STI preventive intervention for methamphetamine-using, black men who have sex with men. *AIDS and Behavior, 15*(8), 1745.

Yancey, E. M., Mayberry, R., Armstrong-Mensah, E., Collins, D., Goodin, L., Cureton, S., . . . Yuan, K. (2012). The community-based participatory intervention effect of "HIV-RAAP". *American Journal of Health Behavior, 36*(4), 555–568. https://doi.org/10.5993/AJHB.36.4.12

16

INCARCERATION

The new slavery

Janeen Cross and Natalie Muñoz

There has never been a time in American history when the economy did not benefit from the forced labor of African Americans (Bauer, 2018). Specifically, in the south many prison systems grew as a direct result of slavery (Bauer, 2018; Hairston, 2013). After slavery was abolished, the cotton and sugar industries struggled economically without the forced labor of African Americans (Bauer, 2018; Hairston, 2013). While the Thirteenth Amendment abolished slavery it also permitted forced labor as a punishment for a crime (Bauer, 2018; Hairston, 2013).

In order to maintain white superiority, Black Codes were passed to outlaw the simplest of activities performed by African Americans (Hairston, 2013). For example, African Americans were imprisoned for trying to board a train, strolling the street in the evening, or for being unemployed (Hairston, 2013). Whites manipulated these unjust paradigms of African men to perpetuate typecasts that framed African American men as lazy (Hairston, 2013). As long as Black men were criminalized, southern states could lease all of their prisoners to private cotton and sugar plantations (Bauer, 2018). Convict leasing also created incentives for governments to arrest and convict newly freed Black men in order to sell their labor to private companies (Hairston, 2013). Convict leasing was the evolution of slavery. In addition, Jim Crow laws placed further restrictions on African Americans to increase the probability of extending this evolutionary form of slavery and reinforcing white superiority and Black inferiority in America (Hairston, 2013). Most importantly, the formalized structure and operations of these systems set the stage for what is now the United States prison system (Hairston, 2013).

Disproportionality, inequality, and oppression

Impoverished people of color have been disproportionately imprisoned in the United States (Crutchfield & Weeks, 2015). Since 1970, the imprisonment rate

DOI: 10.4324/9780429276613-20

in the United States has more than quadrupled (Morsy & Rothstein, 2016). The United States imprisons the highest percentage of its populace as compared to other countries worldwide (Sentencing Project, 2019). Over the last 40 years we've seen incarceration increase by 500%, caging a total of 2.2 million people (Sentencing Project, 2019).

Blacks are the most incarcerated community at 2,200 per 100,000 residents followed by Latino/x at a rate of 1,000 per 100,000 residents (Morsy & Rothstein, 2016). Black men are six times more likely and Latino/x men are 2.7 times more likely to be incarcerated as compared to white men (Morsy & Rothstein, 2016). One out of every three Black men and one in every six Latino/x men will be incarcerated at some point in their lifetime as compared to one in every 17 white men (Sentencing Project, 2019; Morsy & Rothstein, 2016).

Similarly, women have been the most rapidly growing criminal justice population (Hall, Friedman, & Jain, 2015; National Resource Center on Justice Involved Women [NRCJIW], 2016a; Roth, 2012; Swavola, Riley, & Subramanian, 2016). Between 2013 and 2014, 1.2 million women were involved in the overall criminal justice system (NRCJIW, 2016a). The imprisonment rate for African Americans remains two times higher and 1.2 times higher for Hispanic women than Caucasian women (NRCJIW, 2016a). Subsequently, there is an increase in the number of pregnant and parenting women (Minton & Zeng, 2015) with approximately 5% of women known to be pregnant at jail intake and 3–4% at prison intake (Hall et al., 2015). There are 3,000 admissions of pregnant women in state and federal prisons each year and 55,000 admissions of pregnant women to jail each year (Sufrin, Kolbi-Molinas, & Roth, 2015). Most women are entering prison as primary caregivers and planning to return to that role (NRCJIW, 2016a). It is estimated that 65% of women are parents of children under the age of 18 (Roth, 2012).

Currently, Black men and women account for 13% of the American population, but they comprise more than 35% of those incarcerated (Delaney, Subramanian, Shames, & Turner, 2018). Latino/x men and women represent about 20% of the American incarcerated population (Couloute, 2018). Combined, African Americans and Latino/x make up more than 50% of the American prison population (Jones, 2016).

Prison environment for Black and Latino/x men

According to Delaney et al. (2018) American prison systems have three philosophical underpinnings which guide their everyday practices: retribution, incapacitation, and deterrence. These theories subject incarcerated people to "degrading treatment, inhumane conditions, and abusive interactions" (Delaney, 2018, p. 14). One inmate in a *New York Times* interview described prison stressors as daily degradations that grind away at the soul of men (Thompson, 2018). Inmates report social and physical isolation, idleness, antagonistic relationships with guards and inmates, violence, sexual assault, food insufficiency or moldy food, extreme deprivation of privacy, overcrowding, visitation restrictions, little to no natural light or air, loss of meaningful relationships, at risk for higher rates of suicide, and little to no medical services (Delaney, 2018; Massoglia & Pridemore, 2015). One study found that 40% of inmates experienced sexual or physical assault by personnel or another imprisoned person in the last six months (Delaney, 2018). This is ten times the rate of violence experienced outside of prison (Delaney, 2018). These experiences of victimization can cause "deep and long-lasting distrust of others, inability to express or share emotions, feelings of anger, and an outsider-mentality that can make it difficult for people to seek help from others" (Delaney et al., 2018, p. 115).

Poverty and low education

The criminal justice system is also disproportionately representative of low-income people. People in prison report considerably lower incomes prior to imprisonment (Delaney et al., 2018). Before going to prison, imprisoned people earn wages that are 41% lower than people who do not go to prison (Delaney et al., 2018). About 37% of women inmates meet the federal poverty levels, disclosing incomes of less than $600 a month, one-month prior to arrest and 20% of women cited public assistance as their primary income source upon prison entry (NRCJIW, 2016a). Poverty is not only a predictor of incarceration; it is also frequently the outcome, as a criminal record and time spent in prison destroys wealth, creates debt, and decimates job opportunities (Sawyer & Wagner, 2019).

Many imprisoned people of color are undereducated, entering the criminal justice systems at an early age. The majority of imprisoned people do not have a high school education and only one-third will receive one during their sentence (Delaney et al., 2018). There is an overwhelming likelihood of incarceration experienced by young Black men in the United States who do not complete secondary schooling (Pettit & Western, 2004; Western & Wildeman, 2009; Pettit, 2012; Pettit & Gutierrez, 2018). Pettit & Gutierrez, 2018 approximate that 25% of young adults are arrested by the age of 23 years and further research demonstrates that nearly 50% of Black male youth are arrested by the time they turn 23 years old in comparison to 37.9% of white male youth (as cited in Pettit & Gutierrez, 2018).

Mental health and substance use

The pathways to imprisonment include substance use, mental health issues, childhood victimization, and trauma. Imprisoned individuals report higher rates of previous trauma and victimization (Delaney et al., 2018). Many inmates enter prison with drug/alcohol addictions or mental health problems (Crutchfield & Weeks, 2015). Additionally, according to Delaney et al. (2018) more than 50% of imprisoned persons reported mental illness and/or met the criteria for drug abuse/ dependence. Inmates report post-traumatic stress disorder (PTSD) at rates two-to-ten times that of the general populace (Delaney, 2018).

Substance use is the most common disorder for female inmates followed by serious mental illness and trauma (Kraft-Stoler, 2015; Lynch, DeHart, Belknap, &

Green, 2012). Approximately 82% of incarcerated women meet the lifetime criteria for drug and alcohol abuse and substance dependence, 53% of women met the criteria for lifetime PTSD, and 43% met the criteria for lifetime serious mental illness (Hall et al., 2015; Lynch et al., 2012). Incarceration reinforces and perpetuates trauma in a population with existing mental health and substance use concerns. Women are more likely to be sexually victimized in jail with 27% being victimized by inmates and 67% victimized by staff (Swavola et al., 2016). Trauma is often reactivated due to prison policies that permit full body searches and surveillance by male staff for intimate daily routines such as showering and toileting (Swavola et al., 2016).

According to research social work practice intervention includes the need for gender-responsive programs, problem-solving and solution-focused justice systems, and community-based program alternatives to incarceration (Lynch et al., 2012). Interventions need to address substance use, sexual abuse, trauma, post-traumatic stress, and recidivism using multilevel approaches. Direct practice approaches include psychoeducation, cognitive behavioral therapy, relational therapy, and motivational interviewing (NRCJIW, 2016b). Despite these alarming substance abuse and mental health issues, the majority of inmates receive little if any treatment or therapy during their term, due to diminished funding for rehabilitation programs and the closing of mental health facilities (Crutchfield & Weeks, 2015). This is concerning since the daily prison life requires social and psychological adaptations that can pose community reintegration challenges and can compromise interpersonal relationships with friends and family.

Physical health

The health and well-being of partners, children, and communities are also impacted by mass incarceration (Pettit & Gutierrez, 2018). People who are incarcerated have greater risks of sexually transmitted infections and diseases (Pettit & Gutierrez, 2018). These diseases have the potential to translate to their partner in the community. Inmates are the only group with the constitutional right to health care. The Eighth Amendment provides the constitutional right of prison inmates to receive medical care (Roth, 2012), yet pregnant women are not provided access to basic prenatal health care or access to abortion services (Kraft-Stoler, 2015; Roth, 2012; Swavola et al., 2016), contraception, and sanitary napkins (Kraft-Stoler, 2015; Swavola et al., 2016). Additional problems for pregnant and parenting women include hunger, lack of response to medical needs (i.e. labor, bleeding, and hemorrhaging) by prison staff, miscarriage and stillbirth, births inside prison cells, no counseling or post-partum care even after cesarean section (Roth, 2012). When deliveries occur in the hospital, many women are not provided time to spend with their newborn and are required to return to prison within 24 hours of delivery (Kraft-Stoler, 2015; Roth, 2012; Swavola et al., 2016). Currently, there is no reporting requirements on the outcomes for pregnant incarcerated women limiting full understanding of the depth and scope of the problem (Kraft-Stoler, 2015; Roth, 2012).

Reintegration

Current research has proven that the punitive state of prisons results in substantial social, behavioral, and cognitive trauma which hinders the inmate's efforts to reintegrate into their communities upon release (Delaney et al., 2018). In essence, prison jeopardizes their chances for a successful and rewarding life (Delaney et al., 2018). Massoglia (2008) found that returning citizens had increased risks of "(a) being medically diagnosed with stress-related illnesses such as psychological problems, hypertension, and heart disease, and (b) self-reporting stress-related conditions such as chest pain and depression" (p. 11). This results in incarcerated individuals being released back into their old neighborhoods, in many instances, worse off than they were prior to being in prison (Massoglia & Pridemore, 2015). Once they've served their sentences, they are denied social access to public housing, welfare benefits, university loans and grants, voting rights, the right to work or live in certain neighborhoods, and legal requirements to register with local authorities (Crutchfield & Weeks, 2015). Not having access to these support systems during their transition heightens their chances of becoming involved in further criminal activities. Inmates who are re-incarcerated often lose their intimate relationships, access to their kids, and are less likely to find a job (Crutchfield & Weeks, 2015).

Employment

There are limited employment opportunities for returning citizens (Crutchfield & Weeks, 2015). Thus, returning citizens are often limited to low earnings, poor benefits, and no health insurance (Crutchfield & Weeks, 2015; Massoglia & Pridemore, 2015). There is a strong association between incarceration and low earnings growth over an employment career (Massoglia & Pridemore, 2015). Incarceration is partly responsible for aggregate-level ethnic pay inequality in the United States (Massoglia & Pridemore, 2015). Work opportunities in prisons do not prepare incarcerated individuals with new skills or prepare them for the workforce (Delaney et al., 2018). Instead, available jobs in institutional facilities benefit the facilities themselves (i.e. food service, laundry, or janitorial assignment) (Delaney et al., 2018) rather than the individual, reducing the goal of rehabilitation.

For returning citizens who obtain jobs, the average number of hours they work has decreased by half (40 to 20 hours per week) (Delaney et al., 2018). Similarly, their median pay has declined to 86 cents per day (Delaney et al., 2018). Ironically, these returning citizens are often rearrested for failure to pay accumulated court costs, probation fees, or child support (Morsy & Rothstein, 2016). Consequently, the children and families of returning citizens suffer the economic and social consequences of a previously incarcerated parent (Morsy & Rothstein, 2016).

An inmate's inability to successfully reintegrate into his/her family or community has proven to have a negative ripple effect across children, families, and neighborhoods (Goffman, 2009; Lopoo & Western, 2005; Massoglia & Warner, 2011; Turney, Wildeman, & Schnittker, 2012; Western & Wildeman, 2009 as cited in Massoglia & Pridemore, 2015; Pettit & Gutierrez, 2018; Crutchfield & Weeks, 2015).

Family impact

Children of incarcerated African American fathers suffer from lowered cognitive and non-cognitive skills (Morsy & Rothstein, 2016). This may be due to the trauma experienced from the incarceration or loss of a caregiver during critical developmental periods. Research has shown that they are more likely to drop out of school, develop learning disabilities (i.e. ADHD), engage in inappropriate behavior at school, experience homelessness, and suffer from an array of physical (i.e. migraines, asthma, high cholesterol) and mental (i.e. anxiety, depression, PTSD) health challenges (Delaney et al., 2018; Morsy & Rothstein, 2016). Adult daughters of an incarcerated parent have higher risk for heart disease and diabetes (Delaney et al., 2018). This may be caused by adverse childhood experiences that impact overall health outcomes. The intergenerational impact is profound as "an African American child is six times as likely as a white child to have or have had an incarcerated parent" (Morsy & Rothstein, 2016). The homelessness trend for children of incarcerated African American fathers is especially pronounced as their parents experience more economic instability (Morsy & Rothstein, 2016).

Based on these statistics, the mass incarceration of people of color presents a family crisis (Kraft-Stoler, 2015). There are higher stress levels for the parent who is not imprisoned. Consequently, the remaining parent may need to work longer hours to supplement income reducing their availability to attend to their children (Morsy & Rothstein, 2016). It disrupts attachment bonds between parents and their children. Prison policies restricting visitation times and telephone contact further impair attachment between women and their children (Swavola et al., 2016). Mass incarceration of minorities erodes family structures and can permanently damage the family unit.

Prison torture policies

"Sentencing policies, implicit racial bias, and socioeconomic inequality contribute to racial disparities at every level of the criminal justice system" (Sentencing Project, 2019, para 4). The United States' prison system is rooted in a racist slavery system that aims to dismantle Black and Latinx families and perpetuates the overwhelming and unjustified imprisonment of Black and Latino/x fathers. Imprisonment rates disproportionately affect people of color which further support that prisons are the modern-day evolution of slavery.

Solitary confinement is one of the most cruel practices in prisons that contribute to deep depression, anxiety, paranoia, and perceptual disturbances (Equal Justice Initiative [EJI], 2019; Delaney et al., 2018). Currently, approximately 75,000 people are in solitary confinement in the United States (EJI, 2019). Solitary confinement consists of cramped cage-like cells with little to no lighting for 22–24 hours a day (EJI, 2019). Caged prisoners are allowed out of their cell only for brief showers, short exercises, or medical visits (EJI, 2019). Prisoners in confinement are prohibited from receiving telephone calls, participating in group activities, reading books, and family visits (EJI, 2019; Delaney et al., 2018). While prisoners in solitary confinement only make up 3–8% of the U.S. prison population, they account for more than half of prison suicides (EJI, 2019).

While some prisons may argue that it's a safety measure, solitary confinement does not enhance safety. According to Delaney et al. (2018) prisoners may take on the expected demeanor of the security levels to which they are designated. Researchers refer to the labeling theory as evidence that individual behavior is driven by the social expectations of others. This suggests that solitary confinement can actually create or intensify behavioral issues and violence among imprisoned people rather than reduce them (Delaney et al., 2018). Some states and the federal government have enacted reforms to limit solitary confinement for youth and prisoners with mental illness to reduce the maximum length of time that inmates can spend in confinement (EJI, 2019).

Another policy of the criminal justice system is the shackling of prisoners. Most states either allow shackling or have vague laws restricting the practice (Hall et al., 2015). This practice is considered inappropriate and dangerous particularly for pregnant women and their unborn child. Most medical and professional organizations agree that restraining women during childbirth and after is dangerous because it limits balance and mobility, increases the risks of falling (i.e. placental abruption, hemorrhage, stillbirth), blood clots, and interferes with the medical providers' ability to provide care (standard and emergency) (Prison Birth Project & Prisoners' Legal Services of Massachusetts, 2016). Although these risks have been identified by the health care community, many states continue this harmful and potentially life-threatening practice. Many laws limiting and restricting shackling of pregnant women have emerged due to the Second Chance Act in 2008 (Hall et al., 2015). In states that have adopted anti-shackling laws, there is evidence that prisons do not consistently enforce and comply with the provisions of the law (Kraft-Stoler, 2015; Prison Birth Project & Prisoners' Legal Services of Massachusetts, 2016; Swavola et al., 2016).

The death penalty is another heinous practice within the U.S. prison system that has been compared to lynching during the times of slavery (EJI, 2019). Bryan Stevenson, a public interest lawyer and advocate for those unfairly sentenced, describes lynching terrorism as the violence that people of color would experience anytime they did anything to shake or to contradict this ideology of white supremacy and argues that the death penalty is a continuation of that same narrative (EJI, 2019). Since 1976, 34% of those executed have been African American. Currently, 42% of the 2,700 inmates on death row are Black and 97% are male (EJI, 2019; National Association for the Advancement of Colored People [NAACP], 2018). The majority (75%) of cases resulting in execution were Black on white crimes. The death penalty is legal in 29 states across the United States, many of them in the south (Death Penalty Information Center [DPIC], 2019). The overwhelming majority of chief prosecutors in those states are white and only 1% are Black (EJI, 2019). While the use of capital punishment has declined due to research that shows that the system is plagued by racial bias and legal errors, most southern states have continued to execute mass numbers of poor and people of color (EJI, 2019).

The evolution of slavery and its practices along with subsequent retaliatory Jim Crow laws are evident in our current criminal justice system. Approximately, 2.2 million Black citizens are banned from voting (Sentencing Project, 2019). The consequences of incarceration and its subsequent prohibitions, negatively and effectively impacts civic engagement, trust in institutions, and cynicism about society (Weaver & Lerman, 2010). Inmates are often deprived of programs and support services to improve outcomes. Educational and vocational programs decrease violence and improve employment for returning citizens (Delaney et al., 2018). Cognitive behavioral and rehabilitative programs reduce the negative impacts of incarceration and improve post-release employment and earning opportunities. These programs systematically do not exist or are unavailable for inmates (Delaney et al., 2018).

Furthermore, the perpetuation of the "new slavery era" continues in immigration policies. In 1996, the United States passed the Illegal Immigration Reform and Responsibility Act which utilized the same racist logic and infrastructure to criminalize African Americans and imprison over three million immigrants (Sawyer & Wagner, 2019). The existing hostile and political climate has resulted in 13,000 immigrants in federal prisons and 10,600 are being held by U.S. Marshalls for pretrial (Sawyer & Wagner, 2019). The majority are accused of crossing the border without permission (Sawyer & Wagner, 2019). Another 49,000 immigrants are imprisoned in detention centers by U.S. Immigration and Customs Enforcement (ICE) for their undocumented status (Sawyer & Wagner, 2019). Additionally, 11,800 unaccompanied migrant children are detained by the Office of Refugee Resettlement (ORR), awaiting placement with family or friends (Sawyer & Wagner, 2019). Detention centers are operated by for-profit private prisons and mimic punitive prison-like environments. Between 2019 and 2020, seven migrant children have died in the custody of the Department of Homeland Security due to the dire detention conditions (Pompa, 2019).

African-centered perspective

In the African-centered perspective, history and culture are used to interpret social and psychological phenomenon and develop approaches and policies for change (Bent-Goodley, Snell, & Carlton-LaNey, 2017). The U.S. history of slavery, torture, violence, dismantling, and destruction of African families is the foundation and model for our current criminal justice system. Therefore, mass incarceration of men and women of color is the evolution of the inhumane slavery system thus coined the "the new slavery era." Men and women in prison are enslaved with increased risk of chronic health conditions and communicable disease and denied basic physical and mental health care. Men and women of color are denied access to employment and a livable wage with systemic policies that improve the ease of reentry and benefit the slave system through work assignments. In addition, the new slavery is destructive for children and families of color.

The African-centered worldview is not limited to historical oppression but integrates all historical sources of the African experience to develop approaches and patterns that support the philosophical, cultural, and historical heritage of African people (Graham, 1999). The values and principles of the Afrocentric worldview are the interconnectedness of all things; the spiritual nature of human beings; collective/individual identity and the collective/inclusive nature of family structure; oneness of mind, body, and spirit; and the value of interpersonal relationships (Graham, 1999).

Interconnectedness

The consequences of enslavement have repercussions far beyond the enslaved family as its impact on health, wealth, and community are deeply interconnected. This principle of interconnectedness is also reciprocal; therefore the strengths, values, and beliefs of families and communities are interconnected to those individuals who are in prison. As families and communities view their incarcerated members as enslaved, this understanding contextualizes the level of support and emphasizes the need to strengthen family and community bonds. The principles of interconnectedness are empowering as protective factors, family culture, and community systems can impact the individual and enhance resilience and strength of those who are in bondage.

Spirituality

The principle of spirituality views life as a multitude of passages to develop and grow morally, intellectually, and socially within a community (Graham, 1999). Many educational, occupational, mental health/substance use treatment programs are removed or not accessible strategically to prevent spiritual growth in favor of enslavement cognitions and state-of-being. The interconnectedness of enslaved individuals to families and communities allows touchpoints for spirituality. This can be challenging as policies restrict visitation, contacts, and access. As prison policies have become more restrictive over time discouraging the principle of interconnectedness, many persons of color have developed their spirituality by interconnectedness within prison symptoms, fostering group collaborations to strengthen their spirituality in captivity. A person's spirituality is important particularly in enslaved circumstances. Spirituality continues to grow through the principle of interconnectedness via the family, community, and a higher being.

The collective

In the collective African-centered view, the individual is the group in terms of commonalities and experiences (Graham, 1999). This group identity has been discussed throughout the discussion and is the premise for the theme new slavery. The people of color in the United States have a shared history, common ancestral experience, and existing systemic experience with racism and its consequential institutional racism. Most of the people of color in the United States are a byproduct of slavery or directly impacted by the consequences. In this understanding, people are physically enslaved in the criminal justice system and their families and communities directly and indirectly experience the enslavement through extension of the inmates' suffering or experience similar racist and oppressive structures in daily life. As we become more aware of this group identity the stigma related to enslavement dissipates as we realize that we are all victims of slavery.

Oneness and value of interpersonal relationships

Ma'at (truth, justice, righteous-ness, harmony, balance, order, propriety, compassion, and reciprocity) is a principle essential in the development of self-mind, body, and spirit (Graham, 1999). This discussion exemplifies *Ma'at* as it seeks justice and righteousness as it relates to the many men and women of color who are enslaved. An area not discussed but noteworthy is the economic gains of slavery. In the principle of *Ma'at*, the truth can't be ignored that one key driver of slavery historically and today is profits. In 2015, a private contractor with more than half of the private corrections contracts received revenues totaling $3.5 billion (Gotsch & Basti, 2018). Similar to slavery, prison and jail systems are lucrative businesses generating a tremendous amount of revenue.

In the application of the principle of *Ma'at*, the goal is to explore the issue of mass incarceration and its deleterious effects on people of color and locate this phenomenon through an African-centered view which includes its historical foundations. The purpose is to establish harmony, balance, and order by adopting a perspective that enhances conceptual understanding while setting an African-centered foundational framework of support protective factors and strengths inherent in the African group experience.

Conclusion

The incarceration of people of color is the evolution of the historic U.S. slavery system. The mass incarceration of people of color is a social justice issue and crisis for minority families. There are significant disparities in incarceration in terms of race, socioeconomic status, mental health, and substance use populations. Many incarcerated individuals never receive basic health care service or mental health treatment in a trauma-informed environment. In fact, the prison environment, torture tactics, and policies serve to further traumatize those in custody or increase the likelihood of recidivism. Trauma-informed care is a promising intervention and practice for incarcerated individuals but is not efficient to address this complicated issue or the needs of minority men and women. The African-centered perspective and accompanying principles along with trauma-informed care provide a more suitable framework. In applying both principles of trauma-informed care and the African-centered perspectives, policies, practices, and the needs of people of color and their families can be developed to reduce incarceration rates and develop alternative models that are not evolutionary of historic slavery systems.

Supplemental readings

Policies

1. Second Chance Act: https://csgjusticecenter.org/nrrc/projects/second-chance-act/
2. Pretrial Supervision & Release Programs: www.pwcgov.org/government/courts/cjs/pages/pretrial-supervision.aspx
3. Pre-arrest Crisis Intervention Programs: https://store.samhsa.gov/system/files/diversionruralcommunities_002.pdf
4. Problem-Solving Courts: www.ncsc.org/Topics/Alternative-Dockets/Problem-Solving-Courts/Home.aspx
5. National Commission on Correctional Health Care: www.ncchc.org/
6. ACOG Reproductive Health Care for Incarcerated Women and Adolescent Women: www.acog.org/Clinical-Guidance-and-Publications/Committee-Opinions/Committee-on-Health-Care-for-Underserved-Women/Reproductive-Health-Care-for-Incarcerated-Women-and-Adolescent-Females
7. Dignity for Incarcerated Women Act: www.youtube.com/watch?v=SM3mDOHGG3w&feature=youtu.be

Practice

1. Mental Health America, Access to Mental Health Care and Incarceration: www.mhanational.org/issues/access-mental-health-care-and-incarceration
2. Gender-Responsive & Trauma Informed Services: The Importance of Gender Responsive Trauma Informed Care, www.womenshealth.northwestern.edu/blog/importance-gender-responsive-trauma-informed-care

References

Bauer, S. (2018). *American prison: A reporter's undercover journey into the business of punishment.* London: Penguin Press.

Bent-Goodley, T., Snell, C. L., & Carlton-LaNey, I. (2017). Black perspectives and social work practice. *Journal of Human Behavior in the Social Environment, 27*(1–2), 27–35. https://doi.org/10.1080/10911359.2016.1273682

Couloute, L. (2018, January 24). *New poll shows mass incarceration is a Latinx issue.* Prison Policy Initiative. Retrieved from www.prisonpolicy.org/blog/2018/01/24/new-poll-shows-mass-incarceration-is-a-latinx-issue/

Crutchfield, R. D., & Weeks, G. A. (2015). The effects of mass incarceration on communities of color: In poor and disadvantaged communities. *Issues in Science and Technology*, *32*(1), 109–119.

Death Penalty Information Center. (2019). *Death row overview*. Retrieved from https://deathpenaltyinfo.org/state-and-federal-info/state-by-state

Delaney, R., Subramanian, R., Shames, A., & Turner, N. (2018). *Reimagining prison*. Vera Institute of Justice. Retrieved from www.vera.org/publications/reimagining-prison-print-report

Equal Justice Initiative. (2019). *Mass incarceration*. Retrieved from https://eji.org/mass-incarceration

Goffman, A. (2009). On the run: Wanted men in a Philadelphia ghetto. *American Sociological Review*, *74*(3), 339–357. https://doi.org/10.1177/000312240907400301

Gotsch, K., & Basti, V. (2018, August 2). *Capitalizing on mass incarceration: U.S. growth in private prisons*. The Sentencing Project. Retrieved from www.sentencingproject.org/publications/capitalizing-on-mass-incarceration-u-s-growth-in-private-prisons/

Graham, M. J. (1999). The African-centered worldview: Toward a paradigm for social work. *Journal of Black Studies*, *30*(1), 103–122. https://doi.org/10.1177/002193479903000106

Hairston, T. M. (2013). *Black Male incarceration and the preservation of debilitating habits of judgment: An examination of Mississippi* (Publication No. 1545633) (Doctoral dissertation). University of Mississippi. ProQuest Dissertations Publishing.

Hall, R. C., Friedman, S. H., & Jain, A. (2015). Pregnant women and the use of corrections restraints and substance use commitment. *The Journal of the American Academy of Psychiatry and the Law*, *43*(3), 359–368.

Jones, M. (2016). The prison-to-college pipeline. *Washington Monthly*. Retrieved from https://washingtonmonthly.com/magazine/september-october-2018/the-prison-to-college-pipeline/

Kraft-Stoler, T. (2015). *Reproductive injustice: The state of reproductive health care for women in New York state prisons*. Correctional Association of New York. Retrieved from https://static.prisonpolicy.org/scans/Reproductive-Injustice-FULL-REPORT-FINAL-2-11-15.pdf

Lopoo, L. M., & Western, B. (2005). Incarceration and the formation and stability of marital unions. *Journal of Marriage and Family*, *67*(3), 721–734. https://doi.org/10.1111/j.1741-3737.2005.00165.x

Lynch, S. M., DeHart, D. D., Belknap, J., & Green, B. L. (2012). *Women's pathways to jail: The roles and intersections of serious mental illness and trauma*. Bureau of Justice Assistance. Retrieved from www.bja.gov/Publications/Women_Pathways_to_Jail.pdf

Massoglia, M. (2008). Incarceration as exposure: The prison, infectious disease, and other stress-related illnesses. *Journal of Health and Social Behavior*, *49*(1), 56–71. https://doi.org/10.1177/002214650804900105

Massoglia, M., & Pridemore, W. A. (2015). Incarceration and health. *Annual Review of Sociology*, *41*(1), 291–310. https://doi.org/10.1146/annurev-soc-073014-112326

Massoglia, M., & Warner, C. (2011). The consequences of incarceration: Challenges for scientifically informed and policy-relevant research. *Criminology & Public Pol'y*, *10*, 851. https://doi.org/10.1111/j.1745-9133.2011.00754.x

Minton, T., & Zeng, Z. (2015). *Jail inmates at midyear 2014*. Bureau of Justice Statistics. Retrieved from www.bjs.gov/content/pub/pdf/jim14.pdf

Morsy, L., & Rothstein, R. (2016, December 15). *Mass incarceration and children's outcomes: Criminal justice policy is education policy*. Economic Policy Institute. Retrieved from www.epi.org/publication/mass-incarceration-and-childrens-outcomes/

National Association for the Advancement of Colored People. (2018). *Criminal justice fact sheet*. Retrieved from www.naacp.org/criminal-justice-fact-sheet/

National Resource Center on Justice Involved Women. (2016a). *Fact sheet on justice involved women in 2016*. Retrieved from http://cjinvolvedwomen.org/wp-content/uploads/2016/06/Fact-Sheet.pdf

National Resource Center on Justice Involved Women. (2016b). *Evidence based and gender responsive programs for justice involved women: Evaluations findings and resources*. Retrieved from https://cjinvolvedwomen.org/wp-content/uploads/2016/05/EB-GR-Programs-for-Women-4–2016.pdf

Pettit, B. (2012). *Invisible men: Mass incarceration and the myth of Black progress*. New York, NY: Russell Sage Foundation.

Pettit, B., & Gutierrez, C. (2018). Mass incarceration and racial inequality. *American Journal of Economics & Sociology*, 77(3/4), 1153–1182. https://doi.org/10.1111/ajes.12241

Pettit, B., & Western, B. (2004). Mass imprisonment and the life course: Race and class inequality in U.S. incarceration. *American Sociological Review*, 69(2), 151–169. https://doi.org/10.1177/000312240406900201

Pompa, C. (2019, June 24). *Immigrant kids keep dying in CBP detention centers, and DHS won't take accountability*. American Civil Liberties Union. Retrieved from www.aclu.org/blog/immigrants-rights/immigrants-rights-and-detention/immigrant-kids-keep-dying-cbp-detention

Prison Birth Project & Prisoners' Legal Services of Massachusetts. (2016). *Breaking promises: Violations of the Massachusetts pregnancy standard & anti-shackling law*. Retrieved from https://plsma.org/wp-content/uploads/2016/05/Breaking-Promises_May2016.pdf

Roth, R. (2012). *Reproductive laws for the 21st century papers*. Center for Women Policy Studies. Retrieved from www.prisonpolicy.org/scans/CWPS_Roth_Reproductive_Injustice_7_13_2012.pdf

Sawyer, W., & Wagner, P. (2019). *Mass incarceration: The whole pie 2019*. Prison Policy Initiative. Retrieved from www.prisonpolicy.org/reports/pie2019.html

Sentencing Project. (2019). *Criminal justice facts*. Retrieved from www.sentencingproject.org/criminal-justice-facts/

Sufrin, C., Kolbi-Molinas, A., & Roth, R. (2015). Reproductive justice, health disparities and incarcerated women in the United States. *Perspectives on Sexual and Reproductive Health*, 47(4), 213–219.

Swavola, E., Riley, K., & Subramanian, R. (2016). *Overlooked: Women and jails in the era of reform*. Vera Institute of Justice. Retrieved from www.vera.org/downloads/publications/overlooked-women-and-jails-report-updated.pdf

Thompson, H. A. (2018, April 28). Opinion | how a South Carolina prison riot really went down. *The New York Times*. Retrieved from www.nytimes.com/2018/04/28/opinion/how-a-south-carolina-prison-riot-really-went-down.html

Turney, K., Wildeman, C., & Schnittker, J. (2012). As fathers and felons: Explaining the effects of current and recent incarceration on major depression. *Journal of Health and Social Behavior*, 53(4), 465–481. https://doi.org/10.1177/0022146512462400

Weaver, V. M., & Lerman, A. E. (2010). Political consequences of the carceral state. *American Political Science Review*, 104(4), 817–833. https://doi.org/10.1017/S0003055410000456

Western, B., & Wildeman, C. (2009). The black family and mass incarceration. *The ANNALS of the American Academy of Political and Social Science*, 621(1), 221–242. https://doi.org/10.1177/0002716208324850

INDEX